At Century's End

Great Minds Reflect on Our Times

At Century's End

Great Minds Reflect on Our Times

Foreword by
Bill Moyers

Edited by Nathan P. Gardels

A L
T I
PUBLISHING

Library of Congress Cataloging-in-Publication Data
Gardels, Nathan P.
    At Century's End: Great Minds Reflect on our Times / foreword by Bill
Moyers: edited by Nathan P. Gardels. — 1st ed.
        p. cm.
        Compilation of articles from New Perspectives Quarterly.
        ISBN 1-883051-05-3: $24.95
        1. Civilization, Modern—1950–
2. World politics—1945–
I. Gardels, Nathan. II. New Perspectives Quarterly.
CB427.A84 1996
909.82—dc20   95-42855
                                                                                          CIP

ALTI Publishing
Wayne B. Hilbig, President
4180 La Jolla Village Drive, Suite 520
La Jolla, California 92037
U.S.A.
(619) 452-7703

Copyediting: Sherri Schottlaender
Design: Kathleen Thorne-Thomsen

10 9 8 7 6 5 4 3 2 1
Printed in the United States of America

ALTI Publishing wishes to thank
Mr. Manuel Arango of Mexico City
for suggesting this book,
and for his generous support
in making it possible.
We acknowledge the NPQ *staff:*
Leila Conners, Beverly Childers, and Beth Seeley.
Without them, these ideas would
never have hit paper.

TABLE OF CONTENTS

Diversity and Nationalism
after the Cold War

Cultural Currents in the Last Modern Century

How the World Works Now

FOREWORD

I once wrote to *New Perspective Quarterly* that I would be proud to produce on the air what it puts in print. That is true now, more than ever. I have a hard time thinking without it. I sense, though, that we're approaching a Gettysburg, a moment of truth, for quality journalism like that of *NPQ*.

Once newspapers and periodicals drew people to the public square. They provided a culture of community conversation. The purpose was not just to represent and inform, but to signal, tell a story, and activate inquiry. When the press abandons that function, it no longer stimulates what the American philosopher John Dewey termed "the vital habits" of democracy — "the ability to follow an argument, grasp the point of view of another, expand the boundaries of understanding, debate the alternative purposes that might be pursued."

I know times have changed, and so must publishing. I know that it's harder these days to be a publisher, caught between the entertainment imperatives that are nurtured in the cradle and survival economics that can send good publications to the grave. But the effort must go on.

That our system is failing to solve the bedrock problems we face is beyond dispute. One reason is that our public discourse has become the verbal equivalent of mud-wrestling. The anthropologist Marvin Harris says the attack against reason and objectivity in America today "is fast reaching the proportion of a crusade." America, he says, "urgently needs to reaffirm the principle that it is possible to carry out an analysis of social life that rational human beings will recognize as being true, regardless of whether they happen to be women or men, whites or blacks, straights or gays, Jews or born-again Christians." Lacking such an understanding of social life, "we will tear the United States apart in the name of our separate realities."

Taken together, these assumptions and developments foreshadow the catastrophe of social and political paralysis.

People want to know what is happening to them, and what they can do about it. Listening to America, you realize that millions of people are not apathetic; they want to understand the world around them; and they will respond to a press that stimulates the community without pandering to it, that inspires people to embrace their responsibilities without lecturing or hectoring them, and that engages their better natures without sugarcoating ugly realities or patronizing their foibles.

Over the years — a decade now — NPQ has stuck to this high road, defended the high ground. No mud-wrestling here.

The results speak for themselves. This collection reads like a walk through the history of the post–Cold War years with the best minds and most authoritative voices at your side.

NPQ remains a measure for others. Readers will certainly be rewarded for their efforts here.

BILL MOYERS

PREFACE

"To affirm the book," historian and Librarian of Congress Emeritus Daniel J. Boorstin says in his contribution to this volume, "is to affirm the endurance of civilization against the rush of immediacy." For Boorstin, the book is the antidote to the image that dominates the media age because it judges our experience not by the momentary appeal of events, but by their continuing relevance. It is the refuge from the flood of trivia in a world where there is more data than meaning, more information than knowledge.

If information consists of fragments of experience unrelated to each other, knowledge is structured: what cannot be related or is not relevant as time passes is discarded because it lacks meaning.

New Perspectives Quarterly (NPQ) — from which this collection of essays and interviews is selected — was founded ten years ago with precisely these sentiments expressed by Daniel Boorstin in mind. Our working motto (playing off the famous Club Med ad of the 1980s) has been that NPQ is "the antidote to trivialization." Closer to the function of a book than a magazine, NPQ's aim has been to take back the message from the medium in journalism, not reporting the dots but connecting them with perspective. Ahead of their time and tracing the long curve of history, the essays and interviews presented here thus not only endure, but become more relevant as the years go by.

In yet another sense, NPQ is not a magazine. It is an exclusive, ongoing dialogue of the world's best minds and most authoritative voices. In the manner of a Hollywood production, we script the best person anywhere on the globe who can speak with authority on a subject, and don't rest until they appear in print in our pages. NPQ's thematic approach then focuses those minds and voices in a way that connects the topical debates of the day to the deeper issues of civilization at the end of the twentieth century.

No other publication puts it all together in the same way, with contributors who have ranged from Oliver Stone to Aleksandr

Solzhenitsyn, from Richard Nixon to Nelson Mandela, and with an array of issue titles like "Racism Will Always Be with Us," "Superpower Without a Cause," "Looking East: The Confucian Challenge to Western Liberalism," "The Reunification of Japan," "The Post-Atlantic Capitalist Order," or "Brave New Biocracy: Health Care from Womb to Tomb."

The idea of a publication where the big players and big thinkers speak to each other by addressing the same theme emerged, appropriately enough, in that ancient capital of dialogue, Athens. Stanley Sheinbaum — now NPQ's publisher, a onetime Regent of the University of California and L.A. Police Commissioner — and I had gone to Athens in 1984 to interview the Greek prime minister, Andreas Papandreou. In a cafe on Kolonaki Square, Sheinbaum — who had been a fellow of the famed Center for the Study of Democratic Institutions founded by University of Chicago president Robert Maynard Hutchins in the 1950s — lamented the absence of the kind of serious dialogue about the "great ideas" that had characterized the Hutchins think tank. In those days Hutchins had brought big thinkers from around the world together under one roof in the balmy climes of Santa Barbara, California to tackle the issues of the day.

Why not, we asked each other, start a journal that brings the best minds together under one cover instead of one roof? Under the spell of a double espresso, Sheinbaum was seized by the notion and committed on the spot to become publisher. When he returned home to California, he and his wife Betty, an accomplished artist and collector, put their money where their minds were. They auctioned off Willem de Kooning's Pink Lady to finance the pursuit of ideas. Everything that has happened since is a result of their generosity of spirit. In a very real sense this book must be dedicated to them since their dedication to the life of the mind made it all possible. Naturally, much credit also belongs to Richard Dennis and the other NPQ board members.

Ten years on, NPQ is an established critical success. Through our weekly Global Viewpoint column distributed by the Los Angeles Times Syndicate, we have thirty million readers in fifteen languages through many of the world's prestigious papers, ranging from La

Stampa (Italy), El Pais (Spain), Le Figaro (Paris), Tages Anzeiger (Zurich), De Volkskrant (Amsterdam), Berlingske Tidende (Copenhagen), Die Presse (Vienna) and others in Europe to Yomiuri Shimbun (Japan) and the Straits Times of Singapore in Asia to O Estado de São Paulo, Clarin (Buenos Aires), El Mercurio (Santiago), and Mexico City's Excelsior in Latin America. In the Middle East we appear in the Saudi paper Asharq-Al Awsat and Yedhiot Ahronot (Tel Aviv). We are also carried regularly in papers such as the International Herald Tribune and most of the big American regional papers from the Los Angeles Times to the Miami Herald. Such global exposure has earned us a reputation as "the CNN of the print media."

Critical acclaim has come from diverse quarters. Carlos Fuentes, the Mexican novelist, says "NPQ is the only center where the whole intellectual world meets and debates." GBN Book Club says that "NPQ addresses questions others don't even think about. It takes remarkable originality, insight, diversity of thought and depth to identify and address such questions." Henry Grunwald, editor of Time magazine for two decades, has called NPQ "endlessly stimulating, one of the few sources of new ideas around." Media Guide has praised NPQ, saying it has "emerged as one of the most intellectually attractive and stimulating publications in a long time . . . never stuffy or pompous, always tart and vital . . . " The Washington Post says "NPQ is not looking for ideological advantage or smoothing over rough edges. It is actual thought."

In this volume, for the first time, we have collected the most important NPQ pieces from the last decade in book form. If you have known NPQ you will welcome having a copy of this enduring format to go along with the enduring thoughts expressed here. If you haven't known NPQ, there will be no better introduction than this book. Both are designed for that rare, yet essential, moment when you can sit down under the reading lamp to reflect on the swirl of events that sweeps us along in our collective fate.

NATHAN P. GARDELS, *Editor*

Los Angeles, California
November 1995

SOUL OF THE
WORLD ORDER

Just as birthdays remind us of our own mortality and the procession of decades and centuries gives us pause to ponder the direction of our society, the turning of a millennium casts our concerns toward the ages, and the fate of civilizations.

As much as our material ambitions in this secular century may have masked it, the fate of civilizations, as the historian Arnold Toynbee understood, is inherently bound up with the religious imagination. If spiritual vigor and a sense of origins and destiny energize a civilization and drive it toward new heights, senselessness about what it all means leads to demoralization and decline.

The first two contributors in this section — Nobel laureates Aleksandr Solzhenitsyn and Czeslaw Milosz — speak directly to these issues, expressing worry about the nihilism that has consumed the West as a result of the modern excommunication of God. In a mirror image of their concerns, the Islamic scholar Akbar S. Ahmed sees Islam as the one belief system that can resist the radical impiety of the West which, in his view, strikes out at pious people everywhere through the global reach of the mass media. The battle between these two world views is, for Akbar Ahmed, a fight for the soul of the world order.

Zbigniew Brzezinski, the national security adviser to President Jimmy Carter, departs from his normal geopolitical focus and agrees that a spiritually bereft America cannot lead the world. Perhaps the most famous post– Cold War foreign policy intellectual, Samuel P. Huntington, argues that the end of the U.S.–Soviet conflict has revived an old reality in a new context — civilizations that have different values will often be at odds with each other in the global village.

Finally, Ivan Illich, the grand sage and archaeologist of modern certitudes, looks to "those hours that have lost their clock" during the industrial age in order to shed some light on alternative paths not taken.

Reflections on the Eve
of the Twenty-first Century

Aleksandr Solzhenitsyn

*The renowned author of The Gulag Archipelago,
Aleksandr Solzhenitsyn returned in 1994 to live in Russia
after nearly twenty years in exile in the United States. This
article, adapted from a talk at the International Academy
of Philosophy at Schaan, was translated into English by
Yermolai Solzhenitsyn. It appeared in NPQ entitled, "The
Excommunication of God".*

MOSCOW

What is the role, the justifiable and necessary share, of morality in politics? Erasmus believed politics to be an ethical category, and called on it to manifest ethical impulses. But of course that was in the sixteenth century.

And then came our Enlightenment, and by the eighteenth century we had learned from John Locke that it is inconceivable to apply moral terms to the state and its actions. And politicians, who throughout history were so often free of burdensome moral constraints, had thus obtained something of an added theoretical justification. Moral impulses among statesmen had always been weaker than political ones, but in our time the consequences of their decisions have grown in scale.

Moral criteria applicable to the behavior of individuals, families, and small circles can certainly not be transferred on a one-to-one basis to the behavior of states and politicians: there is no exact equivalence, as the scale, the momentum, and the tasks of governmental structures introduce a certain deformation. States, however, are led by politicians, and politicians are ordinary people, whose actions have an impact on other ordinary people. Moreover, the fluctuations of political behavior are often quite removed from the imperatives of state. Therefore, any moral demands imposed by us on individuals, such as understanding the difference between honesty, baseness, and deception, between magnanimity, goodness, avarice, and evil, must to a large degree be applied to the politics of countries, governments, parliaments, and parties.

In fact, if state, party and social policy will not be based on morality, then mankind has no future to speak of. The converse is also true: if the politics of a state or the conduct of an individual is guided by a moral compass, this turns out to be not only the most humane, but in the long run the most prudent behavior for one's own future.

Among the Russian people, for one, this concept, understood as an ideal to be aimed for, and expressed by the term "truth" *(pravda)* and the phrase "to live by the truth" *(zhit' po pravde)*, has never been extinguished. And even at the murky end of the nineteenth century, the Russian philosopher Vladimir Solovyov insisted that from a Christian point of view, morals and political activity are tightly linked: political activity must not be anything but moral service, whereas a politics motivated by the mere pursuit of interests lacks any Christian content whatsoever.

Alas, in my homeland today these moral axes have fallen into even greater disuse than in the West, and I recognize the present vulnerability of my position in passing such judgments. When, in what had been the USSR, seven decades of appalling pressure were followed by the sudden and wide-open unchecked freedom to act, in circumstances of all-around poverty, the result was that many were swept down the path of shamelessness with the unbridled adoption of the worst features of human behavior. It must be noted in this connection that annihilation was not visited upon people in our country in a purely random fashion, but was directed at those with outstanding mental and moral qualities. And so the picture in Russia today is bleaker and more savage than if it were simply the result of the general shortcomings of our human nature.

But let us not partition the misfortune between countries and nations — the misfortune is for all of us to share, as we stand at the end of Christianity's second millennium. Moreover, should we so lightly fling about this term — morality?

Bentham's Behest

The eighteenth century left us the precept of Jeremy Bentham: morality is that which gives pleasure to the greatest number of persons; man can never desire anything except that which favors the preservation of his own existence. And the eagerness with which the civilized world took up so convenient and precious an advice was astonishing!

Cold calculation holds sway in business relations and has even become accepted as normal behavior. To yield in some way to an opponent or competitor is considered an unforgivable blunder for the party having an advantage in position, power, or wealth. The ultimate measure of every event, action, or intention is a purely legalistic one. This was designed as an obstacle to immoral behavior, and it is often successful, but sometimes, in the form of "legal realism," it facilitates precisely such behavior.

We can only be grateful that human nature resists this legalistic hypnosis, that it does not allow itself to be lulled into spiritual lethargy and apathy toward the misfortunes of others. Great numbers of well-to-do Westerners respond with spirit and warmth to far-off pain and suffering by donating goods, money, and not infrequently, expending significant personal efforts.

Infinite Progress

Human knowledge and human abilities continue to be perfected; they cannot and must not be brought to a halt. By the eighteenth century this process began to accelerate and grew more apparent. Anne-Robert Turgot gave it the sonorous title of Progress, meaning that Progress based on economic development would inevitably and directly lead to a general mollification of the human temperament.

This resonant label was widely adapted and grew into something of a universal and proud philosophy of life: We are progressing! Educated mankind readily put its faith into this Progress. And yet somehow no one pressed the issue: Progress yes, but in what? It was enthusiastically assumed that Progress would engulf all aspects of existence and mankind in its entirety. It was from this intense optimism of Progress that Marx, for one, concluded that history will lead us to justice without the help of God.

Time passed, and it turned out that Progress is indeed marching on, and is even stunningly surpassing expectations, but it is only doing so in the field of technological civilization (with special success in creature comforts and military innovations).

Progress has indeed proceeded magnificently, but has led to consequences that the previous generations could not have foreseen.

Progress in Crisis

The first trifle that we overlooked and only recently discovered is that unlimited Progress cannot occur within the limited resources of our planet: nature needs to be supported rather than conquered. We are successfully eating up the environment allotted to us.

The second misjudgment turned out to be that human nature did not become gentler with Progress, as was promised. All we had forgotten was the human soul.

We allowed our wants to grow unchecked, and are now at a loss where to direct them. And with the obliging assistance of commercial enterprises, newer and yet newer wants are concocted, some of them wholly artificial; and we chase after them *en masse*, but find no fulfillment. And we never shall.

The endless accumulation of possessions? That will not bring fulfillment either. (Discerning individuals have long since understood that possessions must be subordinated to other, higher principles, that they must have a spiritual justification, a mission; otherwise, as Nikolai Berdyayev put it, they bring ruin into human life, becoming the tools of avarice and oppression.)

Modern transportation has flung the world wide open to people in the West. Even without it, modern man can all but leap out beyond the confines of his being; through the eyes of television he is present throughout the whole planet all at the same time. Yet it turns out that from this spasmodic pace of technocentric Progress, from the oceans of superficial information and cheap spectacles, the human soul does not grow, but instead grows more shallow, and spiritual life is only reduced. Our culture, accordingly, grows poorer and dimmer, no matter how it tries to drown out its decline by the din of empty novelties. As creature comforts continue to improve for the average person, so spiritual development grows stagnant. Surfeit brings with it a nagging sadness of the heart, as we sense that the whirlpool of pleasures does not bring satisfaction, and that before long, it may suffocate us.

No, all hope cannot be pinned on science, technology, economic growth. The victory of technological civilization has also instilled a spiritual insecurity in us. Its gifts enrich, but enslave us as well. All is interests — we must not neglect our *interests* — all is a struggle for material things; but an inner voice tells us that we have lost something pure, elevated, and fragile. We have ceased to see the purpose.

Let us admit, even if in a whisper and only to ourselves: In this bustle of life at breakneck speed — what are we living for?

The Eternal Questions Remain

It is up to us to stop seeing Progress (which cannot be stopped by anyone or anything) as a stream of unlimited blessings, and to view it rather as a gift from on high, sent down for an extremely intricate trial of our free will.

The gifts of the telephone and the television, for instance, when used without moderation, have fragmented the wholeness of our time, jerking us from the natural flow of our life. The gift of lengthened life expectancy has, as one of its consequences, made the elder generation into a burden for its children, while dooming the former to a lingering loneliness, to abandonment in old age by loved ones, and to an irreparable rift from the joy of passing on their experience to the young.

Horizontal ties between people are being severed as well. With all the seeming effervescence of political and social life, alienation and apathy toward others have grown stronger in human relations. Consumed in their pursuit of material interests, people find only an overwhelming loneliness. (It is this that gave rise to the howl of existentialism.) We must not simply lose ourselves in the mechanical flow of Progress, but strive to harness it in the interests of the human spirit; not to become the mere playthings of Progress, but rather to seek or expand ways of directing its might toward the perpetration of good.

Progress was understood to be a shining and unswerving vector, but it turned out to be a complex and twisted curve that has once more brought us back to the very same eternal questions that had loomed in earlier times — except that facing these questions then was easier for a less distracted, less disconnected mankind.

We have lost the harmony with which we were created, the internal harmony between our spiritual and physical being. We have lost that clarity of spirit that was ours when the concepts of Good and Evil had yet to become a subject of ridicule, shoved aside by the principle of fifty-fifty.

And nothing speaks more of the current helplessness of our spirit, of our intellectual disarray, than the loss of a clear and calm attitude toward death. The greater his well-being, the deeper cuts the chilling fear of death into the soul of modern man. This mass fear, a fear the ancients did not know, was born of our insatiable, loud, and bustling life. Man has lost the sense of himself as a limited point in the universe, albeit one possessing free will. He began to think himself the center of his surroundings, not adapting himself to the world, but the world to himself. And then, of course, the thought of death becomes unbearable: it is the extinction of the entire universe at a stroke.

Having refused to recognize the unchanging Higher Power above us, we have filled that space with personal imperatives, and suddenly life becomes a harrowing prospect indeed.

After the Cold War

The middle of the twentieth century passed for all of us under the cloud of the nuclear threat. It seemed to blot out all the vices of life. All else seemed insignificant: we are doomed anyway, so why not live as we please? And this great threat served also both to halt the development of the human spirit and to postpone our reflection on the meaning of our life.

Paradoxically, however, this same danger temporarily gave Western society something of a unifying purpose of existence: to withstand the lethal menace of communism. By no means did all fully understand this threat, and in no sense was this firmness equally held by all in the West; there were not a few faint hearts thoughtlessly undermining the West's stand. But the preponderance of responsible people in government preserved the West and allowed for victory in the struggles for Berlin, Korea, for the survival of Greece and Portugal. (Yet there was a time when the communist chieftains could have delivered a lightning blow, probably without receiving a nuclear one in return. It may be that only the hedonism of those decrepit chieftains served to postpone their scheme, until President Reagan derailed them with a new, spiralling, and ultimately unbearable arms race.)

And so, at the end of the twentieth century there burst forth a sequence of events, expected by many of my countrymen but catching many in the West by surprise: communism collapsed due to its inherent lack of viability, and from the weight of the accumulated rot within. It collapsed with incredible speed, and in a dozen countries at once. The nuclear threat was suddenly no more.

And then? For a few short months joyful relief swept over the world (while some bemoaned the death of the earthly Utopia, of the socialist paradise on Earth). It passed, but somehow the planet did not grow calmer; it seems instead that with an even greater frequency something flares up here or explodes there; even scraping together enough U.N. forces for pacification has become no easy task.

Besides, communism is far from dead on the territory of the former USSR. In some republics, its institutional structures have survived in their entirety, while in all of them millions of communist cadres remain in reserve, and its roots remain embedded in the consciousness and the daily life of the people.

At the same time, ugly new ulcers have surfaced from years of torment, for instance the current nascent capitalism, fraught with unproductive, savage and repulsive forms of behavior, and the plunder of the nation's wealth, the likes of which the West has not known. This, in turn, has even brought an unprepared and unprotected populace to a nostalgia for the "equality in poverty" of the past.

Although the earthly ideal of socialism-communism has collapsed, the problems that it purported to solve remain: the brazen use of social advantage and the inordinate power of money, which often direct the very course of events. And if the global lesson of the twentieth century does not serve as a healing inoculation, then the vast red whirlwind may repeat itself in entirety.

The Cold War is over, but the problems of modern life have been laid bare as immensely more complex than what had hitherto seemed to fit into the two dimensions of the political plane. The former crisis of the meaning of life and the former spiritual vacuum (which during the nuclear decades had even deepened from neglect) stand out all the more. In the era of the balance of nuclear terror, this vacuum was somehow obscured by the illusion of attained stability on the planet, a stability that has proved to be only transitory. But now the former implacable question looms all the clearer: what is our destination?

On the Eve of the Twenty-first Century

Today we are approaching a symbolic boundary between centuries, and even millennia: fewer than four years separate us from this momentous juncture, which, in the restless spirit of modern times will be proclaimed a year early, not waiting until the year 2001.

Who among us does not wish to meet this solemn divide with exultation and in a ferment of hope? Many thus greeted the twentieth as a century of elevated reason, in no way imagining the cannibalistic horrors that it would bring. Only Dostoyevsky, it seems, foresaw the coming of totalitarianism.

The twentieth century did not witness a growth of morality in mankind. Exterminations, on the other hand, were carried out on an unprecedented scale, culture fell sharply, the human spirit declined. (Although the nineteenth century, of course, did much to prepare this outcome.) So what reason have we to expect that the twentyfirst century, one bristling with first-class weaponry on all sides, will be kinder to us?

And then there is environmental ruin. And the global population explosion. And the colossal problem of the Third World, still called that in quite an inadequate generalization. It constitutes four-fifths of modern mankind, and soon will make up five-sixths, thus becoming the most important component of the twenty-first century. Drowning in poverty and misery, it will, no doubt, soon step forward with an ever-growing list of demands to the advanced nations. (Such thoughts were in the air as far back as the dawn of Soviet communism. It is little known, for example, that in 1921 the Tatar nationalist and communist Sultan Gallev called for the creation of an International of colonial and semicolonial nations, and for the establishment of its dictatorship over the advanced industrial states.)

Today, looking at the growing stream of refugees bursting through all the European borders, it is difficult for the West not to see itself as something of a fortress: a secure one for the time being, but clearly one besieged. And in the future, the growing ecological crisis may alter the climatic zones, leading to shortages of fresh water and suitable land in places where they were once plentiful. This, in turn, may give rise to new and menacing conflicts on the planet —wars for survival.

A complex balancing act thus arises before the West: to maintain a full respect for the entire precious pluralism of world cultures and their search for distinct social solutions, at the same time to not lose sight of its own values, its historically unique stability of civic life under the rule of law — a hard-won stability that grants independence and space to every private citizen.

Self-limitation

The time is urgently upon us to limit our wants. It is difficult to bring ourselves to sacrifice and self-denial, because in political, public, and private life we have long since dropped the golden key of self-restraint to the ocean floor. But self-limitation is the fundamental and wisest aim of a man who has obtained his freedom. It is also the surest path toward its attainment. We must not wait for external events to press harshly upon us or even topple us; we must take a conciliatory stance, and through prudent self-restraint learn to accept the inevitable course of events. Only our conscience, and those close to us, know how we deviate from this rule in our personal lives. Examples of deviations from this course by parties and governments are in full view of all.

When a conference of the alarmed peoples of the earth convenes in the face of the unquestionable and imminent threat to the planet's environment and atmosphere (at the Rio Earth Summit in 1991), a mighty power, one consuming not much less than half of the earth's currently available resources and emitting half of its pollution, insists, because of its present-day internal interests, on lowering the demands of a sensible international agreement, as though it does not itself live on the same earth. Then other leading countries shirk from fulfilling even these reduced demands. Thus, in an economic race, we are poisoning ourselves.

Similarly, the breakup of the USSR along the fallacious Lenin-drawn borders has provided striking examples of newborn formations, which, in the pursuit of great power imagery, rush to occupy extensive territories that are historically and ethnically alien to them, territories containing tens of thousands, or in some cases millions, of ethnically different people, giving no thought to the future, imprudently forgetting that taking never brings one to any good.

It goes without saying that in applying the principle of self-restraint to groups, professions, parties, or entire countries, the ensuing difficult questions outnumber the answers already found. On this scale, all commitments to sacrifice and self-denial will have repercussions for multitudes of people who are perhaps unprepared for, or opposed to them. (And even the personal self-restraint of a consumer will have an effect on producers somewhere.)

And yet, if we do not learn to limit firmly our desires and demands, to subordinate our interests to moral criteria, we, humankind, will simply be torn apart as the worst aspects of human nature bare their teeth. It has been pointed out by various thinkers many times (and I quote here the words of the twentieth-century Russian philosopher Nikolai Lossky): "If a personality is not directed at values higher than the self, corruption and decay inevitably take hold." Or, if you will permit me to share a personal observation: we can only experience true spiritual satisfaction not in seizing, but in refusing to seize. In other words: self-limitation.

Today, self-limitation appears to us as something wholly unacceptable, constraining, even repulsive, because we have over the centuries grown unaccustomed to what for our ancestors had been a habit born of necessity. They lived with far greater external constraints, and had far fewer opportunities. The paramount importance of self-restraint has only in this century arisen in its pressing entirety before mankind. Yet taking into account even the various mutual links running through contemporary life, it is nonetheless only through self-restraint that we can, albeit with much difficulty, gradually cure both our economic and political life.

Today, not many will readily accept this principle for themselves. However, in the increasingly complex circumstances of our modernity, to limit ourselves is the only true path of preservation for us all. And it helps bring back the awareness of a Whole and Higher Authority above us — and the altogether forgotten sense of humility before this entity. There can be only one true Progress: the sum total of the spiritual progress of each individual, of the degree of self-perfection in the course of their lives.

We were recently entertained by a naive fable of the happy arrival at the "end of history," of the overflowing triumph of an all-democratic bliss; supposedly, the ultimate global arrangement has been attained. But we all see and sense that something very different is coming, something new, and perhaps quite stern. No, tranquility does not promise to descend upon our planet, and will not be granted us so easily.

And yet, surely, we have not experienced the trials of the twentieth century in vain. Let us hope: we have, after all, been tempered by these trials, and our hard-won firmness will in some fashion be passed on to the following generations.

The Fate of the Religious Imagination

Czeslaw Milosz

Winner of the 1980 Nobel Prize for literature, Polish-born poet Czeslaw Milosz is the author of The Captive Mind *and* Unattainable Earth. *In the following essay, Milosz considers the historic tension between religious imagination and scientific innovation.*

BERKELEY

How to penetrate what is going on in the minds of our contemporaries? We may know their opinions, their convictions, beliefs, everything that they communicate through language. Yet language is not very reliable, for it usually lags behind the transmutations of a mentality occurring on a deeper level — of not quite conscious adjustments of the mind to the changing world.

I have always been fascinated by the fate of religion in our century; much less, though, by what believers or disbelievers say, much more by what one may guess is behind their pronouncements. I assume we all, living in the same epoch, bear in our heads a set of images of the universe and the place of man in it which might tell us about the workings of the religious imagination, now and in the past. Religious imagination cannot be today the same as it was in the time of Dante, but it also must differ from that of a hundred or two hundred years ago. Certain external signs point to an awareness of this fact; for instance, when going to church, we do not expect to hear a sermon on the sufferings of the damned in Hell amid fire and brimstone, though this once was the normal fare of churchgoers. Such external signs, however, are few, and probably the language of theologians and priests is at a certain variance with the unformulated imaginings of the faithful.

Access to the religious imagination of modern man might be possible only indirectly, through the changing forms of language and also of art and music. Assume all creations of the human mind in a given period are linked in a common *episteme*, so that by looking at a painting or listening to a musical composition we are able to date it quite precisely. Any given *oeuvre* is less an isolated island than it seems. To the contrary, a subterranean bond unites, let us say, Samuel Beckett's desperate vision of the human condition and religious fundamentalism of today, even if in appearance they have nothing in common. Thence the known phenomenon of preachings and writings that are hollow, resembling shells out of which life has escaped.

The scientific revolution has been gradually eroding the religious imagination. First came the Copernican blow toppling the central position of the earth, and then Newton introduced the idea of eternal space and eternal time stretching infinitely. A new cosmology has been victoriously replacing the old one based upon the privileged place of man who was created in the image of God and saved by that very resemblance, i.e., through the Incarnation. The new cosmology somehow dissolved man into the immensity of galaxies, where he became merely a speck arrogantly assigning to himself an exceptional role. Even more destructive proved to be the life sciences. For Descartes, animals were living machines; thus, the barrier between them and humans, endowed with an immortal soul, was still maintained. To abolish that barrier the theory of evolution was needed, and the churches immediately sensed the danger. (To believe an anecdote, Darwin hesitated whether to publish *The Origin of Species* because of the implorations of his pious wife.) As the difference between the "lower" species and man became blurred, grave questions of moral order appeared. If all life is submitted to certain laws, among them the law of the survival of the fittest, the same law also applies to the struggle between men (or classes, or nations), and the moralists' or the humanitarians' tears are of no avail. It is possible that the crime of genocide characteristic of our century has been a side effect of viewing man as a biological entity no less expendable than the myriad of live entities squandered every second by Nature. On the other hand, some questions have been leading us in the opposite direction: if we are so closely related to animals, who are indeed our brothers, should not man in his unrelenting protest against suffering, in his complaint of Job, speak also in the name of all creatures? They suffer, they die, yet they won't receive any recompense. Would it be decent to imagine that only man would receive it?

The progress of science has created a strange duality in the education of the young. They are trained at school in empirical thinking, and receive a more or less coherent vision of the world as governed by chains of material causes and effects. They go out to the street and are surrounded there by products of technology that apply the discoveries of science, and thus confirm the authority of scientific methods. And yet the majority of those students belong, at least nominally, to religious denominations, and have somehow to harmonize two clashing propositions as to the structure of reality, unless — and this happens more and more often — they opt for the scientific variety. Some defenders of religion enter into polemics with scientists and question their theories: for instance, by opposing the theory of evolution. Yet the general line is different: we hear that science and religion cannot clash, for religion is a matter of faith, not of facts. Unfortunately, a need for coherence is our inborn feature, and it is difficult to keep our thought moving constantly on two parallel tracks.

And yet no one would dare today to announce the end of religion, or even the end of Christianity. Such predictions sounded plausible in the nineteenth century when the positivist Auguste Comte went even as far as laying the foundation for "a scientific church." The number of churchgoers may fluctuate, from very high in Catholic countries like Poland, Ireland, and Italy to very low in Catholic France and Protestant Sweden, but the losses in some areas of the globe are compensated for by the ardor of new congregations — in Africa, in Latin America. The travels of Pope John Paul II and the crowds he attracts should give skeptics some food for thought. It is also worth noting that in technologically minded America the people, in their preponderant majority, consider themselves religious — either of Christian orientation, Jewish, or of some Asian faith such as Buddhism. The revival of the Orthodox church in Russia, after persecutions surpassing in their cruelty anything known in the history of Christianity, is another sign of the permanence of human needs.

Obviously, then, the onslaught of science upon the religious imagination, though unquestionable, represents only one element of the problem. It seems to me that by comparing our thinking with that of the eighteenth century, we may receive some hints that can help us avoid simplification. That century has been called the Age of Reason, and our scientific-technological civilization has been traced back to the basic premises laid down by thinkers and scientists of that time. It may appear, though, that by assessing the ways of people who lived then, we fall victim to our propensity to project into the past our own habits. What should surprise us about that century is its optimism, in contrast to the mood of pessimism prevalent today, of which we are not always aware because it so much pervades our thought. Then human reason approached the superabundance of existing phenomena with a confidence in its own unlimited forces because God assigned to it the task of discovering the marvels of His creation. In this sense, it was the Age of *pious* Reason. Isaac Newton was a profoundly believing man. Carolus Linnaeus, the great Swedish botanist who invented the classification of species, opens his *Systema Naturae* with a quotation from a Psalm (in Latin): "O Jehovah! How manifold are thy works! In wisdom hast thou made them all: the earth is full of thy riches!" There is a tendency today to suspect the Age of Reason scientists of duplicity, of using their belief in the Deity as a mask for their basically materialistic philosophy. Yet the atmosphere pervading their writings and the very style of the fine arts and music in that period speak to the contrary. The notion underlying all its artifacts is that of order. God established the immutable laws for the movements of the planets, for the growth of vegetation, for the working of the animal organism, and the life of man on the earth is providentially arranged in accordance with the universal rhythm. Some ideas, like the idea of the inalienable rights of every human being, seem to imply a stability underneath the changing forms of social existence. The *episteme* of the eighteenth century, centered upon order, is best expressed in its music. I believe the greatest music ends around 1800. Those who would disagree must concede, in any case, that around that date music switches to a new direction.

The eighteenth century, let us not forget, brought about in several countries pietistic movements and a spiritual search through free-Masonic lodges (like the lodge in Mozart's *The Magic Flute*), some of which constituted themselves as "mystical lodges." It was also the age of mystical writers — Claude de Saint-Martin, Emanuel Swedenborg, William Blake. Was it so that the full implications of the scientific revolution were not yet grasped (or grasped and fought against, as in

Blake's struggle against the diabolical trinity of Bacon, Newton, and Locke)? That is possible. Be that as it may, by comparing our fate with that of our ancestors, we may draw a lesson as to the simultaneous existence of many trends and inclinations within a given span of time. The next century, the nineteenth, would exacerbate some tendencies of its predecessor, and elaborate what can be called a scientific *Weltanschauung* in fact quite distant from those harmonious visions of the earlier scientists. Destructive of values, it would prompt Friedrich Nietzsche to announce the advent of "European nihilism," in which he cannot be denied a gift of prophecy.

Today as well, many currents, ascending and descending, are at work simultaneously, and in some domains the impact of nineteenth-century science has reached its apogee, while in others it seems to recede. Any literary critic is familiar with the voices of despair, of derision, of universal senselessness uttered by poets and novelists. They are former students who learned to think about the world and human life in the terms of science, which does not offer, however, anything positive in the realm of values. Eminent poets of this age are despairing nihilists, perhaps meriting admiration because of their frankness. To name but a few: Gottfried Benn, Samuel Beckett, Philip Larkin. The enigmatically high number of poets and painters who became marxists is explainable by their search for meaning, which they found through their faith in the earthly salvation of communism: Paul Eluard, Pablo Neruda, Rafael Alberti, Pablo Picasso, and many, many others. Judging by literature and art, the individual existence of a human being is viewed as absurd and devoid of any justification, because life, of which it is a part, made its appearance on the earth not by a decree of a Divinity but by a mere chance. Now, after the breakdown of the communist utopia, we may expect the intensification of the mood of hopelessness, going together with rapacious consumerism.

In such a predicament, people may turn to religion in the first place because they search for a *moral* order. In this respect the shift of emphasis in the teachings of the Roman Catholic Church is highly significant. A hundred or two hundred years ago, the basic topic of sermons was the salvation of the soul; in the last decades one hears more and more about man's participation in society, often to such an extent that the zeal of the clergy seems to be directed mainly toward various social "causes" like the emancipation of the poor, national independence, or obsessive anti-abortion campaigns. Religion, which traditionally was vertically directed, becomes horizontal, probably because the images founding Christian metaphysics are lacking. Yet that horizontal orientation often makes the words of preachers sound hollow, for they are too much social activists to intimate they are also men of contemplation and faith.

Religion as a social institution is not identical with a deeper spiritual life, and can even prosper for a time when such a life is lacking. The basic question that confronts us today is whether there are signs indicating that the religious imagination, devastated by the onslaught of nineteenth-century science, can revive. Transformations of mentality proper to a given moment in history are usually slow, and even now, at the very end of the century, it is difficult to disentangle the crisscrossing multiple trends often opposing each other. And yet we are not at the same point as, let us say, in 1900. I would be wary in joining all those who hail the new physics as the beginning of an era of recovered harmony—like Fritjof Capra's *The Tao of Physics* (what, after all, is Tao if not a sense of the universe as harmony?). Yet I am more cynical when, in the biochemist Jacques Monod's *Chance and Necessity,* I find his desperate statement about the one-way path we are launched on by science: "A track which nineteenth-century scientism saw leading infallibly upward to an empyrean noon hour of mankind, whereas what we see opening before us today is an abyss of darkness." I think Jacques Monod was writing a dirge to bygone attitudes, while science now again stands before a breathtaking, miraculous spectacle of unsuspected complexity, and it is the new physics that is responsible for this change of orientation. After all, William Blake was right when he denounced the absolute space and absolute time of Newton, and he would have greeted Einstein's relativity as a discovery liberating the human spirit from the oppressive images of the void completely "objective" and thus torn off from the human mind. The universe so conceived was for Blake "the land of Ulro," the realm of Death, in which all things are mere "spectres," dead to Eternity. The theory of quanta, independently of conclusions drawn from it, is antireductionist, for it restores the mind to its role of a co-creator in the fabric of reality. This favors a shift from belittling man as an insignificant speck in the immensity of galaxies to regarding him again as the main actor in the universal drama — which is a vision proper to every religion (Blake's Divine Humanity, Adam Kadmon of the Cabbalah, Logos Christ of the Christian denominations).

For a believer, such as myself, the key to the mystery of the universe is the mystery of man — not vice versa; or rather, every part of the mystery is a function of the other. The enthusiasm of the eighteenth-century scientists who searched for an objective order looks naive today, yet I sense at the end of our century something like a renewal of a hopeful tone. One possibility should not be excluded in advance: that science will move away from the reductionism and crude materiality of scientism, and yet, that state of affairs would not help the religious imagination at all. Science may explore a world become again miraculous but use a language inaccessible to the public and untranslatable into any visualization; once, science was potent enough to attract converts to its myth.

In such a case, various religious denominations will become more and more horizontal, captive as it were of local, national, and social surroundings, and allied with political forces. It seems to me American fundamentalism could be one example of such a development, and I am afraid Roman Catholicism in Poland, though in many respects different, has some components announcing a similar future. Or should we look at Latin America? Ireland? The fate of Shintoism in Japan as a national religion? It is safer not to make predictions. Much depends on the number of serious religious thinkers in every country — not religiously minded social reformers who everywhere abound — but those who would try to deal with the basic enigmas of Being, in the present conditions when all the premises have to be restated anew.

Media Mongols at the Gates of Baghdad

Akbar S. Ahmed

A Pakistani scholar currently in residence at Selwyn College at the University of Cambridge, Akbar S. Ahmed is author of Discovering Islam *(Routledge) and, most recently,* Postmodernism and Islam *(Routledge, 1993), which is a longer version of this article.*

CAMBRIDGE

A political cartographer with a bold eye for simplification would reject the clumsy apparatus of global classification that has prevailed so far — First, Second, Third World, North-South, East-West, and so on. He would divide the world map in the 1990s into two major categories: the civilizations that are exploding — reaching out, expanding, bubbling with scientific ideas, economic plans, political ambitions, cultural expression — and those that are imploding, collapsing in on themselves with economic, political, and social crises which prevent any serious attempt at major initiatives. The former are, above all, exploding with optimism, with sights firmly fixed on the future; the latter are weighted down by their history, traditions, "certainties," their ethnic and religious hatreds.

Western, or global civilization — in essence the G-7 — is exploding; much of the rest of the world is imploding.

This exploding-imploding world is so shrunk by the ubiquitous media that defines our postmodern era, so interlinked and so claustrophobic, that elbowroom on this planet is ever more scarce. We have all been shoved face to face with each other. As the exploding West continues through its domination of the media to expand its cultural boundaries to encompass the world, traditional civilizations will resist in some areas, accommodate to change in others.

In the main, only one civilization, Islam, will stand firm in its path. Only the Muslim world, poised both to implode and explode, offers a global perspective with a potential alternative role on the world stage. Islam, therefore, appears to be set on a collision course with the West. More than a clash of cultures, more than a confrontation of races, the collision between the global civilization emanating from the West and Islam is a straight-out fight between two approaches to the world, two opposed philosophies. Under the layers of history and the mosaic of cultures, we can simplify in order to discover the major positions. One is based in secular materialism, the other in faith; one has rejected belief altogether, the other has placed it at the center of its world view.

While conflict has long brewed between the traditional religious precepts of Islam and the materialism and scientific reason of modernity, the challenge postmodernism presents is more decisive for the ultimate fate of Islam.

While Muslims appreciate the spirit of tolerance, optimism, and the drive for self-knowledge in postmodernism, they also recognize the threat it poses to them with its cynicism and irony. This is a challenge to the faith and piety that lie at the core of their world view.

Pious Muslims know that the problem with the G-7 civilization is the hole where the heart should be — the vacuum inside, the absence of a moral philosophy. What gives the West its dynamic energy is individualism, the desire to dominate, the sheer drive to acquire material items through a philosophy of consumerism at all costs, to hoard. Such frenetic energy keeps society moving.

Patience, pace, and equilibrium, by contrast, are emphasized in Islam. Haste is the devil's work, the Prophet warned. But the postmodern age is based on speed. In particular, the media thrive on and are intoxicated by speed, change, news. The unceasing noise, dazzling color, and restlessly shifting images of the MTV culture beckon and harass. Silence, withdrawal, and meditation — advocated by all the great religions — are simply not encouraged by the media.

The African and South Asian are dazzled with images of *Dallas*- and *Dynasty*-like plenty, of a cornucopia. But they have no access to such a reality. These tantalizing images are thus no more than dangerous illusions for the majority of the people on the planet. They cannot solve anything; but they can, through the envy and desire they spread, spoil a great deal of contentment, patience, and balance — the virtues of traditional societies, which no longer have the power to soothe or mollify.

Nothing in history has threatened Muslims like the Western media; neither gunpowder in the Middle Ages, which Muslims like Babar used with skill on the fields of Panipat, thus winning India for his Mughal dynasty; not trains and the telephone, which helped colonize them in the last century; nor even planes, which they mastered for their national airlines earlier this century. The Western media are ever present and ubiquitous, never resting and never allowing respite. They probe and attack ceaselessly, showing no mercy for weakness and frailty.

The powerful media offensive is compounded for Muslims: they appear not to have the capacity to defend themselves. Worse, they appear unable even to comprehend the nature and objectives of the onslaught. The empty bluster of the leaders and the narrow-minded whining of the scholars make them appear pitiful, like pygmies arguing among themselves while the powerful giant of an enemy is at the gate.

It is the ordinary Muslim who senses the immensity of the danger. He is conscious of the potential scale of the battle and the forces arrayed against him; his tension is made worse because he has so little faith in his own leaders.

It must have been something like this in 1258 when the Mongols were gathering outside Baghdad to shatter forever the greatest Arab empire in history. But while the Abbasids remained in ruins, other, equally significant structures with glorious edifices were created: the Fatimids in Egypt, the Umayyads in Spain, and later, the Saffavids in Iran, the Mughals in India.

This time the decision will be final. If Islam is conquered, there will be no coming back.

The Media is Power

It is the American mass media that have achieved what American political might could not: the attainment for America of world domination. Hollywood has succeeded where the Pentagon failed. The link between the two is established in the fact that films and defense equipment are the two largest export earners in the U.S. economy. J. R. Ewing has triumphed in a way John Foster Dulles could not even dream. The world watches with hypnotic fascination the rerun episodes of American soaps: across the world people ask "Who shot J. R.?" in *Dallas* or "Who killed Laura Palmer?" in *Twin Peaks*. The American dream is seen as irresistible.

The demise of communism and the collapse of its monolithic state structures are widely considered as the Western media's greatest victory. With their incessant propaganda, their capacity to satirize and ridicule, the Western media made deep inroads into the communist world, dooming it years before Gorbachev and his successors arrived.

Muslims ask: now that the Western media have helped conquer communism, who will be their next opponent? It is not difficult to guess: Islam. We have here a thesis in need of investigation: the more traditional a religious culture in our age of the media, the greater the pressures upon it to yield.

All traditional religions, whether Buddhist, Hindu, Muslim, or Christian, encourage piety, contemplation, and mysticism. In contrast, as I indicated earlier, the full-scale onslaught of the media is an obscene cry for noise, materialism, for consumerism and *blague*. The seductive ads, the glamorous stars, all drown thoughts of piety and austerity. Then it robs human beings of that most delicate of crowns, dignity. In the knockabout irreverence and turbulence of the postmodern wit there is no dignity allowed anyone.

The purity of the past can no longer be guaranteed under such relentless assault. It is thus understandable why Muslims reject postmodernism as nihilism and anarchy.

For the Western media, civilizations "out there" tend to be shown in stereotypes. Islam continues to be marginalized and degraded. In a hundred hours of CNN or other television coverage, Islam might get ten minutes of projection, which will be Muslims burning books or expressing rage in a threatening mob. Hinduism and Buddhism are shown to be holy priests, half-naked and meditating, to be dismissed in the popular media as exotic relics of the past.

What I wish to emphasize here is the concept of media as power, as assertion of cultural superiority, as extension of political arguments, indeed, as the main player. Through the media the opposing position can not only be triumphed over but also, by denying it access, it can cease to exist altogether. The media is thus one of the most important weapons in the arsenal of any country. This is the paramount lesson of our times.

While triumphant on the world stage, the basic unit of human organization, the family, is in grave danger in Western civilization. One of the main quarrels Muslims have with contemporary Western culture concerns the disintegration of the Western family, whose authoritative function in the moral formation of the person has been eroded by the invasion of the media in the home.

In the Islamic family, integrity, unity, and stability are the ideal. Muslims thus see the pressures of the consumerist culture of the West — the promiscuity, the drugs, the high expectations — as taking their toll on Western marriages with about half of them falling apart. They fear that these pressures are now being brought to bear on Muslim homes. They fear *din* (religion) is in danger of being totally submerged under *dunya* (the world). This would be catastrophic to the Muslim concept of a just and balanced order.

Muslim parents blanch at the modern Western media because of the universality, power, and pervasiveness of their subversive images, and because of their malignity and hostility toward Islam.

The images on television that come nonstop at the viewer are of couples performing sex, men inflicting terrible pain, limbs and guts dismembered, *disjecta membra* everywhere. The videocassettes that accompany pop songs produce ever more bizarre images, from Madonna masturbating to Michael Jackson's transmogrification into a panther.

They blot out other images, whether the *gravitas* of the serious documentaries or the false conviviality of the chat shows. The VCR is a trapdoor to the darkest, most depraved images humans can possibly conjure up. Anything and everything is available. Even a Marquis de Sade would be satisfied at what he could find here.

These intrusions corrode the innermost structure of balance and authority in that crucible of all civilization, the family, adding to the crumbling authority structures of the West that have been under attack now for the last two generations.

Take the case of Britain. The father at home, the bobby in the street, the teacher at the school, and the monarchy and politicians in public life are all the subjects of constant media ridicule. In particular, men are singled out. To be a male in authority is to be suspect.

People in authority were the special target of the brainless marxist intellectual brigade of the last generation. The media took over after them. In the West, stories of political corruption in public life, incest at home, ritual satanic abuse in the schools, and so on, have finally ended whatever little respect remained for authority. In the place of the old structures is a vacuum.

If the power of the Western media dictated the 1980s social agenda — feminism, homosexuality, AIDS — we are, in the 1990s, already discussing post-feminism, post-homosexuality, and post-AIDS.

Many of the issues that Islam never conceded, such as the abuse of alcohol and drugs, are now being widely reaccepted in the West. Many in the West are also now reevaluating divorce, the challenge to parental authority, the marginalization of the elderly, the regular relocation of the home because of work and related issues. All are devastating to the family. The legitimate questions being raised by Muslims are the following: Why should they be dragged along the path of social experimentation which they know diverges from their own vision of society? Why should they disrupt their domestic situation for temporary values, however overpowering in their immediate and glamorous appeal?

Why is a religion advocating goodness, cleanliness, tolerance, learning, and piety so misunderstood and reviled? Many of the currently accepted social positions in the West — the undesirability of cigarettes, drugs, and alcoholism, and the promotion of family life — have always been advocated by Islam. *Jihad* has become a dirty word in the media, representing the physical threat of a barbaric civilization. Yet the concept is noble and powerful. It is the desire to improve oneself, to attempt betterment, and to struggle for the good cause. It is Tennysonian in its scope: to strive, to seek, and not to yield.

Busting Muslim Stereotypes

I wish to avoid what I see as sterile sexist and religious polemics about Muslim women. But I feel it necessary to point out in passing the wholly incorrect, negative media stereotype of women as inanimate objects, submissively attending to the needs of their lord and master, locked away in darkened homes. I believe this is a stereotype partly reflected from the poor opinion, bordering on misogyny, that Western society (inspired by the ancient Greeks), holds of women.

The potential of women in Islam is far superior to anything offered by Confucius in China or Aristotle in Greece, or to what Hindu or Christian civilizations offered. Muslim women are central to family affairs, from domestic decision-making to rituals. Where their lot is miserable and they have virtually no rights, as in certain tribal areas, it is to be attributed to Muslim male tyranny, not Islamic advice, and is in need of urgent redress.

We know that the modern political life of many Muslim nations has been enriched by the contributions of women. Miss Fatimah Jinnah, the sister of the founder of Pakistan, mounted the most severe political challenge to the military dictatorship of Ayub Khan in the 1960s. Two decades later, Benazir Bhutto followed the same pattern, challenging General Zia and succeeding in becoming the first female Muslim prime minister, one of just a handful of women premiers in the world until that time. Begum Khalida Zia in 1991 continued the trend by becoming the first female prime minister of Bangladesh.

Muslims also face dilemmas in education. Away from the educated scholars, in the villages of Asia, Islamic scholarship faces serious problems. In lengthy and intimate discussions with orthodox religious scholars this was made plain to me. To them the outside world simply does not exist. The works of Marx or Weber are unknown. Faith and fervor are sufficient to carry all before them. This blocking-out provides Muslims with their supreme confidence but also poses the most formidable threat to them. And the threat is felt most sharply at the moment of realization that there are other, outside systems. It was first heard in the plaintive complaint of Aurangzeb, the Mughal emperor, to his tutor. The Emperor chided his tutor for filling his head with the most exaggerated notions of the Mughal Empire, and for dismissing the European kings as petty *rajas*. The same questioning is heard today among the more honest and intelligent *ulema*, the religious scholars.

These dilemmas provoke passionate responses. There is an interesting parallel in recent history that illustrates the principle prompting Muslim action against Salman Rushdie. A century ago, advancing European imperialism met Muslim resistance determined to defend the traditional way of life, from Sudan in Africa to Swat in Asia. The picture that symbolizes the clash is that of illiterate tribesmen crying "Allah-u-Akbar" (God is most great), waving swords blessed by holy men, charging at the formations of European infantrymen firing the latest most deadly guns. The slaughter did little to dim Muslim commitment.

In our times, the one picture that perhaps best symbolizes a similar clash between the West and Islam is that of the burning of Rushdie's book; it is the contemporary equivalent of the nineteenth-century charge. This time Muslims, once again convinced that they were protesting against an attack on their beliefs, shouted "Allah-u-Akbar," brandished matches endorsed by elders, and marched toward the waiting media. Once again the most advanced Western technology met Muslim faith; once again it was a massacre, this time of the Muslim image in the West. We witness again two mutually uncomprehending systems collide: monumental contempt and arrogance on one side, blind faith and fury on the other.

Muslim Anguish

It is the nature of this complex historical encounter, exacerbated by each incident, that feeds into the Muslim incapacity to respond coolly and meaningfully. Muslims being killed on the West Bank or in Kashmir, their mosques being threatened with demolition in Jerusalem or in Ayodhya, India, are seen throughout the Muslim world on television and cause instant dismay and anger. The threat to the mosques has deep resonances in Muslim history. The one in Jerusalem is named after Umar, one of the greatest Muslims and rulers after the Prophet, and the one in India after Babar, the founder of the Mughal dynasty. One is over a millennium in age, the other almost half a millennium.

It is a milieu of distrust and violence within which Muslims see their lives enmeshed. The recent killings of Muslims by Muslims across the world — a vice chancellor in Kashmir, an Imam in Belgium, an aged writer in Turkey — is one response. It demonstrates the attempt to force greater commitment on the community, to push people off the fence, to obliterate the moderate and reasonable position; it also demonstrates desperation.

Muslims throughout the world cite examples of gross injustice, particularly where they live as a minority in non-Muslim countries. This group forms a large percentage of the total number of Muslims in the world today. Their problems in non-Muslim countries stem as much from their powerlessness as from the shortsightedness of those dealing with them. Repeated shootings and killings have led to desperation among Muslims. The state appears to have few answers besides the bullet and the baton. Lord Acton would have sneered; repression tends to corrupt, and absolute repression corrupts absolutely.

However, Muslims themselves are not blameless. Muslim leaders are failing in the need to feed and clothe the poor. The greatest emphasis in Islam is given to the less privileged. This, alas, remains a neglected area of attention as leaders prefer to fulminate against their opponents.

Muslim leaders are also failing in another crucial area. Those Muslims living in the West and complaining about racism would do well to turn their gaze on their own societies. Pakistanis have been killing Pakistanis on the basis of race, in the most brutal manner possible, for years in Sind province; political messages are carved into the buttocks of ethnic opponents. Kurds have been gassed and bombed in Iraq by fellow Muslims for decades. The sordid and all but forgotten matter of the future of almost half a million Biharis living in the most wretched camps in the Dhaka remains unresolved. The Biharis, demoted to the status of alien creatures, maintain they are legitimate citizens of Pakistan. Their sin was the belief in an Islamic, united Pakistan. After 1971, in Bangladesh, they were seen as a fifth column. Islamic Pakistan is reluctant to allow residence to these Muslims — its legitimate citizens — and Islamic Bangladesh is equally reluctant to own them, so their lives remain suspended in the squalor and filth of the refugee camps. The concept of *ummah* (the Muslim brotherhood) is an excellent one; but it remains inchoate and needs to be pursued with more vigor than that presently exhibited by Muslims.

In this period, many Muslim leaders and heads of government across the Muslim world have met a violent end by shooting (Sadat, Faisal, Mujib, and, starting with Daud, too many to name in Afghanistan). They have been hanged (Bhutto), or even blown up in the air (Zia). What Muslims have done to their leaders is more than matched by what the leaders did to their Muslim followers. Nightmare images are seared in the mind. State power — the army and police — has been responsible for the massacre of innocent country-folk, and even entire towns in Syria, in East Pakistan (now Bangladesh), in Iraq, and in Iran.

Furthermore, large proportions of the unprecedented wealth from oil revenues have been squandered on an unprecedented scale, in an unprecedented style. Call girls in London and casinos in the south of France, ranches in the United States and chalets in Switzerland diverted money that could have gone into health-care provision, education, and the closing of the vast gaps between the rich and poor. In Islamic countries, oil money created an arrogance among some Muslims who cherished a sense of special destiny around their family or clan. These antics provided legitimate ammunition for the Western satirists wishing to lampoon Muslims; they became the caricature of a civilization. Ordinary Muslims, therefore, have good cause to complain.

Also in need of pursuit is the notion of a just and stable state. Contemplating the prospects for the twenty-first century, some Middle East experts conclude that the lack of "a civil society" is the great bane of the Muslims. Repression and stagnation — in spite of a certain record of durability in some states — mark their society. Lawyers and journalists are unable to work freely, and businessmen operate in an economy that may be labeled "socialist" or "capitalist" but, in either case, is controlled by the state. Nevertheless, the picture is not entirely pessimistic. As has been noted by British scholars, Egypt has developed and maintained elements of a civil society and separation of powers within the state in spite of its long tradition of authoritarianism— from the Pharaohs, through Muhammad Ali and Cromer, to Nasser and Sadat.

The Muslim Response

The main Muslim responses appear to be chauvinism and withdrawal; this is both dangerous and doomed. The self-imposed isolation, the deliberate retreat, is culturally determined. It is not Islamic in spirit or content. Muslims who are isolated and self-centered sense triumph in their aggressive assertion of faith. They imagine that passionate faith is exclusive to them. Yet a similar religious wave exists also in Christianity, Hinduism, and Buddhism. Preferring to ignore this, Muslims will point out that the Western world is intimidated by them, and fears their zeal. That Rushdie was driven underground is cited as one proof of this. It seems that Muslim spokesmen are in danger of being intoxicated by the exuberance of their own verbosity.

Because orthodox Muslims claim that Islam is an all-pervasive, all-embracing system, this affects the way in which Muslim writers and academics think. The increasing stridency in their tone is thus linked to the larger Muslim sense of anger and powerlessness. They advocate confrontation and violence, an eye for an eye, a tooth for a tooth; this attitude confirms the stereotypes of Muslims in the West. They argue that moderation has failed and that extremism will draw attention to their problems. Perhaps in the atmosphere of violence and blind hatred, of injustice and inequality, they have a certain logic in their position. At least they will be heard. They will force Muslim problems onto the agenda where more sober voices have failed, and because we live in an interconnected world, no country can isolate itself from — or immunize itself against — Muslim wrath. Nevertheless, violence and cruelty are not in the spirit of the Qur'an, nor are they found in the life of the Prophet, nor in the lives of saintly Muslims.

Locating the Essence of Islam

The Muslim voices of learning and balance — whether in politics or among academics — are being drowned by those advocating violence and hatred. Two vital questions arise with wide-ranging, short- and long-term implications: In the short term, has one of the world's greatest civilizations lost its ability to deal with problems except through violent force? In the long term, would Muslims replace the central Qur'anic concepts of *adl* and *ahsan* (balance and compassion), of *ilm* (knowledge), and *sabr* (patience), with the bullet and the bomb?

Islam is a religion of equilibrium and tolerance, suggesting an encouraging breadth of vision, global positions, and the fulfillment of human destiny in the universe. Balance is essential to Islam, and never more so than in society, and the crucial balance is between *din* (religion) and *dunya* (world); it is a balance, not a separation, between the two. The Muslim lives in the now, in the real world, but within the frame of his religion, with a mind to the future afterlife. So, whether he is a businessman, an academic, or a politician, he must not forget the moral laws of Islam. In the postmodern world, *dunya* is upsetting the balance, invading and appropriating *din*.

Yet the non-Muslim media, by their consistently hammerheaded onslaught, have succeeded in portraying a negative image of it. They may even succeed in changing Muslim character. Muslims, because of their gut response to the attack — both vehement and vitriolic — are failing to maintain the essential features of Islam. Muslim leaders have pushed themselves into a hole dug by themselves in viewing the present upsurge simplistically as a confrontation with the West. They are in danger of rejecting features central to Islam — such as love of knowledge, egalitarianism, tolerance — because they are visibly associated with the West. In locating anti-Islamic animosity firmly in the West, they also implicitly reject the universalism of human nature.

But Allah is everywhere. The universal nature of humanity is the main topos in the Qur'an. God's purview and compassion take in everyone, "all creatures." The world is not divided into an East and a West: "To Allah belong the East and West: whithersoever Ye turn, there is Allah's countenance" (Surah 2:115). Again and again God points to the wonders of creation, the diversity of races and languages in the world. Such a God cannot be parochial or xenophobic. Neither can a religion that acknowledges the wisdom and piety of over 124,000 "prophets" in its folklore be isolationist or intolerant. With its references to the "heavens" above, the Qur'an encourages us to lift up our heads and look beyond our planet, to the stars.

The divine presence is all around; it can be glimpsed in the eyes of a mother beholding her infant, the rising of the sun, a bird in flight, the first flowers of spring. The wonders and mystery of creation cannot be the monopoly of any one people. The Sufis — like Iqbal — see God everywhere, even among the godless, not only in the mosque. In their desire for knowledge, compassion, and cleanliness, many non-Muslims possess ideal Muslim virtues. We note goodness and humanity in people like Mother Teresa, Mandela, and Havel. Islam has always shown the capacity to emerge in unexpected places and in unexpected times. The true understanding of Islam will therefore be critical in the coming years — and not only for Muslims.

What Can Islam Give
to the Global Civilization?

On the threshold of the twenty-first century, what can Islamic civilization contribute to the world? The answer is a great deal. Its notion of a balance between *din* (religion), and *dunya* (the world), is a worthy one. It can provide a corrective and a check to the materialism that characterizes much of contemporary civilization, offering instead compassion, piety, and a sense of humility. The philoprogenitivity of Muslims is a social fact. The qualities mentioned above underline the moral content of human existence; they suggest security and stability in family life, in marriage, and in care for the aged. Recent signs in Western societies indicate that perhaps the time is ripe to readmit care and compassion into human relations; here too, postmodernist sensibilities can help.

In its abjuration of materialism, Sufism provides a balance to the dominant values of Western civilization, although many see the impact of Sufism as limited in our world. Especially in the Sufistic message of *sulh-i-kul* (peace with all), Islam has a positive message of peace and brotherhood to preach. This message is irrespective of color or creed, and has stood the test of time. Not surprisingly, Sufistic Islam has made significant inroads in the West, especially among European converts.

Islam places knowledge at the highest level of human endeavor. Repeatedly the Qur'an and the sayings of the Prophet urge the acquisition of knowledge. Indeed, the word knowledge (*ilm*), is the most used after the name of God in the Qur'an. The Prophet urged his followers to "seek knowledge, even unto China." Human beings are asked in the Qur'an to think of and marvel at the variety confronting them: "And among His signs is the creation of the heavens and the earth, and the variations in your languages and your colors" (Surah 30:22).

Change and reinterpretation are embedded in Islamic history and text. The following discourse between the Prophet and Muadh ibn Jabal, a judge, on his way to the Yemen clearly indicates the principle:

Prophet: How will you decide a problem?

Muadh: According to the Qur'an.

Prophet: If it is not in it?

Muadh: According to the *sunna* [Islamic custom].

Prophet: If it is not in that either?

Muadh: Then I will use my own reasoning.

The Islamic principles that encourage flexibility and rational choice are reflected in the exchange: *ijtihad* (independent judgment), *shura* (consultation), and *ijma* (consensus). Clearly, rationality and man's own judgment play a part in arriving at decisions.

You Can't Flee CNN

The Muslim response to postmodernism, unfortunately, is the same as it was a century ago: retreat accompanied by passionate expressions of faith and anger. From the Sanusi in North Africa to the Mahdi in Sudan to the Akhund in Swat, Muslims appeared to challenge the European imperialist and, under fire, disappeared back into the vastness of their deserts and mountains. In the mountains and deserts was escape from the colonial European; there lay the strength of tradition, the integrity of custom, and the promise of renewal. For the European, the Muslim, in the vastness of his mountains and deserts, had secured a place out of his reach, free from his rules and administrators; the Muslim reverted to the past as if the present did not exist.

But there is one significant difference today. Whereas a century ago Muslims could retreat so as to maintain the integrity of their lives, their areas are now penetrated, and technological advances have made escape impossible: the satellite in the sky can follow any camel across any Arabian desert, the laser-guided missile can land in any home in any remote Afghan mountain valley, and the VCR is available in the desert tent as well as the mountain village.

The Muslim tribesman has always possessed a shrewd eye for strategy — more so than his compatriot in the city. He was quick to identify the media as a source of potential disruption to traditional life. Consequently, until a few years ago, a radio, as a symbol of modernity, was ritually shot to pieces in Tirah, deep in the inaccessible Tribal Areas of Pakistan. The rejection was a clear message for the young with ideas of change in their minds.

Today, however, the media cannot be stopped; they can penetrate the most remote home, and no place could be more remote than Makran, in the Baluchistan Province of Pakistan. Makran is one of the most isolated and inaccessible parts of the Muslim world. It is a vast, sparsely populated area and still without electricity, and therefore, television. No highways or railways connect it to the rest of the country. There are only a few miles of blacktop road in the main town. The rest are dirt tracks that shift with the sands. Little has changed in Makran since Alexander, returning from his Indus adventure, got lost there.

Even Islam is twisted according to local tradition and clouded in ignorance: the Zikris, an autochthonic sect, possess their own Makkah, Arafat, *haj*, Kaaba, and prophet. Their physical isolation allows them to escape the wrath of the orthodox in Pakistan. Yet the latest foreign films are freely available through the miracle of diesel-powered generators and the VCR, which are among the first possessions of those who can afford them; these were commonly owned in the most distant villages, which I visited as Commissioner of Makran in 1985. What impact contemporary values are making on these societies that are centuries old has not yet been studied. We are left with conjecture, with stories of tension and clash in society. In Makran, traditional values are coeval with the most up-to-date ones; Alexander's age runs parallel to the post-McLuhan era.

Similarly penetrated is the secure, comfortable, and timeless Muslim middle-class urban life as depicted so well by Naguib Mahfouz, for instance, in his 1990 novel, *Palace Walk*. His story is set in Cairo, but it could be Marrakesh in the extreme west of the Muslim world, or Kuala Lumpur in the extreme east. The frequent references in conversation to the Qur'an, the underlying class and color prejudices, the simmering sexual and political tensions, are authentic. But this cocooned, privileged timelessness is now shattered; it is irretrievably lost with the invasion of the Western media. By the late 1980s, CNN and the BBC, the Western media's stormtroopers, were preparing to broadcast directly, via satellite, to the Muslim world. Neither Cairo nor Marrakesh nor Kuala Lumpur is inviolate.

The age of the media in Muslim society has dawned. Muslims need to face up to the fact that there is no escape now, no retreat, no hiding place, from the demon.

The postmodernist age in the 1990s hammers at the doors of Muslim *ijtihad*, or reasoned innovation within the faith. Muslims ignore the din at their peril. Before they creak open the doors, however, they must know the power and nature of the age, and for that they must understand those who represent it. These include figures they do not admire, like the singer Madonna and the writer Salman Rushdie. More important, Muslims must understand why these figures represent the age. The onslaught comes when Muslims are at their weakest; corrupt rulers, incompetent administrators, and feeble thinkers mark their societies. For all the rhetoric and symbolic form, the spirit of Islam is often palpably missing from their endeavors, while, more than ever, *ijtihad* is urgently needed where women, education, and politics are involved. The old methods and the old certainties will not hold the forces swirling and eddying around Muslim societies; there can be no evolution of Muslim society without a comprehension of the non-Muslim age we live in.

Another Muslim ponders on *ijtihad*. The fate of the Muslims in Spain makes the Aga Khan thoughtful. He talks of the loss of vigor, the drying-up of initiative, the emphasis on empty dogma as causes of the Muslim downfall. The Aga Khan sees parallels in our times:

> Those who wish to introduce the concept that you can only practice your faith as it was practiced hundreds of years ago are introducing a time dimension which is not a practice of our faith. Therefore what we have to be doing, I think, is to

be asking as Muslims how do we apply the ethics of our faith today? This is a matter for Muslims to think about and it is a very delicate issue whether it is in science, in medicine, in economics.

In our postmodern age, rigid boundaries are no longer easy to maintain. A person can, and does, possess overlapping identities. He can be both a devout Muslim and a loyal citizen of Britain. Multiple identities mean eclecticism, which requires tolerance of others. In such a world, the confrontation between Islam and the West poses terrible dilemmas for both.

The test for Muslims is how to preserve the essence of the Qur'anic message, of *adl* and *ahsan, ilm* and *sabr*, without it being reduced to an ancient and empty chant in our times, and how to participate in the global civilization without their identities being obliterated.

It is an apocalyptic test: the most severe examination. Muslims stand at the crossroads. If they take one route they can harness their vitality and commitment in order to fulfill their destiny on the world stage. If they take the other they can dissipate their energy through internecine strife and petty bickering. The choice is between harmony and hope versus disunity and disorder.

The challenge for those in the West is how to expand the Western idealistic notions of justice, equality, freedom, and liberty beyond their borders to all humanity without appearing like nineteenth-century imperialists, to reach out to those not of their civilization in friendship and sincerity.

The logic of this argument demands that the West use its great power — which includes the media — to assist in solving some of the long-festering problems, most urgently of the Palestinians and the Kashmiris, that plague Muslim society. There is the need to push unwilling rulers who subsist on Western arms and aid toward conceding democracy and a fairer distribution of wealth, and of ensuring the rights and dignity of women and children, the less privileged, and those in the minority. The problems are interwoven, binding Muslims and non-Muslims together. There can be no viable world order if these wrongs are not redressed.

Into the predicament postmodernism has plunged us all, there is also promise. Such a conclusion might appear illogically optimistic, but it is understandable in the context of the Islamic vision, which is rooted firmly in history and belief. That vision has much to offer a world saturated with disintegration, cynicism, and loss of faith.

However, regaining integrity and overcoming cynicism will only be possible if there is a universal tolerance of others among Muslims and non-Muslims alike placed at the top of the agenda in preparation for the next millennium, embraced both as personal philosophy and national foreign policy. This, too, is the largesse of postmodernism.

Weak Ramparts of the Permissive West

Zbigniew Brzezinski

National security adviser to President Jimmy Carter,
Zbigniew Brzezinski warns in his most recent book, Out of
Control *(1993), that the "permissive cornucopia" of*
American culture undermines the ability of the United
States to play a leadership role in the post–Cold War era.
NPQ *Editor Nathan Gardels spoke with him in*
Washington.

NPQ

You have said that the key issues of world affairs in this time after the Cold War are more philosophical and cultural than ideological or national. Does that mean the traditional geopolitical way we have looked at international relations — balances of power among nations or blocs — is being supplanted by a geocultural set of conflicts, by a "clash of civilizations?"

Zbigniew Brzezinski

The world has become much more intimate. Yet, at the same time, the issues that infuse passion into politics have become more differentiated. In the advanced world, the old conflicts of public life that involved national frontiers or competing ideological systems are giving way to issues pertaining more to definitions of the "good life," and even, ultimately, to questions about the scope of the "human authenticity" of the individual.

Take, for example, our own society. Matters that evoke the greatest passion are matters that pertain to the definition of when life begins or when life should end, and who has the right, in either case, to make that choice. Issues such as abortion, euthanasia, and, increasingly, self-alteration (everything from plastic surgery to genetic engineering), are becoming central. In a way, the paramount issues today are more about the boundaries of the person than about the boundaries of nation-states.

Inevitably, there are, and will be, conflicts as we cope with these philosophical challenges, not only within societies but between different cultures, linked as they are by trade, travel, and communications.

NPQ

Isn't there already geocultural conflict? Neither the Islamic cultures, which call for submission of the individual, nor Confucian cultures, which call for "hammering down all nails" and loyalty to authority—"soft authoritarianism" — are commensurable with Western liberalism's ethos of individual liberation.

Brzezinski

Even human rights cannot any longer be defined purely in political terms, as they were when the world was still largely dominated by the challenge of totalitarianism.

The substantive discussion of human rights itself already involves the complex question of how one defines the meaning of the "good life." Today that definition necessarily involves "soft" issues like the overall quality of life, which cannot be limited to either the political or to the material dimensions alone. The definition of the "good life" should deal with deeper commitments of virtue, moral order, and spiritual belief.

NPQ

These fresh philosophical issues about the human condition come to the fore even as the old issues of the second half of the twentieth century have still not been resolved.

Referring to the pressure put on China to improve the human rights situation after the Tiananmen massacre, Deng Xiaoping says, "There is a new Cold War going on between America and China." Malaysian Prime Minister Mohammed Mahathir objects outright to what he calls the "human rights imperialism" of the West.

Brzezinski

Some of that conflict is still a residue of the older era in which the political definition of human rights was part and parcel of the ideological conflict.

As important as that may be, I am convinced that in the West we are moving beyond such conventional disputes to the much more complex question of what really is the human being, and thus what really defines the scope of human rights.

Here we do have to address the kind of questions I have already raised: Who has the right to end a life, whether in the womb or in the hospital bed? A mother, a priest, a doctor, the state, or the church? What about genetic self-alteration? Who has the right to enjoy the benefits of it, and who does not? Who has the right to determine its scope and its limits? A scientist or a theologian? These are the new dimensions of human rights.

NPQ

One can already imagine the coming cultural conflicts. Messing around with the genetic integrity of a person is one thing in the Judeo-Christian West, where the individual is viewed as a discrete entity that ends in the finality of death.

But how will genetic self-alteration be viewed in Japan, where Shinto belief holds that the soul is immortal, cyclically recurring in life from ancestors to descendants?

For all intents and purposes, America's two-hundred-year-old multiracial society already approaches Jose Vasconcellos's idea of "*la raza cosmica*." But the Japanese imperial family traces its continuous genetic lineage back 2,600 years!

Brzezinski

I think we can see in these examples that we will soon feel nostalgia for how comparatively straightforward our moral dilemmas were during the middle part of the twentieth century.

NPQ

On Islam, you have said the global political awakening that erupted after the fall of communism "is taking place in a philosophical context largely bereft of any deeper commitments — apart from Islam." The rest of the global political scene, you say, is "dominated by rhetoric and values that are primarily consumption-oriented and stress personal self-gratification."

From only a slightly different angle, Octavio Paz has made the same observation: "Without the reconciliation of faith with science in Islam," the Mexican poet says, "there will be great conflict with the vast relativist civilization that now stretches through most of Asia, across the Americas and Europe."

Given the materialist and value relativist outlook of the West, are we headed for a civilizational conflict with Islam?

Brzezinski

I think we have to be very careful not to adopt a position that Islam is automatically our enemy or that Islam is automatically against human rights as politically defined.

If one looks at human rights in the broader sense we are beginning to define, one can also make the case that a deeply religious society in which Islamic moral precepts are respected is ultimately a society that also respects the "humanness" of the person as a whole being, not just a political or economic subject.

Certainly, militant Islamic actions, like the condemnation of Salman Rushdie, cannot be accommodated. But it would be a self-fulfilling prophecy to castigate Islam generally and try to impose on it our purely political definition of human rights, while at the same time, in the cultural domain, propagate a kind of material hedonism which, in the final analysis, is much more detrimental to the spiritual dimension of the human being.

NPQ

That is precisely why a clash seems inevitable, and not just with militant edges of Islam. In a world that is linked by commerce and telecommunications, pious societies are necessarily on a collision course with the radical impiety of the modern West, especially as their belief system inherently challenges the materialist underpinnings of secular liberalism.

Brzezinski

I don't think Western secularism in its present shape is the best standard-bearer for human rights. It is essentially a cultural wave in which hedonism, self-gratification, and consumption are the essential definitions of the meaning of the "good life." The human condition is about more than that. The defense of the political individual doesn't mean a whole lot in such a spiritual and moral vacuum.

The out-of-control secularism of much of the West contains within it the seeds of cultural self-destruction. That is why I am worried that the underpinnings of American superpower status are somewhat fragile.

A culture of permissive cornucopia in America is inimical to the transformation of American power into any kind of globally respected moral authority, because it makes efforts to promote the superiority of liberalism worldwide look hypocritical and empty.

NPQ

No doubt this weakness of the West explains the increasing appeal of Islam in destitute places like Sudan where the economic gap with the West just can't be closed. Perhaps some kind of spiritually reinforced subsistence will emerge as an alternative to an American-led world order in places like Africa?

Brzezinski

What worries me most is not that we may not be able to provide a satisfactory answer to the cravings of politically awakened peoples now turning, for example, to a more militant Islam. What worries me most is that our own cultural self-corruption may undercut America's capacity to sustain not just its position in the world as a political leader, but eventually even as a systemic model for others.

NPQ

The potential surely exists for geocultural conflict between the liberal West — in both its strengths and weaknesses — on the one hand, and the soft-authoritarian societies of East Asia and militant Islam on the other.

Is there cause for concern that such cultural conflicts may one day take on a military dimension? I'm thinking here of the sale of missiles, and possibly nuclear components, by China to Iran.

Harvard political scientist Samuel Huntington, who postulates a coming "clash of civilizations," notes this Confucian-Islamic connection as a challenge to the West.

Brzezinski

One has to consider the possibility of China, leading an alliance that includes Iran and Russia, posing a challenge to the existing hierarchy of global power led by the United States.

That challenge would be only in part geopolitical. It would also be very much a cultural challenge and a socioeconomic challenge. China might well conceive its emergent role as the articulator of a "third way," that is, rejecting the old communist command style, but also rejecting the laissez-faire economics and political liberalism of the West.

At the same time, it might want to project an alternative cultural-philosophical model in which Western-style hedonism and materialism are resisted and constrained.

Such an alliance would stand astride a vast whirlpool of violence that stretches in an oblong shape across the map of Central Asia. It extends from east to west, from the Adriatic Sea next to the Balkans all the way to the border of China at Sinkiang province; from south to north it loops around the Persian Gulf, embracing parts of the Middle East, then Iran, Pakistan, and Afghanistan in the south, all along the Russian-Kazakh frontier to the north, and all the way along the Russian-Ukrainian border.

There are close to thirty countries, most in the early stages of nation building, and almost four hundred million people in this area. Already, violence based on religious, tribal, and ethnic differences has broken out, and promises to intensify with ever greater ferocity.

Seized by political awakening and possessed with ethnic and religious fervor, this region is a geographical vortex of clashing civilizations. While on a global scale I do not think that Confucian or Islamic or Christian civilizations are cohesive enough to enter into conflict, I do believe that on this smaller scale, as we've seen in Yugoslavia, such clashes are very real indeed.

It is thus no coincidence that of all the states seeking, or that have already acquired, weapons of mass destruction, half of them are located within this Eurasian area. The Chinese weapons connection to this region is thus very worrying.

NPQ

The nuclear explosions at Hiroshima and Nagasaki introduced the era of Pax Americana. Is use of the bomb by warring tribes or religions in this Eurasian cauldron the likely event that will finally break us epistemically from the past order and decisively introduce the era of pandemonium?

Brzezinski

That's right. I think this region is where we are likely to see the next use of nuclear weapons.

NPQ

This postmodern political awakening of arming tribes raises the question of just how enduring are the universal claims of such Western values as the freedom of the individual or separation of temporal and spiritual authority. In many ways, liberalism has the same problem marxism did. Marxism had no political theory about how different parts of society would relate to each other under communism because it assumed a universal class that would one day be triumphant and eliminate all conflicts.

Similarly, liberalism has assumed the universality of its values, and thus has no political theory about how incommensurable civilizations can coexist in a new world order. Don't we need such rules of engagement now as pandemonium descends on the post–Cold War world? Do we attempt to impose these values, for example, through "the right to interfere" as the former French minister for humanitarian affairs has proposed?

Brzezinski

I don't think we can do it. The West has neither the force nor the public will to do so. That would entail sacrifices that are out of the question in today's comfortable consumer societies.

However, this reality is in conflict with the universalist predisposition of liberalism. Its precepts are assumed to be inherently universally valid. Obviously there is a conflict between that implication and the restraints of reality.

Moreover, at this stage, I think we have to recognize that just as marxism made a false claim to universality — because it reflected a particular phase in history and was deeply conditioned by European experience — so too liberalism as a philosophy may be limited in terms of historical time and its European origin. Its universal validity is today in question.

The great success of the societies of East Asia certainly puts a large question mark on the universal claims of the Western liberal model. Though nominally considered to be liberal democracies, they are in fact, with their deep Confucian influences, something systemically quite different.

NPQ

Takeshi Umehara, the Japanese philosopher, has similarly argued that the failure of marxism, a side current of modernity, was only the precursor to the collapse of liberalism, modernity's main current. Both, Umehara says, invited failure because they excommunicated spiritual life from their secular societies. Do you agree?

Brzezinski

I would put it this way: the collapse of marxism revealed the global limitations of liberalism. Liberalism was viewed as universal in part because marxism had universalist pretensions that threatened the human condition. In response, liberalism was posited as the universal alternative as part of that contest.

Now that the contest is over and marxism is dead, it is no longer dangerous nor politically costly to acknowledge the limitations of liberalism. We're entering that phase now. Absent the danger of totalitarian utopia, it is easier to see the dangers of permissive cornucopia for our liberal societies. But the shakedown process is likely to be prolonged, painful, and difficult.

NPQ

Isn't the "permissive cornucopia" undermining our society the ethos that emerges inexorably from a procedural republic embedded in a consumer culture?

In such a society, the concept of "negative liberty" protects the values of all with equal indifference, leaving no positive guides for behavior, be it traditional religion or natural law.

Brzezinski

Maybe. That certainly is the case today, with a large role being played by mass communications, particularly television, which has replaced the family, the school, and the church — in that order — as the principal instruments for socialization and transmission of values. In replacing these three previously decisive institutions of value transferral and continuity, television has been driven by its equivalent of Gresham's law: bad programming pushes out good programming since the broadest common appeal is not to the noblest in man, but to his lowest prurient interests and morbid fears and anxieties. Television has thus become an instrument for the dissemination of corruptive, demoralizing, and destructive values.

Precisely the values that have been considered throughout civilized history by all societies and all religions to be destructive and disintegrative — greed, debauchery, violence, unlimited self-gratification, absence of moral restraint — are the daily fare glamorously dished up to our children.

If that reality does not alarm us, the soul of the leading nation of the world order has already rotted beyond repair.

NPQ

Western liberalism is thus a weak rampart against the passions of ethnic cleansing and religious fundamentalism or the challenge of proto-authoritarian Confucian prosperity. . . .

Brzezinski

Absolutely. This self-indulgent, hedonistic, consumption-oriented society cannot project a moral imperative onto the world.

NPQ

Such morally flabby indifference can't stand up to multiculturalism in the university any more than it could stand up to ethnic cleansing in Bosnia.

Brzezinski

Exactly. And for the same reason: our moral consciousness has been corrupted by consumerism and the equal indifference we assign to all values as if they were competing products on the supermarket shelf.

NPQ

The policy paralysis we have witnessed in Washington and Europe over Bosnia in some way reveals the paralysis of the Western soul, the fatigue of its moral vigor.

Brzezinski

It shows that there are no moral imperatives guiding the conduct of the West, and that slogans are essentially rituals of self-congratulation.

Since the end of World War II, the slogan "never again" has been invoked as a call to resistance against another holocaust.

But what does "never again" mean operationally today? It means opening museums and watching genocidal slaughter on television.

Even in saluting the memory of the Jewish holocaust we are essentially engaging in an act of hypocrisy that is self-gratifying. We are elevating ourselves morally over those who failed to act in the 1940s, but in so doing we self-righteously ignore our own inaction now. What else is self-deceptive hypocrisy if not this?

NPQ

Is it going too far to say that marxism collapsed because the Soviet Union failed and that liberalism may collapse because the permissive cornucopia of America triumphed?

Brzezinski

Marxism died because it was irrelevant to the needs of people, it was wrong, and it was, in practice, criminal. Permissive cornucopia is infecting triumphant liberalism with a potentially fatal disease that can still be resisted.

Permissive cornucopia does not yet define the essence of America, though the dangerous trends we have discussed are leading in that direction.

If permissive cornucopia in fact becomes the defining reality of America, then I don't think liberalism or American authority will be sustainable on a global scale.

NPQ

Poets like Octavio Paz and Czeslaw Milosz have long warned that the nihilism and value indifference of the West are every bit as deadly as totalitarianism. Both extinguish the soul. . . .

Brzezinski

Yes, but I would not equate the two. If liberalism becomes defined by permissive cornucopia, it will produce a kind of corrupt asphyxiation of the soul, whereas totalitarianism brutally kills it and stomps on it.

NPQ

How then does a liberal society arm itself against the morally corrosive inroads of permissive cornucopia?

Brzezinski

The place to start for America (as well as the liberal societies of Western Europe) is the development of moral consciousness: to

become more aware of the desirability and utility of moral imperatives, and through that to adopt an ethos of self-restraint instead of
self-indulgence.

If we fail to do so, we will not have any operational criteria for
defining what is right or wrong and thereby will slide into self-
destruction.

Of course, these moral criteria can't just be invented. They are
inherent in the values of which we partake traditionally in the three
great religions — Christianity, Judaism, and Islam. All contain certain precepts that a secular society can also adopt — certain notions
that right and wrong should be internalized in instinctive feelings;
that there is such a thing as an absolute right and absolute wrong;
that everything cannot be relativized. . . .

NPQ

The dilemma for liberal societies is how to do this when the political structure of the state guarantees the relativism of all values
through constitutional protections.

Brzezinski

It was possible when the traditional socializing institutions — the
family, the school, and the church — were fully intact. They provided a moral grounding, a counterbalance to the indulgent propaganda of the mass media. As the traditional institutions weakened,
the culturally subversive media strengthened, leaving the neutral
state as a legal referee, not a moral one.

There are signs that the need for self-restraint is of necessity reemerging to contain indulgent consumerism. The ecology movement is probably the most important example here that resists the
reigning mindset that more of everything is inherently considered a
good thing.

In the end, we need to restore the self-conscious transmittal of
absolute values in our society through the primary institutions of
socialization. The order of influence on society of those institutions

ought to be family, school, church — and then mass media, not the other way around.

In other words, we need to rebalance our lives to cope with the global crisis of the spirit. It is time to recognize that the spiritual dimension of life is as important as the material. In the twentieth century, we have already seen that "never again" too easily can become reality once again. If humanity is to reassert command over its destiny in a contingent world, moral imperatives have to be central.

Civilizations at Odds

Samuel P. Huntington

One of America's leading foreign policy intellectuals, Samuel Huntington served at the White House under President Carter as coordinator of security and planning for the National Security Council. He now heads the Olin Institute for Strategic Studies at Harvard University.

Huntington is author of the seminal book Political Order in Changing Societies *(1968) and, most recently,* The Third Wave: Democratization in the Late Twentieth Century *(1991). He spoke with* NPQ *Editor Nathan Gardels in the summer of 1993.*

NPQ

First Francis Fukuyama declared an "end to history." Now, important foreign policy intellectuals in the United States who became prominent during the Cold War, such as yourself and Zbigniew Brzezinski, are declaring an end to modern geopolitical conflict.

Brzezinski says that international issues now are primarily cultural and philosophical. You similarly argue that geocultural friction — the clash of civilizations — will be the dominant source of international conflict in our future.

Samuel P. Huntington

Let me first of all emphasize that I am elaborating a plausible hypothesis about the likely course of world affairs, not making an absolute prediction. But there is plenty of reason to expect that the fault lines between civilizations — for example between the West on one hand and the Confucian societies of East Asia and the Muslim world on the other — will be the battle lines of the future.

Such civilizational conflicts are the latest phase in the evolution of conflict in the modern world. The conflicts within the modern international system that emerged with the Peace of Westphalia in 1648 were first among princes, then among nation-states and, in this century, among ideologies. These conflicts, including the long Cold War between liberal democracy and Marxism-Leninism, have been aptly described as "Western civil wars."

Now that the Cold War has ended, international politics is moving out of its Western phase. From now on, the core of global politics will be the interaction between the West and non-Western cultures.

These fault lines of future conflict can be seen clearly in Eurasia. As the ideological division of Europe has disappeared, the cultural division of Europe among western Christianity, Orthodox Christianity, and Islam has reemerged. Today the most significant dividing line in Europe may be that identified by the British scholar William Wallace — the eastern boundary of Western Christianity in the year 1500.

The prospering Protestants and Catholics on one side of that line share a common history running from feudalism to the Renaissance and the Reformation to the Enlightenment, the French Revolution, and the Industrial Revolution. On the other side of that line the economically less advanced Orthodox and Muslim peoples belonged to the Ottoman and Tsarist empires. They were barely touched by the modernizing experiences to their west in Europe.

Though Western mass culture can be spotted across most of the earth's surface, Western concepts of individualism, liberalism, human rights, equality, liberty, law, democracy, free markets, and separation of church and state differ fundamentally from those prevalent elsewhere in Islamic, Confucian, Hindu, or Buddhist cultures.

The propagation of Western values as "universal" helps stimulate reactions such as the religious fundamentalism taking hold in many Islamic societies. And reacting to human rights pressure from the West after the Tiananmen showdown, Deng Xiaoping warned of a "new Cold War" with America. It is not difficult here to see the emergence of a dynamic of conflict that pits, in the words of Kishore Mahbubani, "the West against the rest."

NPQ

The Japanese management guru Kenichi Ohmae has argued the opposite: rather than breaking up, the world will integrate where it can into a global consumer marketplace. In the end, he says "people want Sony not soil" — meaning they prefer consumer goods over indigenous culture.

What in your view reinforces the tendency of cultural conflict over the desire for harmonious consumerism?

Huntington

People want both Sonys and soil. They want the benefits of modernity and the identity provided by their own culture and values. There are several reasons why civilizational conflict is a probable future.

To start with, civilizations have different views on the relations between God and man, the individual and the group, the citizen and the state, parents and child, husband and wife, liberty and authority, rights and responsibilities, equality and hierarchy.

The increasing contact between cultures brought about by the media and travel has intensified consciousness of the awareness of differences between civilizations as well as commonalities within civilizations. The economic modernization and social change driving and accompanying this growing contact between cultures have separated people from their traditional local identities, weakening the state as the primary source of that identity in the postcolonial era. Religion and a return to roots have moved to fill in the gap in most places.

In Japan one hears talk about "re-Asianization." Nehru's multicultural secularism threatens to be supplanted by the fervor of "Hinduization" of India. The failure of Arab nationalism and socialism fuels the burgeoning movement for "re-Islamization" in the Middle East.

Significantly in all of these places, just as the masses are beginning to tune in to American television and videos, the elites are becoming "indigenized," reversing the pattern of the long colonial and postcolonial periods. To the extent people are becoming consumers, economic regionalism is gaining in East Asia, Europe, and North America. Successful economic regionalism will build on and reinforce civilizational consciousness.

NPQ

So Islam, Confucian authoritarianism, and ethnic fundamentalism are the challenges Western liberalism faces in this coming conflict of civilizations?

Huntington

Those are certainly the three central challenges, to which I would add a fourth: the decay of Western liberalism in the absence of a cohesive ideological challenge by a competing ideology, such as Marxism-Leninism. Fragmentation and multiculturalism are now eating away at the whole set of ideas and philosophies that have been the binding cement of American society. We have been able to manage tremendous diversity and ethnicity in the past because we accepted the basic political principles of the American Creed: liberty, equality, democracy, and individualism.

NPQ

Much focus has been given to the challenge militant Islam poses to the universal realization of Western liberal values. But the conflict with soft-authoritarian and communitarian East Asian cultures seems just as great. How will the world order reconcile the mythic emblem of the West, "the Lone Ranger," with the guiding ethos, for example, of "hammer down all nails," as they say in Japan?

Huntington

In recent months I have been to two conferences involving the discussion of human rights and democracy between Asians and Americans. The more militant Asians, of course, attack America for "human rights imperialism." But even among the most reasonable people there are significant differences.

For example, a very distinguished Singaporean said,

> Look, in Singapore a policeman has the right to ask any citizen to come in immediately for a urine test if he is suspected of using drugs. If he tests positive for drug use, that person is given compulsory treatment and rehabilitation. That would be unthinkable in America. But in Singapore, we accept it and value it as bringing order, security and cohesion to our society. Consequently, I can walk around the streets of Singapore anywhere, at any time, and be safe from assault. Name one American city in which I could do that?

NPQ

Even Francis Fukuyama admits that the soft-authoritarian regimes of those East Asian countries influenced by Confucian values are an alternative to Western liberalism at the "end of history." Lee Kuan Yew is the answer to Friedrich Hegel.

Huntington

Exactly, but Islam too offers an alternative. There is a continuity that has existed in Islam since its founding. It is a militant religion in which there is no distinction between what is religious and what is secular. The idea of "render unto Caesar what is Caesar's, render unto God what is God's" is totally antithetical to Islam. This theocratic proclivity makes it extraordinarily difficult for Islamic societies to accommodate non-Muslims. It makes it very difficult for Muslims to easily fit into societies where the majority is non-Muslim.

NPQ

The looming question is whether these civilizational conflicts will, so to speak, come to blows. You have spoken of an Islamic-Confucian connection in military terms.

Huntington

Yes, connection. I was very careful not to use the word "alliance" or anything meaning more than the connection for mutual convenience that is now present. One cannot know where it will lead in the future. For the moment it is a connection that clearly serves the purposes of China and North Korea on the one hand, and several Middle Eastern states on the other.

Significantly, Western countries, and Russia, are reducing their military power in the post–Cold War period while the Islamic, Confucian, Hindu, and Buddhist countries are increasing their military power.

At the moment, the conflict between the West and the Confucian-Islamic states focuses largely on nuclear, chemical, and biological weapons, ballistic missiles, and sophisticated guidance systems. While the West promotes nuclear nonproliferation as a universal norm, these nations assert their right to acquire and deploy whatever weapons they think necessary for their security.

China already has nuclear weapons; Pakistan has the capability to deploy them. North Korea, Iran, Iraq, Libya, and Algeria appear to be attempting to acquire them. A top Iranian official has declared that all Muslim states should acquire nuclear weapons, and in 1988 the president of Iran reportedly issued a directive calling for development of "offensive and defensive chemical, biological, and radiological weapons."

China's role is critical to the development of these counter-West military capabilities. It is at present strengthening its army. It is purchasing weapons from the former Soviet states; it is developing long-range missiles. China is also a major exporter of arms and weapons technology that can be used to manufacture nuclear weapons and missiles, especially to Libya and Iraq.

China has helped Algeria build a nuclear reactor suitable for nuclear weapons research and production; it has sold nuclear technology to Iran which American officials believe could only be used to create weapons. North Korea has had a nuclear weapons program and, ominously, has threatened off and on to withdraw from the nonproliferation treaty. It has sold advanced missiles and missile technology to Syria and Iran.

NPQ

This may not be an alliance or an active axis, but what nonetheless connects the arms suppliers of East Asia and their Islamic customers is philosophical opposition to Western liberalism.

Huntington

That is right.

NPQ

Does Western liberalism, which assumed its values to be universal, have a political theory of how to deal with these contending civilizations?

Huntington

The West has to try to defend itself, defend its values and maintain its position. We especially need to develop cooperative relations with what I call the "torn countries" in this conflict of civilizations — such as Russia — who have good economic and security reasons not to join any anti-West bloc. In Russia there are some, thankfully not in leadership positions just now, who want to turn away. They want Russia to once again become a Eurasian power, fulfilling its historic mission as the center of the Slavic Orthodox civilization. And there are those in Japan who want it to once again "look east."

Over the longer term, the West is going to have to learn how to adapt to a world in which, despite its current preponderance in economic and military power, the balance of power is shifting into the hands of others.

NPQ

What does "adapt" mean specifically? Let's take the case of the Islamic movement in Algeria that was prevented from taking power through elections by a military coup instigated by the secular government.

Officially, the U.S. has said that it does not support the idea of "one man, one vote, one time" in a place like Algeria, referring to the presumed suspension of the constitution if Islamic forces won the government.

Some have gone so far as to argue that the U.S. should not support elections in these countries, but only human rights. Elections would lead to majoritarian rule by those who might impose the theocratic *shari'a*.

Huntington

I don't agree with that line. The best way to protect human rights in the long run is to push a country toward democratization. I served in the National Security Council during the Carter presidency. We helped free thousands of political prisoners around the world, but we were rightly criticized by the incoming Reagan administration for only promoting human rights, not democracy. Inevitably, the human rights guarantees would not last; after a time, the authoritarian government would pick up the freed prisoners again, so we must promote democracy. Clearly there will be pitfalls and dangers to such a policy. You mentioned Algeria. My own view is that the military coup that prevented the Islamic Front from coming to power was most unfortunate. There are three arguments that come to mind that argue against this idea of preventative coups.

What would have happened in any case if that movement came to power? First, there is no assurance that a government that comes to power through an election is going to act the same way as a government that comes to power through a revolution, as in Iran, or in a coup d'état, as in the Sudan. Playing by the rules of the democratic game can moderate extremists.

Second, the new Algerian government would have wanted to maintain close relations with France, the European Union, and the U.S., and would remain as dependent upon trade and investment with those countries as it is now. That would further constrain its behavior.

Third, if the Islamic Front had won and imposed religious repression, the Algerian army would have remained and could have ousted them, just as the Chilean army did with Salvador Allende.

As a result of preventing the Islamic Front from coming to power by the rules of democracy, what do we have now? An organized militant movement aimed at overthrowing the government by force. We can be sure there will be no democracy and no human rights in Algeria under these conditions.

NPQ

Let's take an example from the Confucian side: China. The late Richard Nixon argued from the basis of economic determinism: only the development of a bourgeoisie as in Europe will ensure the endurance of human rights. Therefore, he argued, keep open trade relations, which is the engine of prosperity and the rise of a Chinese middle class.

Huntington

There is little doubt that if China has a substantial private sector — much of the economy is now in private hands — it will take a democratic direction over time. Without question, it would be counterproductive to take any action that diminished the growth of the private sector. At the same time, there ought to be ways to punish the government by imposing some penalties for violation of human rights.

NPQ

Bernard Kouchner, the French minister of humanitarian affairs under the last Socialist government, argues that the West should be more aggressive in this conflict of civilizations, taking upon itself the "right to interfere" to prevent the violation of human rights. He argues, for example, that if a woman in the Sudan asks for protection against a clitorectomy, the West should come to her aid.

Do you agree?

Huntington

Where there are sustained, gross violations of human rights, I agree. The U.N. sanctioned such intervention to help the Kurds, and in Somalia. But, for now, there is no general support for such a "right to interfere." But there is another type of intervention that I believe may be more acceptable, and with which I agree: the right of the global democratic community to prevent the reversion of what has become a democratic country to authoritarianism. It is a kind of "democratic Brezhnev doctrine."

In practice, such a democratic Brezhnev doctrine cannot, of course, be a hard and fast rule. What would happen, for example, if India were to become a Hindu authoritarian state? But such a policy does establish a clear goal for the U.S. and other powerful democratic nations: sustain democracy in countries where the people have adopted it.

The Shadow Our Future Throws

Ivan Illich

*Because of his groundbreaking critique of industrial soci-
ety well over a decade ago in such books as* Energy and
Equity, Medical Nemesis: The Expropriation of Health,
and Toward a History of Needs, *the philosopher Ivan
Illich is widely regarded as a founding thinker of the ecology movement. He is often thought of as "the prophet of
an era of limits."*

NPQ *Editors Nathan Gardels and Marilyn Berlin Snell
spoke with Illich in the spring of 1989 at his home in a
small village on the slopes of the Sierra Madre some sev-
enty miles from Mexico City.*

NPQ

Because of your radical critiques of industrial society fifteen and twenty years ago, you are widely regarded as a founding thinker of the environmental movement. Now, many of your concepts have entered the vocabulary of the established institutions of industrialism and development: the World Bank now talks about "sustainable development" and incorporates ecological concerns into their sponsorship of economic development; world leaders worry publicly about the ozone layer and promise "an environmental agenda." What's changed?

Ivan Illich

What has changed is that our common sense has begun searching for a language to speak about the shadow our future throws.

The central thesis that ran through much of my early work was that most man-made misery — from the suffering of cancer patients and the ignorance of the poor, to urban gridlock, housing shortages, and air pollution — was a byproduct of the institutions of industrial society originally designed to protect the common man from the environment, improve his material circumstances, and enhance his freedom. By breaching the limits set on man by nature and history, industrial society engendered disability and suffering in the name of eliminating disability and suffering.

In this early critique, I recalled Homer's warning of the doom of Nemesis. Driven by *pleonexia*, or radical greed, Prometheus transgressed the boundaries of the human condition. In *hubris*, or measureless presumption, he brought fire from the heavens and thereby doom onto himself. He was chained to a rock, an eagle preyed on his liver, and heartlessly healing gods kept him alive by regrafting the liver each night. The encounter of Prometheus with Nemesis is an immortal reminder of inescapable cosmic retribution.

Common to all preindustrial ethics was the idea that the range of human action was narrowly circumscribed. Technology was a measured tribute to necessity, not the implement to facilitate mankind's chosen action. In more recent times, through our inordinate attempt to transform the human condition with industrialization, our whole culture has fallen prey to the envy of the gods. Now Everyman has become Prometheus, and Nemesis has become endemic; it is the backlash of progress. We are hostage to a lifestyle that provokes doom.

Man cannot do without his CO_2-belching cars or the chlorofluoro-carbon deodorant sprays that destroy the biosphere. He can't do without his radiation therapy, his pesticides, or his nonbiodegradable plastic bags at the supermarket. If the species were to survive, I argued in my early work, it could do so only by learning to cope with Nemesis.

For a seminar in the summer of 1970, I gathered a reading list on "environmental issues." It included several of the first studies on genetic changes in children born into the fallout from atomic experiments at the Bikini Atoll; a study on the pesticide residues in the human liver; and the very first study of its kind on DDT residues in mothers' milk. At that time, I was widely criticized for engaging in "apocalyptic randiness."

Now, two decades later, a woeful sense of imbalance has dawned on the common sense. The destruction of the ozone layer, the heating up of the earth's atmosphere, the nonreversible and progressive depletion of genetic variety — all these things bring to consciousness the consequences of our Promethean transgression.

There is a generalized sense now that the future we expected is not working, and that we are in front of what Michel Foucault has called an "epistemic break" — a sudden image-shift in consciousness in which the unthinkable becomes thinkable. Until the French Revolution, for example, it was simply not thinkable that a king could be beheaded. Then, suddenly the king was beheaded, and a dramatically new image of the common man's role in society emerged. A language was invented which spoke in new, previously unimaginable, terms about the order of society.

Similarly, it is no longer tolerable for us to think of nuclear bombs as weapons; now they are known as tools of self-annihilation. The disintegrating ozone layer and warming atmosphere are making it intolerable to think of industrial growth as progress; now it appears to us as aggression against the human condition. Perhaps for the first time, we can now imagine that, as Samuel Beckett once put it, "this earth could be uninhabited."

What is new is not the magnitude, not even the quality, but the very essence of the coming rupture in consciousness. This rupture is not a break in the line of progress to a new stage; it is not even the passage from one dimension to a new dimension. We can only describe it as a *catastrophic* break with industrial man's image of himself.

NPQ

When Norwegian Prime Minister Brundtland's World Commission on Environment and Development called for "sustainable development," they both contributed to and detracted from a language that speaks to the future's shadow. "Sustainable" is the language of balance and limits; "development" is the language of the expectation of *more*.

Illich

Although Brundtland exposed the detrimental side effects of industrial progress, and told the rich nations they must bear the burden of saving the planet, she remained firmly within the "development" discourse. While Ms. Brundtland is quite capable of delinking the pursuit of peace and justice from the nineteenth-century dream of progress, the underlying critique of the concept of development still remains outside her thinking. The outer forms are crumbling, but the conceptual underpinnings of "development" remain vigorous.

The pressing questions today are: "After development, what? What concepts? What symbols? What images?" In order to find an alternative language, one must return to the past — to discover the history of those invented certitudes that are the mythological crystallization points around which modern experience is organized, certitudes like "need," "growth," "participation," "development."

To paraphrase the Chilean poet Vicente Huidobro, insight into alternatives not chosen can be found by remembering "those hours which have lost their clock."

For example, before Cortez, a unique Indian corn seed made up of at least 150 distinct genetic strains came into existence. It was uniquely adapted to the microclimate of the area where I live. When ground into meal, the corn was the characteristic blue color of local flowers, different from those ten miles east or west of here. Religious festivals, marriage customs, ovens, and diet were shaped by that crop.

Then came Dr. Bourlag's "miracle" seed, with government subsidies for fertilizer, insecticides, and fungicides. In the first few years, the fields produced fantastic returns. But then, within less than a decade, the terraces that had covered this region from pre-Columbian times, left uncultivated, were all washed out. Now, the young people here no longer work in the fields. They seek work in larger towns, repair old cars, or try to earn some money peddling household appliances. The tools and donkeys of their fathers have disappeared. These changes occurred so rapidly that the "blue corn" festivals are still celebrated.

Only by reentering the present moment with knowledge of the lost time of the blue tortilla — to extend this example — will it be possible to establish a new way of seeing and a new set of terms that can guide sustainable "policies" without recourse to "development."

NPQ

What is the history of the term "development?" How has it transformed our relationship to nature?

Illich

The "human condition" once described a way of life bound by immutable necessities. Each culture cultivated commonly shared desires or projects of a symbolic nature. In the instance I just described, before transportation and refrigeration, or scientifically produced seed strains, great varieties of food, like blue corn, were grown, complex diets formalized, and seasons ritualized. "The Good" was defined within the "commons" and bounded by accepted limits.

"Development," on the other hand, is one of those modern terms that expresses rebellion against the "necessity" that ruled *all* societies up to the eighteenth century. The notion of "development" promises an escape from the realm of necessity by transforming the "commons" into "resources" for use in satisfying the boundless wants of the possessive individual.

"Development" combines a faith that technology will free us from the constraints that bound all past civilizations with the root certainty of the twentieth century: evolution. As interpreted by optimistic politics, "evolution" becomes "progress." The term "underdevelopment," in fact, was first used by Harry Truman in 1949, when the colonialism shattered by World War II "revealed" a world that was not on the track of industrial growth.

Parallel to the construction of this idea of industrial progress, another concept, which implied the assent of the "masses" to development, came into vogue: participation. Since development reduces the constraints of necessity, people must, for their own good, transform their vague and sometimes unconscious desires into "needs," which then must be fulfilled.

"Needs" redefine "wants" as "lacks" to be satisfied by "resources." Since "wants" are boundless, resources become "scarce" because of the value "lack" places upon them. This is the basis for the insatiable demand for *more*.

"Needs" are not "necessities." They are "wants" that have been redefined as claims to commodities or services delivered by professionals from outside the vernacular skills of the community. The universal appearance of "needs" during the past thirty years thus reflects a redefinition of the human condition and what is meant by "the Good."

For example, in Mexico City today, the burgeoning population *needs* to be provided with food because fewer people in absolute numbers can grow their own food. More people in Mexico City *need* public transport or recycled American cars because they have no choice but to commute in order to work in the market economy. More housing, with water and electricity, *needs* to be provided by borrowing from North American banks because there is less space suited for self-built shacks, and because people have lost the skills necessary to pour a roof slab.

NPQ

So, at the root of environmental destruction and the depletion of finite resources is a drive for economic growth stimulated by transformation of *the human condition ruled by necessity into the reign of "needs."* If that is so, then the path "after development," in your view, would involve a return to subsistence and restoration of the commons?

Illich

Yes, exactly. Sustainability without development, or subsistence, is simply living within the limits of genuinely basic needs. Shelter, food, education, community, and personal intimacy can all be met within this framework.

NPQ

A renunciation of economic growth hardly seems capable, at the moment, of garnering much political support. And, in modern times, where political will lacks, technology substitutes. Indeed, one wonders why we can't move on to "postscarcity" instead of "subsistence." Why not go the route of ecological modernization? If energy is finite, why not resource-efficient technology? If petroleum-powered cars pollute, why not switch to methanol? If passenger miles are excessive for the commute to the office, why not stay at home and work on the computer?

Illich

The Information Revolution has injected new life into what would otherwise have been the exhausted logic of industrial development.

It encourages expectations that, through his tools, man can escape the limits of his condition.

On the other hand, subsistence assumes a context of commonly defined needs balanced against the limits of nature. The social awareness that distinguishes between postscarcity and subsistence rests upon historical knowledge that the human condition is precarious.

NPQ

With the technologies of the Information Age, especially bioengineering, I suppose it is even more crucial to see attempted escape from the human condition as a transgression. In your terms, this delusion is all the more dangerous for seeming all the more possible. Does this make you more or less hopeful about the future?

Illich

I distinguish between the attitudes of hope and expectation. "Expectation" is based on a belief in instruments and the naive acceptance of socially constructed certitudes. "Hope" is based on historically rooted experience. To face the future freely, one must give up both optimism and pessimism and place all *hope* in human beings, not *trust* in tools.

I, for one, see unsquashable signs of hope in the lifestyles of subsistence peasants or in the network of activists who save trees here, or plant them there. But, I admit that I am still unable to envisage how, short of a devastating catastrophe, these hope-inspiring acts can be translated into "policy."

NPQ

Surely, when the revenge of the cosmos crystallizes in the ruin of an ancient metropolis like Mexico City — where the fetuses of the unborn are poisoned by lead from the air their mothers breathe — its ruins will stand, like Prometheus, as a testament to the curse of Nemesis. Then, perhaps, "policy" will desert development and new forms of organizing life will take hold.

Illich

Mexico City is beyond catastrophe. It is a metaphor for all that has gone wrong with development. That ancient city, founded on a lake in the pristine air of a high mountain valley, will have no clean air or water by the year 2000. But what is marvelous about Mexico City is *why* the city survives at all.

Why are people there not dying from thirst? Of the enormous amount of water pumped over the mountains from the country-side, 50 percent goes to less than 3 percent of the households, and 50 percent of the households get less than 3 percent of the water. That means the latter 50 percent gets only enough water to drink, cook, and wash, and then flush away only every seventeenth s---!

The fact is that dilution of feces in water is totally unfeasible in Mexico City. Yet, the 5.5 million people who have no stable place for s------g somehow keep even this aspect of their life under control.

So, Mexico City is also a symbol of the stability of neighborhood equilibrium beyond catastrophe. In such a world as this, I see frightening but effective forms of self-government emerging that keep government and the development institutions out of people's everyday affairs. Most of this new activity emerged after the earth-quake in 1985 when the government was paralyzed and unable to aid recovery. Today, demands for self-governance are formulated routinely by the Assembly of *Barrios* (neighborhoods) in discussions like these:

"How can there be enough water in Mexico City for everyone? Let us build the water tanks, fill them, and then we will distribute the water in our own *barrio*."

"How to avoid gridlock and traffic jams and lower the lead level in the air? No trucks on Mexico City streets during the day. During the night food can be brought to central markets in each of the *barrios* and then hauled from there to neighborhoods by pushcart."

Now, there are even demands for the self-management of their own s---! And, in many *barrios*, there is an increasing number of places where the police are barred because they are considered a menace.

These are practical indications that people can invent alternatives to a concept of development that has thrown the whole nation into a debtor's prison. Self-management of genuinely basic needs is what occurs here.

NPQ

So, new forms of living emerge out of the ruins of development?

Illich

Some novelists, like Doris Lessing in *The Fifth Child*, create a sense of the emergent future, of what kinds of relationships are possible in the ruins. There is a sense in Lessing's writings of the frightening beings who have survival capacity.

It is fascinating to discover this shared experience of outsiders in post-earthquake, pre-ecological-apocalypse Mexico City. There is something here of the taste of the gang, the ragpicker, the garbage- dump dweller. Our difficulty is finding a language to speak about this alternative, because contrary to professional wisdom, people with unmet basic needs are surviving with new forms of conviviality.

Perhaps we can think of them as the *technophagic majority* of the late twentieth century — people who feed on the waste of development. This population comprises, for example, half of Chicago's inner-city youth, who have dropped out of school, as well as two-thirds of Mexico City's dwellers, whose excrement goes untreated. From New York's underclass to Cairo's "city of the dead" where people live in the cemeteries, these survivors are the spontaneous architects of our postmodern "future."

NPQ

Roadwarriors is the image that springs to mind. . . .

Illich

Guilty of the crime of "social disillusionment," these survivors reassert unsquashable hope with the chilling character of the gang. As outlaw communities that have no diplomatic consistency, their experience is barred from the Brundtland discourse except as recalcitrant, "needy" clients who require the kindness of strangers.

Yet, as living renunciations of the "future," these survivors somehow show the way forward. Their willingness to engage in communitarian exercises, outside "development," makes us smile about the pompousness of professionals plotting humanity's next step.

NPQ

You've sketched a path beyond development and outside the dominant debate now shaped by the idea of sustainable development. What is the next move within that discourse?

Illich

It is clear to me that an administrative-intensive global ecology follows logically from the utilitarian ethic of management that undergirds Brundtland.

Originally, utilitarianism was conceived as an attempt to give the most good to the largest number of people. Then, sometime in the 1970s, it came to mean the least pain for the largest number of people. This medical metaphor illuminates the next step after Brundtland: not the greatest good, nor the least pain, but the greatest *pain management* for the species.

NPQ

In effect, hooking up the earth to a respirator and supplying it with drugs. . . .

Illich

Precisely. After Brundtland, I envision management of the depletion of the commons, not restoration of the common environment to culturally bounded, politically sanctioned limits to growth. In this ectopia, we will see the technologically assisted management of man from sperm to worm, including rates of reproduction.

NPQ

Would you then welcome the emergence of a new ecological world view that focuses man's attention on restoring the natural equilibrium? Might that be the new universal ethos that ties this fragmented planet together?

Illich

You must understand that the concept of ecology is deeply related to the concept of "life." "Life" cannot be understood apart from the "death of nature." In a continuous thread that runs back to Anaxagoras (500 – 428 B.C.) and up through the sixteenth century, an organic, whole conception of nature was a constant theme in the West. God was the pattern that connected the cosmos. With the Scientific Revolution, a mechanistic model came to dominate thinking. As the object of man's will, nature was transformed into dead material. This death of nature, I would argue, was the most far-reaching effect of the radical change in man's vision of the universe.

Now, this artificial character of "life" appears with special poignancy in the ecological discourse. The pattern that connects living forms and their habitat — God — is dissolved into the cybernetic concept of an "ecosystem" which, through multiple feedback mechanisms, can be regulated scientifically if the inputs are chosen properly by intelligent man. Man, the agent of disequilibrium, projects upon himself the task of restoring equilibrium to nature. Ecological man protects "life" and defends resources from depletion.

The self-regulating system of "life" thus becomes the model for opposing industrial destruction. It is a very seductive idea and it simplifies everything. In an attempt to come to grips with Nemesis, man expands his presumption to managing the cosmos! In the name of nature, ecology idolizes Promethean man.

DIVERSITY AND NATIONALISM AFTER THE COLD WAR

Though it is by now a cliché that ethnicity and nationalism have returned with a vengeance after being frozen by the Cold War and the modern faith in rationalism, it is nonetheless a truth that will be with us into the twenty-first century.

As much as we all laud cultural self-determination, pluralism, and diversity, at the same time we fear the intolerance and discrimination that have historically fortified the identity of human communities.

Isaiah Berlin, the Oxford historian of ideas, opens this section with an examination of nationalism, good and bad, and what it bodes for the times to come.

Pierre Trudeau, the flamboyant former premier of Canada, strenuously rejects the idea of ethnic-based rights as a backward step for humanity. Carlos Fuentes, the Mexican novelist, makes the case for federalism. Felipe Gonzalez, the prime minister of Spain, warns against sanctifying the principle of self-determination. Both men have struggled mightily when in power to keep their countries from fragmenting. Hans Jurgen Syberberg, the controversial German director of Hitler: A Film from Germany, *candidly argues that Germany invites the worst of the past to return if it continues to repress its own cultural identity.*

The fashionable nouvelle philosophe *from France, Bernard Henri-Levy, maintains that the West has lost the courage of its convictions by failing in Bosnia to defend the idea of modern Europe: multiculturalism and the universal rights of man. Nigerian Nobel laureate Wole Soyinka makes a similar case about the genocide of the Tutsi in Rwanda. The writer V. S. Naipaul expresses his faith that modern, tolerant India will overcome the revived hatred of Hindus and Muslims, while the foremost chronicler of the postcolonial Third World, Ryzsard Kapuscinski, looks to the multicultural superpower, America, as a premonition of the relatively harmonious cosmic culture that could characterize a new global civilization.*

Futurists Alvin and Heidi Toffler look at another phenomenon dividing the post–Cold War world: the revolt of the rich.

Return of the Volksgeist:
Nationalism, Good and Bad

Isaiah Berlin

Perhaps the West's foremost political philosopher, Sir
Isaiah Berlin is a fellow at All Soul's College, Oxford.
Born in Riga, Latvia, in 1909, he is author of Karl Marx,
The Age of Enlightenment, Four Essays on Liberty, *and*
Vico and Herder. *A selection of Sir Isaiah's essays, entitled*
The Crooked Timber of Humanity: Chapters in the History
of Ideas, *was published in 1991.*

NPQ *editor Nathan Gardels talked with Sir Isaiah at the*
end of the summer of 1991 in Portofino, Italy.

NPQ

According to Harold Isaacs, author of *Idols of the Tribe*, today we are witnessing a "convulsive ingathering" of nations. Open ethnic warfare rages not far from here in Yugoslavia. The Soviet Union has been rent asunder by resurgent nationalist republics. The new world order built from the rubble of the Berlin Wall has already gone the way of the Tower of Babel. What are the origins of nationalism? Whence this ingathering storm?

Isaiah Berlin

The Tower of Babel was meant to be unitary in character; a single great building, reaching to the skies, with one language for everybody.

The Lord didn't like it.

There is, I have been told, an excellent Hebrew prayer to be uttered when seeing a monster: "Blessed be the Lord our God, who introducest variety amongst Thy creatures." We can only be happy to have seen the Soviet Tower of Babel collapse into ruin, dangerous as some of the consequences may turn out to be — I mean, a bitter clash of nationalisms. But, unfortunately, that would be nothing new.

In our modern age, nationalism is not resurgent; it never died. Neither did racism. They are the most powerful movements in the world today, cutting across many social systems.

None of the great thinkers of the nineteenth century predicted this. Saint-Simon predicted the importance of industrialists and bankers. Fourier, who understood that if glass was made unbreakable there could be no business for the glazier, grasped the contradictions of capitalism. Karl Burchhardt predicted the military-industrial complex. Not very much of what Marx predicted turned out to be true, except the vitally important insight that technology transforms culture. Big Business and class conflicts are among its results.

They all thought that the imperial regimes of the great states were a central problem of their century. Once these tyrannical conglomerations — the British Empire, the Austro-Hungarian Empire, the Russian Empire—were, together with colonialism, destroyed, the peoples under their heels would live peacefully together and realize their destiny in a productive and creative manner. Well, they were mistaken.

Although most liberal philosophers of the nineteenth century opposed the cruel exploitation of the "dark masses" by imperialism, in no case did any of them think that black, Indian, or Asian people could ever have states, parliaments, or armies — they were completely Eurocentric.

That, I suspect, changed with the Russo-Japanese War of 1904. The fact that an Asiatic nation defeated a great European power must have produced an electric shock in the minds of many Indians, Africans, and others, and given a great fillip to the idea of anti-imperialist self-assertion and national independence. In the twentieth century, left-wing movements might not have succeeded in Asia or Africa — in Indo-China, Egypt, Algeria, Syria, or Iraq — unless they went arm in arm with nationalist feeling.

Nonaggressive nationalism is another story entirely. I trace the beginning of that idea to the highly influential eighteenth-century German poet and philosopher Johann Gottfried Herder.

Herder virtually invented the idea of belonging. He believed that just as people need to eat and drink, to have security and freedom of movement, so too they need to belong to a group. Deprived of this, they felt cut off, lonely, diminished, unhappy. Nostalgia, Herder said, was the noblest of all pains. To be human meant to be able to feel at home somewhere, with your own kind.

Each group, according to Herder, has its own *Volksgeist*, or *Nationalgeist* — a set of customs and a lifestyle, a way of perceiving and behaving that is of value solely because it is their own. The whole of cultural life is shaped from within the particular stream of tradition that comes from collective historical experience shared only by members of the group.

Thus one could not, for example, fully understand the great

Scandinavian sagas unless one had oneself experienced (as he did on his voyage to England) a great tempest in the North Sea. Herder's idea of the nation was deeply nonaggressive. All he wanted was cultural self-determination. He denied the superiority of one people over another. Anyone who proclaimed it was saying something false. Herder believed in a variety of national cultures, all of which could, in his view, peacefully coexist.

Each culture was equal in value and deserved its place in the sun. The villains of history for Herder were the great conquerors such as Alexander the Great, Caesar, or Charlemagne, because they stamped out native cultures. He did not live to see the full effects of Napoleon's victories — but since they undermined the dominion of the Holy Roman Empire, he might have forgiven him.

Only what was unique had true value. This is why Herder also opposed the French universalists of the Enlightenment. For him there were few timeless truths: time and place and social life — what came to be called civil society — were everything.

NPQ

And yet, Herder's *Volksgeist* became the Third Reich. And today, the Serbian *Volksgeist* is at war with the Croatian *Volksgeist*, and the Bosnian Muslim way of life. The Armenians and the Azeris have long been at it, and, among the Georgians and Russians — and even the Ukrainians and the Russians — passions are stirring.

What transforms the aspiration of cultural self-determination into nationalist aggression?

Berlin

I have written elsewhere that a wounded *Volksgeist*, so to speak, is like a bent twig, forced down so severely that when released, it lashes back with fury. Nationalism, at least in the West, is created by wounds inflicted by stress. As for Eastern Europe and the former Soviet empire, they seem today to be one vast, open wound. After years of oppression and humiliation, there is liable to occur a violent counterreaction, an outburst of national pride, often aggressive self-assertion, by liberated nations and their leaders.

Although I am not allowed to say this to German historians, I believe that Louis XIV was principally responsible for the beginnings of German nationalism in the seventeenth century. While the rest of Europe — Italy, England, Spain, the Low Countries, above all France — experienced a magnificent renaissance in art and thought, and political and military power, Germany, after the age of Dürer, Grünewald, Reuchlin, became (with the exception of architecture) a relative backwater. The Germans tended to be looked down upon by the French as provincials, simple, slightly comical, beer-drinking yokels, literate but ungifted.

At first, there was naturally much imitation of the French, but later, as always, there was a reaction. The pietists asked, "Why not be ourselves? Why imitate foreigners? Let the French have their royal courts, their salons, worldly abbés, soldiers, poets, painters, their empty glory. It's all dross. Nothing matters save a man's relation to his own soul, to God, to true values, which are of the spirit, the inner life, Christian truth."

By the 1670s a pietist-national countermovement was under way; this was the spiritual movement in which Kant, Herder, Hamann, the sages of East Prussia, grew up. The pietist attitude was, "We don't require what Paris offers. It is all but worthless. Only inner freedom, purity of the soul, matter." It was a grand form of sour grapes.

That is when nationalist self-assertion begins. By 1720 Thomasius, a minor German thinker, dared to give university lectures in his own tongue, in German, instead of Latin. That was a major departure. The corresponding consequences of the deeper German humiliations — from the Napoleonic wars to the Treaty of Versailles — are only too obvious.

Today, Georgians, Armenians, and the rest are trying to recover their submerged pasts, pushed into the background by the huge Russian imperial power. Persecuted under Stalin, Armenian and Georgian literature survived: Isakian and Yashvili were gifted poets; Pasternak's translations of Vaz Pshavela and Tabidze are wonderful reading — but when Ribbentrop went to see Stalin in 1939, he presented him with a German translation of the twelfth-century Georgian epic *The Knight in the Tiger Skin* by Rustaveli. Who, in the West, knew of later masterpieces?

Sooner or later, the backlash comes with irrepressible force. People tire of being spat upon, ordered about by a superior nation, a superior class, or a superior anyone. Sooner or later they ask the nationalist questions: "Why do we have to obey them?" "What right have they . . .?" "What about us?" "Why can't we . . .?"

NPQ

All these bent twigs in revolt may have finally overturned the ideological world order. The explosion of the Soviet system may be the last act of deconstruction of the Enlightenment ideals of unity, universality, and rationalism. That's all finito now.

Berlin

I think that is true. And Russia is an appropriate place to illuminate the misapprehensions of the *lumiéres*. Most Russian westernizers who followed the eighteenth-century French thinkers admired them because they stood up to the church, stood up to reactionary tendencies, stood up to fate. Voltaire and Rousseau were heroes because they enlisted reason, and the right to freedom, against reaction.

But even the radical writer Alexander Herzen, my hero, never accepted, for example, Condorcet's claims to knowable, timeless truths. He thought the idea of continuous progress an illusion, and protested against the new idolatries: the substitute for human sacrifice (the sacrifice of living beings to new altars); abstractions (like the universal class or the infallible party or the march of history); and the victimization of the present for the sake of an unknowable future that would lead to some harmonious solution.

Herzen regarded any dedication to abstract unity and universality with great suspicion. For him, England was England, France was France, Russia was Russia. The differences neither could nor should be flattened out. The ends of life were life itself. For Herzen, as for Herder and the eighteenth-century Italian philosopher Giambattista Vico, cultures were incommensurable. It follows, though they do not spell it out, that the pursuit of total harmony, or the perfect state, is a fallacy, and sometimes a fatal one.

Of course, nobody believed in universality more than the Marxists: Lenin, Trotsky, and the others who triumphed saw themselves as disciples of the Enlightenment thinkers, corrected and brought up to date by Marx.

If one were to defend the general record of communism, which neither you nor I would be willing to do, it would have to be defended on the basis that Stalin may have murdered forty million people — but at least he kept nationalism down and prevented the ethnic Babel from anarchically asserting its ambitions. Of course, Stalin did keep it — and everything else — down, but he didn't kill it. As soon as the stone was rolled away from the grave, it rose again with a vengeance.

NPQ

Herder was a *horizontal critic*, if you will, of the French *lumiéres* because he believed in the singularity of all cultures. Giambattista Vico also opposed the Enlightenment idea of universality from a *vertical*, or historical perspective. As you have written, he believed each successive culture was incommensurable with others.

Berlin

Both rejected the Enlightenment idea that man, in every country at every time, had identical values. For them, as for me, the plurality of cultures is irreducible.

NPQ

Does the final breakup of communist totalitarianism, a creature of the ideal of universality, suggest that we are living out the final years of the last modern century?

Berlin

I accept that, almost. The ideal of universality, so deeply perverted that it would utterly horrify the eighteenth-century philosophers who expounded it, evidently lives on in some form in the remote reaches of Europe's influence: China, North Korea, Cuba.

NPQ

One can only imagine how differently the twentieth century would have turned out had Vico and Herder prevailed rather than the French philosophers or Hegel and Marx — if the local soul had not been overrun by the world soul. We might have had a century of cultural pluralism instead of totalitarianism.

Berlin

How could that have happened? Universalism in the eighteenth century was the doctrine of the top nation, France. So everyone tried to emulate its brilliant culture.

Perhaps it was much more the rise of the natural sciences, with the emphasis on universal laws, and nature as an organism or a machine, and the imitation of scientific methods in other spheres, which dominated all thinking.Fuelled by these ideas, the nineteenth-century explosion of technology and economic development isolated the intellectual stream deriving from such nonquantitative — indeed, qualitative — thinkers as Vico and Herder.

The temper of the times is illustrated in a story told in one of Jacob Talmon's books. He writes of two Czech schoolmasters talking with each other around the early 1800s. "We're probably the last people in the world to speak Czech," they said to each other. "Our language is at an end. Inevitably, we'll all speak German here in Central Europe, and probably the Balkans. We're the last survivors of our native culture."

Of course, such survivors are today in the saddle in many lands.

NPQ

What political structure can possibly accommodate this new age of cultural self-determination, preserve liberty, and perhaps stem some of the bloodshed?

Berlin

Cultural self-determination without a political framework is precisely the issue now, and not only for the East. Spain has the Basques and Catalans; Britain has Northern Ireland; Canada the Quebecois; Belgium has the Flemings; Israel the Arabs, and so on. Whoever in the past would have dreamed of Breton nationalism or a Scottish national party?

Idealists like Herder evidently didn't consider this problem. He merely hated the Austro-Hungarian empire for politically welding together incompatible elements.

In Eastern Europe they really do seem to loathe each other: Romanians hate the Hungarians, and Hungarians have for years disliked the Czechs in a way the Bretons can't pretend to hate the French. It is a phenomenon of a different order. Only the Irish are like that in the West.

Only in America have a variety of ethnic groups retained their own original cultures, and nobody seems to mind. The Italians, Poles, Jews, and Koreans have their own newspapers, books, and I am told, TV programs.

NPQ

Perhaps when immigrants forsake their soil, they leave behind the passionate edge of their *Volksgeist* as well. Yet even in America, a new multicultural movement has emerged in academia that seeks to stress not what is common in the curriculum but what is not.

Berlin

Yes, I know. Black studies, Chicano studies, and the rest. I suppose this too is a bent twig revolt of minorities that feel disadvantaged in the context of American polyethnicity. Polyethnicity was not Herder's idea. He didn't urge the Germans to study Dutch, or German students to study the culture of the Portuguese.

In Herder, there is nothing about race and nothing about blood. He only spoke about soil, language, common memories, and customs. His central point, as a Montenegrian friend once said to me, is that loneliness is not just absence of others, but living among people who do not understand what you are saying; they can truly understand only if they belong to a community where communication is effortless, almost instinctive.

Herder looked unkindly on the cultural friction generated in Vienna, where many nationalities were crammed into the same narrow space. It produced men of genius, but with a deeply neurotic element in a good many of them — one need only think of Gustav Mahler, Ludwig Wittgenstein, Karl Kraus, Arnold Schoenberg, Stefan Zweig, and the birth of psychoanalysis in this largely Jewish, particularly defenseless, society.

All that tremendous collision of not very compatible cultures — Slavs, Italians, Germans, Jews — unleashed a great deal of creativity. This was a different kind of cultural expression from that of an earlier Vienna, that of Mozart or Haydn or Schubert.

NPQ

In grappling with the separatist Quebecois, Pierre Trudeau often invoked Lord Acton. He felt that wherever political boundaries coincided with ethnic ones, chauvinism, xenophobia, and racism inevitably threatened liberty.

Only individual constitutional rights in a federal republic — equal citizenship rights for all, despite ethnicity — could protect minorities and individuals. "The theory of nationality," Trudeau quoted Acton as saying, "is a retrograde step in history."

Berlin

Lord Acton was a noble figure, and I agree with him. Yet we have to admit that, despite Trudeau's efforts, the Quebecois are still seeking independence. In the grand scale of things, one has to consider that, despite royal and clerical monopolies of power and authority, the Middle Ages were, in some ways, more civilized than the deeply disturbed nineteenth — and worse still, our own terrible century, with widespread violence, chauvinism, and in the end mass destruction in racial, and Stalin's political, holocausts.

Of course, there were ethnic frictions in the Middle Ages, and persecution of Jews and heretics, but nationalism as such didn't exist. The wars were dynastic. What existed was the universal church and a common Latin language. We can't turn history back. Yet I do not wish to abandon the belief that a world that is a reasonably peaceful coat of many colors, each portion of which develops its own distinct cultural identity and is tolerant of others, is not a utopian dream.

NPQ

But of what common thread can such a coat be spun? In a universe of autonomous cultural worlds, each in its own orbit, where is the sun that keeps the various planets from colliding with the others?

Berlin

The idea of a center can lead to cultural imperialism again.

In Herder's universe, you didn't need a sun. His cultures were not planets, but stars that didn't collide. I admit that, at the end of the twentieth century, there is little historical evidence for the realizability of such a vision.

At eighty-two, I've lived through virtually the entire century. I have no doubt that it is the worst century that Europe has ever had.

Nothing has been more horrible for our civilization. In my life, more dreadful things occurred than at any other time in history. Worse even than the days of the Huns.

One can only hope that after the peoples get exhausted from fighting, the bloody tide will subside. Unless tourniquets can be applied to stop the hemorrhaging, and bandages to the wounds so that they can slowly heal (even if they leave scars), we're in for the continuation of a very bad time.

The only nations about which one need not wring one's hands are the sated nations, unwounded or healed, such as the liberal democracies of North America, Western Europe, Australia, New Zealand, and one hopes, Japan.

NPQ

Perhaps the two futures will live, decoupled, side by side. A civilization of the soil, so to speak, and a civilization of the satellite. Instead of the violent splintering of nations, the sated nations will become a small world after all, with the passions of blood and soil drained away by homogenizing consumerism and mass entertainment. Perhaps that is the price of peaceful integration. As Milan Kundera has recently written, frivolous cultures are anthropologically incapable of war. But they are also incapable of producing Picassos.

Berlin

As for that, I don't believe that only tragic events and wounds can create genius. In Central Europe, Kafka and Rilke bore wounds. But neither Racine nor Moliére nor Pushkin nor Tolstoy — unlike Dostoyevsky — bore deep wounds. And Goethe seems completely free from them. The fate of the Russian poets of our century is another, gloomier, story.

Without doubt, uniformity may increase under the pressure of technology, as is already happening with the Americanization of Europe. Some people hate it, but it clearly can't be stopped.

As we discussed, it is possible, as in the Austro-Hungarian empire, to have political and economic uniformity, but cultural variety.

That is what I ultimately visualize. A degree of uniformity in the sated nations, combined with a pleasing degree of peaceful variety in the rest of the world. I admit that the present trend is in the opposite direction: sharp, sometimes aggressive self-assertion on the part of some very minor human groups.

NPQ

What about the emergence of a new set of common values — ecological rights and human rights — that can to some degree unite all these erupting cultures without cramping their style?

Berlin

At the present, there don't seem to be accepted minimum values that can keep the world straight. Let us hope, one day, that a large minimum of common values, such as the ones you mention, will be accepted. Otherwise we are bound to go under.

Unless there is a minimum of shared values that can preserve the peace, no decent societies can survive.

NPQ

The liberal dream of cosmopolitanism, even in the sated world, is not on the agenda as far as you are concerned?

Berlin

Like Herder, I regard cosmopolitanism as empty. People can't develop unless they belong to a culture. Even if they rebel against it and transform it entirely, they still belong to a stream of tradition. New streams can be created — in the West, by Christianity, or Luther, or the Renaissance, or the Romantic movement — but in the end they derive from a single river, an underlying central tradition, which, sometimes in radically altered forms, survives.

But if the streams dry up, as for instance, where men and women are not products of a culture, where they don't have kith and kin and feel closer to some people than to others, where there is no native language — that would lead to a tremendous desiccation of everything that is human.

NPQ

So, for you, Vico and Herder, the apostles of cultural pluralism, are the philosophers of the future?

Berlin

Yes, in the sense that we are all affected by a variety of values to some degree. From the Greeks and the Hebrews to the Christian Middle Ages to the Renaissance and the Enlightenment of the seventeenth and eighteenth centuries, unity was the great virtue. Truth is one, many is error.

Variety is a new virtue, brought to us by the Romantic movement, of which Herder and Vico, whom I regard as the prophets of variety, were an important part. After that, variety, pluralism (which entails the possibility of many incompatible ideals that attract human devotion), sincerity (not necessarily leading to truth or goodness) — all these are thought to be virtues. Once pluralism of ways of life is accepted, and there can be mutual esteem between different, uncombinable outlooks, it is difficult to suppose that all this can be flattened by some huge, crushing jackboot.

On this score, let me make a prophecy for the twenty-fifth century. Aldous Huxley's *Brave New World* could perhaps be established, in part as an irresistible response to the endless ethnic violence and nationalist rivalry at the turn of the millennium. Under this system, everyone would be clothed and fed. All would live under one roof, following one single pattern of existence.

But, sooner or later, somebody will rebel, somebody will cry for room. Not only will people revolt against totalitarianism, but against an all-embracing, well-meaning, benign system as well. The first terrible fellow to kick over the traces will be burned alive. But other troublemakers will be sure to follow. If there is anything I'm certain about, after living for so long, it is that people must sooner or later rebel against uniformity and attempts at global solutions of any sort.

The Reformation was such a rebellion against claims to universal authority. The domination of the vast territories of the Roman Empire collapsed in due course. So, too, the Austro-Hungarian Empire. The sun set on the British Empire. And now the Soviet empire. There is a Russian story about a sultan who decided to punish one of his wives for a misdeed and ordered her sealed, with her son, in a barrel with little holes for air. The sultan set them afloat at sea to perish. After several days the son said to the mother "I can't bear being so cramped. I want to stretch." "You can't," she responded, "you'll push out the bottom, and we'll drown." Several days later, the son protested again, "I long for room." The mother said, "For God's sake, don't do it, we'll drown." The son then said, "So be it, I must stretch out, just once, and then let it come." He got his moment of freedom, and perished.

The Russian radical Herzen applied this to the condition of the Russian people. They were bound to strike out for freedom — no matter what came after.

NPQ

In Herder's day, we might have been unable to grasp the masterpiece of a Scandinavian saga without experiencing a North Sea tempest, but today, through MTV, teenagers from Beijing to Moscow to Los Angeles can share the same thrill of watching a Madonna concert. What can cultural self-determination mean in such an age?

Berlin

All the same — past differences take their toll: the spectacles through which the young of Bangkok and Valparaiso see Madonna are not the same. The many languages of the islands of Polynesia and Micronesia are said to be totally unlike each other; this is also true of the Caucasus. If you think that all this will one day give way to one universal language — not just for learned purposes or politics or business, but to convey emotional nuances, to express inner lives — then I suppose what you suggest could happen: this would not be one culture, but the death of culture. I am glad to be as old as I am.

Against Nationalism

Pierre Trudeau

Pierre Trudeau was prime minister of Canada from 1968 to 1979, and again from 1980 to 1984. He composed this article in response to NPQ's *Spring 1990 issue about the end of the Cold War, entitled "The New World Disorder."*

MONTREAL

Without the cold breath of ideological hostility between blocs, ethnic nationalism reminiscent of Central Europe before Yalta or the Soviet Union before 1917 is again beginning to smolder. From Georgia and Azerbaijan to the former Yugoslavia and Russia, from the new Czech and Slovak Federal Republic to Hungary and Romania, from Germany to Quebec, the approaching twenty-first century is beginning to look alarmingly like the nineteenth.

At such a pivotal moment in history, it seems oddly necessary to restate the modern, liberal principles of statehood once so widely accepted in the West — principles that led us away from the bloody disasters of nationalistic and ethnic-based politics of the past.

As the prime minister who pressed for enactment of the Canadian Constitution Act of 1982, which eschewed "distinct society" status for Quebec in favor of a federalist solution, I think there is universal value in the Canadian experience — and logic in the liberal political approach — for all states grappling with the reemergent issue of ethnic-based nationalism. For, if six million Canadians of French origin cannot manage to share their national sovereignty with twenty million Canadians of British and other origins, there is very little hope for far less privileged regions of the world, such as Nagorno-Karabakh, where deprivation fuels age-old enmities.

Throughout history, when a state has taken an exclusive and intolerant idea such as religion or ethnicity as its cornerstone, this idea has more often than not been the very mainspring of violence and war. In days gone by, religion had to be displaced as the basis of the state before frightful religious wars came to an end. And there will be little hope of putting an end to wars between nations until in some similar fashion the "nation" in ethnic terms ceases to be the basis of a state.

Whether we look at Nazi Germany, Fascist Japan or Islamic Iran, a state that defines its function essentially in terms of ethnic or religions attributes inevitably becomes chauvinistic and intolerant. Nationalists, whether of the left or right, are politically reactionary because they are led to define the common good as a function of an ethnic group or religious ideal rather than in terms of "all the people" regardless of individual characteristics. This is why a nationalistic government is by nature intolerant, discriminatory, and when all is said and done, totalitarian.

As Lord Acton wrote as early as 1862, the nation as an ideal unit founded on race

> overrules the rights and wishes of its inhabitants, absorbing their divergent interests in a fictitious unity; sacrifices their inclinations and duties to the higher claim of nationality, and crushes all natural rights and all established liberties for the purpose of vindicating itself. Whenever a single definite object is made the supreme end of the State, the State becomes for the time being inevitably absolute.

Thus, a truly democratic government, whether provincial or federal, cannot be "nationalist" because it must pursue the good of all its citizens regardless of sex, color, race, religious belief, or ethnic origin. Democratic government stands for good citizenship, never nationalism. This is not to say that the state must disregard cultural or linguistic values. Among the many values that a political society must protect and develop, these have high priority. It is therefore entirely desirable that a state ensure, through its Constitution and legislation, the protection of such values.

Moreover, it is inevitable that its policies will serve the interests of ethnic groups, and especially of the majority group; but this will happen as a natural consequence of the equality of all its citizens, not as a special privilege such as "a distinct society" of the largest group in a given territory. I entered federal politics in Canada precisely for the purpose of carrying out these principles in practice. I believed strongly then, as I do now, that federalism is a superior form of government by definition because it is more pluralist than monolithic, and therefore respects diversity among people and groups. In general, freedom has a firmer foundation under federalism than in any kind of unitary nation-state.

In the grand tradition of the 1789 Declaration of the Rights of Man and the Citizen, and the 1791 Bill of Rights of the United States, the Canadian Charter thus implicitly established the primacy of the individual over the state and all government institutions, and in so doing, recognized that all sovereignty resides in the people as equal citizens.

Clearly, the very adoption of a constitutional charter is in keeping with the purest liberalism, according to which all members of a civil society enjoy certain fundamental, inalienable rights, and cannot be deprived of them by any collectivity (nation, ethnic, or religious group).

By this conception, all individual members of civil society are "human personalities"— that is, beings of a moral order, free and equal among themselves, each having absolute dignity and infinite value. As such, they transcend the accidents of place and time, and partake in the essence of universal Humanity. They are therefore not coercible by any ancestral tradition, being vassals neither to their race, nor to their religion, nor to their condition of birth, nor to their collective history.

It follows from this that only the individual, not the ethnic group, is the possessor of rights. A political collectivity can exercise only those rights it has received by delegation from its members. The spirit and substance of the Canadian Charter is thus clear to protect the individual against not only the tyranny of the state, but also any other tyranny to which the individual may be subjected by virtue of his belonging to a minority group.

Having reviewed these principles, it should be manifestly clear how the notion of regarding any group within a political entity as a "distinct society," wherein individual rights are subordinated to collective rights, opens up the dangerous doors of Balkanization and threatens to undermine the very foundation of a liberal state. The return of such a perspective into the mainstream of political thought presages a return to premodern conflicts once thought to have passed into history.

If the nineteenth century is what awaits us at the opening of the twenty-first, it behooves us to listen once again to Lord Acton, one of the great thinkers of the nineteenth century, who described with extraordinarily prophetic insight the errors of nationalism that were to soak the twentieth century with so much blood and acrimony:

> A great democracy must either sacrifice self-government to unity or preserve it by federalism. The coexistence of several nations under the same State is a test, as well as the best security of its freedom. It is also one of the chief instruments of civilization. . . .

> The combination of different nations in one State is as necessary a condition of civilized life as the combination of men in society. Where political and national boundaries coincide, society ceases to advance, and nations relapse into a condition corresponding to that of men who renounce intercourse with their fellow men. . . . A State which is incompetent to satisfy different races condemns itself; a State which labors to neutralize, to absorb, or to expel them is destitute of the chief basis of self-government. The theory of nationality, then, is a retrograde step in history.

The Federalist Way

Carlos Fuentes

Carlos Fuentes, the Mexican novelist, is perhaps Latin America's most enduring literary talent. His many works over the decades have included The Death of Artemio Cruz, Terra Nostra, *and* Return to Mexico: Journeys Behind the Mask. *Fuentes lives in Mexico City and London.*

This article first appeared in the NPQ *Winter 1991 issue entitled "Post-nationalist Mexico," and was adapted to include a later passage from an interview with Fuentes about the Chiapas revolt of 1994.*

MEXICO CITY

The cat is out of the bag and is roaming a world of instant communications, available information, and visual vocabulary. The new political grammar transforms walls into air, and iron curtains into windows of irony.

The trilogy of economic interdependence, technological progress, and instant communications can, conceivably, lead us all — from Moscow to Madrid to Mexico City — to a better world order of shared plenty. But hardly has this door been opened, than in much of the world the problems of culture have, riotously, stepped in to break up the celebration.

The paradox is this: if economic rationality tells us that the next century will be the age of global integration of the world's national economies, cultural "irrationality" steps in to inform us that it will also be the century of ethnic demands and revived nationalisms.

How can you quicken the step toward global integration if you have Ukranians and Lithuanians, Georgians and Armenians, Moldavians and Azerbaijanis yapping at your heels, denying the very principle of a worldwide integration of productive forces?

This is where political and cultural imagination must join together to ask: Can we reconcile global economic demands with the resurrection of these nationalistic claims?

Both reason and imagination tell us that the name of the solution, that point where you can balance the demands of integration and those of the nationalities, is federalism. My hope is that we shall witness a reevaluation of the federalist theme as a compromise between three equally real forces: the region and the world, passing through the nation.

To this end, the North American book *The Federalist Papers*, written by Hamilton, Madison, and Jay, should be distributed in the millions. Although two hundred years old, it may hold the secret to making the new world order work.

The applicability of their eighty-five essays is, of course, neither universal, nor restricted to conditions in 1787. Madison addressed the human tendency toward factionalism. While clearly understanding that its causes were difficult to uproot, he proposed to control its effects. How? Through a seeming paradox: a strong national government, but controlled by checks and balances, separation of powers, and federal diffusion of power. "You must first enable the government to control the governed; and in the next place oblige it to control itself." Thanks to *The Federalist Papers*, thirteen factious little colonies of the English New World became a great modern nation.

As the United States, Canada, and Mexico today are building a North American free-trade area, one wonders about the fate of the Ibero-American republics to the south of the United States. Do they pose problems comparable to those we are seeing in the Balkans, Central and Eastern Europe — not to mention Ireland and the Basque country, Brittany, and Quebec?

The world change has caught Latin America in a vicious crisis — political, social, economic — with scant resources with which to make ourselves actively present in the new multipolar order substituting the dead bipolar structure. Yet our contemporary crisis has made us realize that one thing stands on its own feet in the midst of our political and economic failures. And this is our cultural continuity, the multiracial and pluralistic culture we have created during the past five hundred years. Contrary to current revindications in Europe and Asia, cultural demands in Latin America do not disrupt the national or even the global rationalities. They reinforce them.

This has proven true despite the events in Chiapas in 1994, which reminded us that Mexico is a multiethnic, multicultural country. Mexico has the desire to be, and regards itself as, a *mestizo*, or mixed-race, country. But that does not mean simply putting aside the fact that there are ten million Indians in Mexico whose first language is not Spanish, and who often suffer the hardest brunt of social injustice. The challenge for *mestizo* Mexico after Chiapas is to come to grips with this multicultural and multiethnic reality, with stricter laws and protections for the indigenous cultures within the extant federal context. This must be done without closing the door on greater Indian integration into the *mestizo* mainstream, but at the pace determined by the Indian communities, and under a far more vigorous national compromise on democracy and social justice throughout Mexico.

If in Eurasia the problem is the conciliation of international integration with ethnic demands through a new federalist regime, in Latin America the problem is to conciliate economic growth with social justice through, again, a democratic federalism. This is the case, in particular, in Chiapas.

Latin America has a peculiar advantage over other areas of today's world. Our national cultures coincide with the physical limits of each one of our nations, even as our larger cultural boundaries embrace the Iberian peninsula (Spain and Portugal), and through them, Europe, and even as our internal diversification includes the Indian and black cultures.

The important thing is that no local separatisms menace our national unity or our neighbor's territorial integrity. Our culture, precisely because it is so varied — European, Indian, black — does not propose religious fundamentalisms or ethnic intolerance. As the Venezuelan author Arturo Uslar Pietri puts it, even when we are purely white in Latin America (and whites are a minority), we are Indian and we are black. Our culture cannot be understood without all three components. We are *mestizo*: a mixture of tastes, mores, memories, and accents.

What we do bear is profound social injustice. But because the national cultures are contained within the national boundaries, it is up to each of us to solve this problem through local politics. It is here that the federalist idea is quite relevant for Latin America.

Traditionally, we have been ruled from the center and from the top. Today, the emergence of new civil societies from Mexico to

Argentina proposes rule from the bottom and from the outskirts of society. To conciliate both movements is the mission of Latin American democracy. We are trying to "extend the republic," as Madison put it.

Even as Latin America organizes her democratic existence and reforms her economic life, she has a great contribution to make to international relations. The end of the Cold War creates a new international context that demands cooperation, but refuses intervention. Few regions in the world have a greater experience in diplomatic negotiation than Latin America as a result of our difficult dealings with our powerful northern neighbor. This has created a cultural tradition that stresses peaceful solution of controversies, diplomacy, and adherence to international laws and treaties.

If the federalist spirit becomes successfully ingrained at the national level in Latin America, it can perhaps then play a role in uniting our republics in response to collective external challenges.

The Limits to Self-Determination

Felipe Gonzalez

The prime minister of Spain, Felipe Gonzalez has been called "the only true European." He was interviewed at the Moncloa Palace in Madrid by NPQ *Editor Nathan Gardels in the winter of 1992. The following is an excerpt from that interview.*

NPQ

Yelena Bonner, the human rights activist and widow of Andrei Sakharov, has said that each nationality has a right to its own state. Self-determination, she says, is the most fundamental human right. Do you agree with this view?

Felipe Gonzalez

As a declaration of principle, I agree. But first of all we have to define exactly what each "people" is within this maze of nationalities. How far does self-determination go?

In Yugoslavia, is the "self" determined by the Croatians or the Serb minority that lives within Croatia? Is it something that can be decided by the Albanians who live in Kosovo? Is self-determination up to the Lithuanians only, or it is also up to the Russians who live in Lithuania? Or the Poles who live in Lithuania?

What is the limit to self-determination? Where do we draw the line?

Also keep in mind that all these people who want self-determination also want to be part of something bigger with someone else. "I want to break with my neighbor, even though I share large minorities with my neighbor, in order to join up with my neighbor's neighbor." That's the logic.

If we were to take this issue to its ultimate consequence, we could say that each minority has the right to self-determination in that place where it lives.

For these reasons, I believe self-determination as a principle ought to be a matter that is only agreed to and regulated internationally. Otherwise, it will be an extremely dangerous situation for Europe because there will be no end to the splintering. If we enter into a process of unlimited change of boundaries in Europe, we will be entering a period of tremendous risks.

I'm a great admirer of Abraham Lincoln. Lincoln democratically and legitimately followed the United States Constitution, not the desires of individual states for secession. His reading of the Constitution in

1861 was that the overriding principle was that it was better for freedom for all to hang together than each one for himself.

That is why America exists as successfully as it does today. And that is why I fully understood — and supported — the positions of President Bush and U.S. Secretary of State James Baker just after the collapse of the Soviet Union. Prudently, they did not look at Europe as if it were a jigsaw puzzle where the pieces can be shuffled at will. "Careful," they said. "Let us not play on divisions, because changes of borders and conflict may happen."

NPQ

Isn't the best guarantee of freedom a federal constitution where each individual has the same rights under the law? In the European context, isn't "European citizenship," not a proliferation of new states, the best course?

Gonzalez

Aside from being a citizen of one's own country, I believe each individual in Europe should become a citizen with equal rights under the law.

But it is very touchy to try to label it by calling it "federal." The Britons ask, for example, what would happen to their institutions under federalism. I don't care what you call it. I care about what it means practically as a guarantee of liberty.

NPQ

Union, constitution, individual rights under the law, not self-determination of any ethnic group that seeks it. Is that the Spanish approach? And does this apply not just to the former Soviet Union, or eastern and central Europe, but to Catalonia or the Basque areas as well?

Gonzalez

The Spanish constitution says, in the first place, that sovereignty is deposited in the national parliament. It also recognizes individual rights for all people, but admits cultural peculiarities, both linguistic and historical.

Therefore, the constitution does not establish a centralized state, but a state established on the basis of "autonomous communities."

To take Catalonia as merely one example, it has its own parliament, its own government, and its own exclusive areas of competence, as well as those it shares with Madrid.

In today's rather confusing international situation, people often tend to forget basic principles. They say to me, "you tell me, no self-determination." But that is not the point. It is not a question of self-determination or no self-determination. It is a question of limits. And in Spain, self-determination is limited by the constitution. If anybody wants to change the constitution, they must change it constitutionally, not by force.

The constitutions in most of the former Eastern-bloc countries were not democratically voted on, in the first place. That must happen first. In the case of Yugoslavia, that country reached a point of no return. It can only now come up with a new structure. There is no going back.

Croatia is never going to come up with a solution unless it keeps in mind the Serbian minorities in Croatia. So some type of accommodation must be made between Serbs and Croats, not Croats and Croats, or Serbs and Serbs. The cradle of Serbian culture is Kosovo, but the people who live there now are Albanians!

As in all civil wars, it is basically an absurd situation. Yugoslavia was a federation. Perhaps the solution is for it to break up and form a confederation — basically the same thing all over again. So, we have to keep in mind that, whether or not they become independent republics or a confederation, or whatever, they are going to have to set their own limits to self-determination, because there are so many minorities in each of these republics that they are going to have to allow each one to breathe.

In the meantime, Europe has to be extremely cautious with regard to what it does.

The worst thing would be to start recalling historic zones of influence, talking about what belonged to whom and when, and recognizing new states on that basis. Let's remember that communism in Czechoslovakia, for example, lasted for fifty years. But Czechoslovakia has a thousand-year-old history. So we have to compare nine hundred-fifty years of turmoil and change there to fifty years of communism. Let us not despise the profound history of Europe, but let us also not stir up the conflicts of the past. The cauldron is already at a boiling point. We are going to have be very cool, calm, and collected in Europe.

Germany's Heart:
The Modern Taboo

Hans Jurgen Syberberg

Filmmaker, dramatist, essayist, and consummate cultural critic, Hans Jurgen Syberberg is the man German intellectuals and politicians love to hate. Hitler: A Film from Germany *and* Parsifal *are among his best known films.*

NPQ *Senior Editor Marilyn Berlin Snell met with Syberberg on a rainy Munich afternoon in the winter of 1993 to discuss his views on the German essence, and the resurgence of neo-Nazi youth gangs.*

NPQ

Much of your work has been devoted to celebrating German culture and reclaiming its lost purity — an essence that was co-opted and soiled not only by Hitler but, according to your views, by the entire Enlightenment project, and by the seductions of a soulless material culture. As a longtime interpreter of the German *zeitgeist*, how do you explain the dark renaissance of anti-Semitic and antiforeigner violence in Germany today?

Hans Jurgen Syberberg

First, I have to tell you that no German would ever ask me this question. I hold a very special position here. For twenty-five years now, German intellectuals have treated me as if I were an enemy. They do not want to hear about what I believe lies at the heart of German identity. This is a real problem, and not just for me. It is emblematic of a general tendency for Germans, especially German intellectuals, to repress important aspects of our history — political, artistic, and cultural — which has only succeeded in nurturing the growth of ugly, right-wing street gangs.

NPQ

What is it exactly that, to your mind, has been repressed?

Syberberg

After the war, intellectuals stood on the tradition of the Enlightenment and a hegemonic rationalism that focused on the head at the expense of the heart. But the heart of Germany, like that of Russia, is very special, very different. Culture is built from the light on the trees, the way the heavens look at night from a particular plot of land. The light and the heavens are different here than elsewhere. Our perspective, our feelings, therefore, are different. Yet we have felt compelled in postwar Germany to repress this uniqueness. We feel safe excelling in mathematics, physics, business. Our people, dominated by facts and figures, are satisfied to dance around the golden calf of materialism. We are very efficient and methodical. But where is the heart?

This has been my artistic project: to focus on the heart, the modern German taboo. And I see that the repression of this aspect of the German identity has cultivated a very negative reaction.

I have warned in the past of the dangers of "repressed irrationalism." Right-wing extremism in Germany today is indeed the result of repression, but I would now revise my terminology. Today, though I use the word "rationalism" to characterize the postwar intellectual tradition, l do not mean that the contrary is necessarily "irrationalism." The distinction between the "head" and the "heart" does not translate to "rationalism" versus "irrationalism." The artistic and intellectual form this took in Germany in the past was idealism, as opposed to the later materialism of the nineteenth century.

As to the question of the right-wing uprising on the streets, I see it resulting from a kind of postwar democratic repression. These youths represent the German wound. They are very vulgar, ugly, and sometimes just banal. But in the end they are merely a function of our postwar democracy. In history, haunting Erinyes are never nice or beloved.

Let me give you an example of what I mean by "democratic repression." Recently, after a right-wing leader appeared on a late-night television show, the entire country went into an uproar over the fact that this man was given a platform to air his views.

Every newspaper, large and small, editorialized about how right-wing views should not be allowed, with the argument that he spoke too cleverly. And now, popular opinion — or should I say official media opinion — has it that this man and his viewpoint should be silenced. Yet we cannot eradicate our little Hitlers by refusing to give them the microphone. If people want a Hitler, one cannot prevent them from having him. And, in fact, the repression of these views may only increase their seductiveness among those who feel left out of society already.

In a historical sense, Hitler interests me because he came out of the heart of the German people. A man without a heart; this was the tragedy for them. But this awareness does not help me with our current crisis in the streets. The man I just mentioned, the right-wing extremist who will no longer be allowed to speak his views publicly, does not spring from the heart of the people. Rather he is the product of democratic repression. The threat he poses, however, is no less great for this fact.

This is a new era for Germany, with new dangers. Certainly we must be concerned about the extremists who burn down the houses of foreigners; and we must be concerned with a justice system that reacts too slowly and too late. But we must also go beyond these symptoms of the postwar German wound and get to its cause.

When people support neo-Nazi leaders today, they are not necessarily supporting the message. These people are wounded, and they see that their pain and their fear are better represented by extremist leaders than by German politicians and intellectuals. But frankly, I don't think these young men are really interested in following anybody. They have no ideology, neo-Nazi or otherwise. They only make fire. Violence is their form of anarchic expression. We should ask ourselves what they are expressing. What went wrong?

Our political leaders can try to extinguish these flames with laws and decrees. They may succeed in putting out a few small fires, but we know from personal and historical experience that it is very unwise to stifle expressions of discontent. Psychoanalysis and Weimar should be our guides here.

Every society constructs its antithesis, and in certain revolutionary moments it bursts upon the scene. In our society today, where money is so central, where the minister of finance holds a position of importance the defense minister held in times past — in a time where money has such incredible power — we would be well-advised to pay attention to what springs up where there is no money or business interests.

What today is finding success with the young generation has nothing at all to do with money. They make music called "Oi," whose sales are prohibited in stores; they have concerts that can't be advertised. They don't make money; they don't spend money. They just gather, and the gatherings are getting larger. They are part of a real underground, like the early Christians in the catacombs in Rome.

And the German media are going crazy. They are saying that this trend is worse than Hitler and Himmler combined! But the German press probably just wants to please people abroad with this kind of coverage.

NPQ

Isn't it disturbing to you, as well?

Syberberg

It's a wound. And because it has been covered up, suppressed all this time, it has now become infected and is oozing the pus out into society. But this is a reaction to something else; it is not springing fully formed from the heart of the German people.

NPQ

But you are describing this phenomenon of racist extremism as though it were somehow healthy for Germany — a healthy reaction to the soulless market culture that now prevails.

Syberberg

No. This extremism frightens me, too. These youths are bloodthirsty, aggressive. When one sees clips of them on television, their faces are contorted like wild animals. But there they are: the new German underground. It's really like the first Christians, in the belly of the golden calf.

Moreover, my role as an artist is not to judge but to discover how and why it is happening. There is something wrong with my country. Maybe these youths don't understand who Hitler was. Maybe they don't know history; they only use Hitler for shock effect. I want to know what it is in the air that nourishes this behavior. It's not just because these young men are poor and without work. And it's not just a violent protest against their fathers, against capitalism or democracy. There is something more.

What permeates the air in Germany also exists in Poland, Italy, Hungary, France, Scandinavia, and elsewhere. It has the odor of anti-Semitism, in part. After Auschwitz, the Jewish position was a moral one, which developed over time into a kind of moral hegemony. But there is a danger inherent in any kind of hegemony: it eventually engenders resentment on the part of the weaker player. People don't like to be told over and over that they are morally inferior. They bear it for a certain time, but then there comes a point when the children refuse to continue paying their fathers' debts. European culture has reached this breaking point. Not the intellectuals, of course; they are professionals at maintaining their equanimity. But that is not the case in the streets.

The rebellion does not come from the head, but from the gut, and in all countries of Europe. It is a rebellion of the Erinyes — ugly, brutal. The Greeks depicted them in mythical images as something barbaric.

But this said, there is also another picture of Germany: thousands taking to the streets — the majority; one sees them on television, in the newspapers. They are shocked. Never before have so many in Germany declared their support for foreigners, and so selflessly. They show their solidarity for the foreigners in Germany, just as they did last winter for Russia or for Yugoslavia, in numbers greater than in any other country in the world. Those who lay the fires are a fringe group of a special kind.

NPQ

Your analysis has the effect of transforming victims into antagonists — culprits in their own victimization.

Syberberg

People are always very quick to make that argument. But in this historical moment the Jews are not victims; they are victors, morally speaking. This has been the case since the end of the war. And not only in Jerusalem or in Germany, but worldwide. But we cannot freeze historical moments. History moves. Fifty years after Hitler, a whole new generation has taken the stage. They behave differently than their guilt-ridden parents. They don't see the young Jew as a victim. They see in him someone like themselves.

What one is concerned with now is finding a new definition: the cards of world history have been reshuffled since the fall of the Wall with the ending of the East-West conflict. People are looking in history, in the future and in art for new identities. This is the case for people in other parts of Europe, in the U.S. and in Germany — and, one hopes, this is also the case for the Jews.

The reason I defend my position in Germany so vehemently may, I believe, be found in the fact that my enemies today would in many cases have been my enemies in the Nazi era, too. Just as they are yes-men today, so they would have been collaborators under Hitler. I am, therefore, doing battle for their souls, and I do so with a certain sadness. I see the way they behave, so loud and righteously as democrats, and yet I recognize in them antidemocrats possessing the same characteristics I knew during my school days in eastern Germany under Stalin. My work, then, is a labor of mourning, and it is aimed at present-day symptoms of the "ugly German" as Holderlin once described him, or Thomas Bernhard in Austria.

So, one should not be so quick with judgments. It would be more productive just to look at and attempt to understand what is happening. My personal concern is where art moves now. For too long, art has been regressing, stuck repeating an old postwar aesthetic.

Germany has been left in the postwar world to be picked at by vultures, both internally and abroad. I use the example of Kleist, whose plays have been consistently misinterpreted in postwar Germany. For instance, in one of his plays the actor can say either "dirt" or "pain," at a very important moment in the piece. Today, the writing is always interpreted as "the *dirt* of my heart" rather than "the *pain* of my heart." It is instances such as this that underscore Germany's postwar aesthetics of polemics, self-flagellation, and ugliness.

Ugliness exists, and that fact should not be avoided in art. But my solution has been to place the ugliness in a larger universe, so that it doesn't consume the moment. Indeed, the most noble goal of art in the German tradition was and is the elevation of reality as an achievement of precisely this art.

I find that my colleagues in stage or film too often roll themselves in ugliness, but in doing so they betray the function of art, which is to move through the facts of the world to another point to travel through. And in Germany, the artists are guilty of something else as well. There has been a certain demonization of the purely aesthetic as something tainted by fascism. This, of course, is part of Hitler's legacy. His aesthetic, which was a reaction against the German expressionist art of the prewar period, celebrated German myth and glorified rural life as the embodiment of German blood and soil. In effect, Hitler co-opted the beauty of German myth and history. Part of Hitler's blood and soil aesthetic is also his curse of scorched earth, which he wanted to leave behind. And that has been tragically accomplished in the burned-out hearts of my generation.

NPQ

Is it possible to retrieve what has been despoiled by Hitler's legacy?

Syberberg

Yes. But it is very difficult, not least because of the way Germans use democracy to stifle discussion of these issues — both in politics and in art.

My strength, if I have one, is that I understand that the truth lies on the other side of the past. I want my art to pass through it, to overcome the ugliness that so much of postmodern society and art dwells upon. I think that's what art should do.

NPQ

The sociologist Ralf Dahrendorf has made the argument that liberal democracy is government by conflict. In the U.S., though many may not like it, the Ku Klux Klan has a right to march in the street and proselytize its racist philosophy. Germany, on the other hand, legislates against discord in politics, and from what you have been saying, strongly discourages it in art. Why do you think this is the case? Are Germans somehow uniquely unqualified to maneuver in the chaotic, uncomfortable, and often uncontrollable structures of liberal democracy?

Syberberg

The problem is that Germans are too well organized for the messiness of liberal democracy. We attempt to organize democratic opinion, to keep the system running smoothly and efficiently. When something disrupts the system, or doesn't fit where it's supposed to, there are problems.

The concentration camps also belong to this chapter of German thoroughness, of starting from basics, thinking radically, totally, absolutely, getting to the very root of things. Expressed in vulgar terms, this means German orderliness (or security or cleanliness or industry) is capable of transforming itself in everyday life into something bureaucratic, ideological, racial; or it finds itself realized in the concrete form of a perverted political "work of art" (Plato) matching Kafka's vision. Other peoples in Europe are also familiar with these tendencies toward obliteration in pogroms, but it was allotted to Germany to carry it out with thoroughness.

NPQ

The philosopher Ivan Illich spoke of the earthy virtue of soil — his form of *heimat* perhaps — of tradition, community and memory. . . .

Syberberg

Hitler talked about soil too — blood and soil. . . .

NPQ

That's the point: Is it possible to have a notion of *heimat* without it devolving into nationalism and antimodernism in Germany?

Syberberg

First, why is *heimat* experiencing such a renaissance in contemporary Germany? *Heimat* was one of the aesthetic subjects that was forbidden territory after the war. But fifteen million people came out of the Eastern provinces that now no longer exist, and they have a strong feeling of *heimat* because they have lost their homeland. People need food and shelter, but they also need love, community, a home. This is part of the natural function of being human.

Instead of being worried about making the neighbors nervous, we should rather be taking a look at ourselves. We behave like postmodern animals in a cave of our own denaturalized creation. We are afraid to sing our grandfather's songs; we are afraid to appreciate Wagner, even to mourn the theft of our myths and fairy tales by history. We live in cities with fouled air, water, and soil — completely detached from ourselves and our cultural heritage — and become these neurotic beings.

Contrary to popular opinion, I think that the urge to retrieve what it is we have lost — water we can drink, fresh corn out of our own garden plots, our songs, our Teutonic fantasies — is healthy. This longing for *heimat* is not a longing for Hitler. Germany is capable of benign nostalgia. But we must be allowed to long.

These are the wounds of Germany. When you look into the face of the nineteen-year-old who threw the firebomb at the home of immigrant Turks in Moelln, you see that he's not working for himself, nor for a political party, but for something else. He's really the victim of a certain situation.

NPQ

But what about individual responsibility? Maybe that young man is a victim of something, but he killed three people.

Syberberg

Yes, of course. But my point is that we should not be focusing on what propelled the firebomb but what propelled the man. He is not yet part of a group that cannot be changed. This is not 1933, but post-1945! Then, popular discontent went like the ghost of the world into the grave of our culture, but today I don't see it like that.

Flaubert said of his time that "the thought of the future torments us and the past holds us back. And that is why the present is slipping from our grasp." This seems to be the curse of Germany — in art as well as in politics and morality. Part of the problem is that Germany cannot free itself from the dialectics of guilt, atonement, and resentment, while the Jews cannot escape the backlash that arises from their moral hegemony. We are fixed to each other like two sides of the same coin.

Germany became the nostalgic venue of the culture of the emigrants and their children, as Jerusalem was once for German Christians. The only question is: which Germany? I believe that if those who go to see my films or stage projects or who read my writing were to perceive the reality of Germany today they would be extremely disappointed.

In the end, however, Germany's self-flagellation just becomes a sordid form of big business. The German artist who touches Auschwitz or Hitler in the appropriately chaste way immediately finds open doors worldwide. There is something sickening about this.

But I can only see this changing through some sort of catastrophe. What we see in the streets now are just little catastrophes, which only tie us more tightly to the past. I think art could play an important role in untangling the death grip of the German and the Jew. But today, unfortunately, all real art is demonized, while this subject in particular remains taboo.

German artists must turn their energies toward investigating the German identity. The more blood that has flowed, the more art will be necessary: as catharsis, for atonement. And what the contemporary practitioners fail to achieve, the children will have to continue, for the sake of purification, as a ritual. This is a goal that cannot be set too highly. Only those artists and artworks will survive in history that are capable of achieving this goal.

Bosnia and the Diet Coke Civilization

Bernard Henri-Levy

One of France's leading "nouvelle philosophes," Bernard Henri-Levy is author of, among other works, Barbarism with a Human Face. *A close acquaintance of the Bosnian Muslim president, Alija Izetbegovic, Henri-Levy convinced French President François Mitterrand to make a surprise visit to Sarajevo in 1992, thus focusing world attention on the need to open that city to the delivery of humanitarian supplies. He spoke with* NPQ *editor Nathan Gardels at the Cafe de Flore in Paris in January 1993.*

NPQ

What does it mean that the West has left Sarajevo — the very emblem of the idea of Europe — to die?

Bernard Henri-Levy

It means many things. First, I think we are witnessing the revival in a soft and sated Europe of what in the 1930s was called the "mentality of Munich," the mentality of appeasement and compromise with evil.

Second, the West is very shortsighted. It seems to think that its interests are at stake only when oil is involved. In Sarajevo, there is no oil. There is only an idea that is the essence of Europe: tolerance and coexistence. Unfortunately, today we have political leaders who don't understand that the interests of the West are far more threatened in Sarajevo than in the oil fields of the Gulf. In starving and besieged Sarajevo, the European idea itself has been mortally wounded.

Third, I have the horrible suspicion that, in the cynical depths of power, European governments agree that ethnic cleansing and segregation into ethnic-based nation-states is the final answer for the Balkans. Our diplomats have long regarded the Balkans as an eternal mess. For over a century the Balkans have been beset by disorder and chaos. The Balkan conflict ignited the First World War.

I fear that the diplomats think, without expressing it, that "here we have a barbarian, a madman — Milosevic (the Serbian leader.) But this murderer does the job. He does it with cruelty and is spilling too much blood, of course. But he is doing what has to be done. So, let us close our eyes. Let us look aside. But let us not get in his way." I fear this is the subconscious motive for not standing up to Milosevic.

The West could not be making a bigger mistake by living with ethnic cleansing. If it wins in Sarajevo, it will win everywhere else, in Georgia, in Azerbaijan, in Armenia, in Transylvania. Ethnic cleansing is a temptation waiting to happen in Rostock, in Italy north of the Lombard line, and elsewhere. The fuse of racial hatred is long, and winds through all of Europe.

Not to stand firm against this assault on the very idea of Europe is not a decision for peace. It is a decision for war. Sarajevo stands for a universalist, open, and tolerant Europe, the Europe of Maastricht. I said during the French referendum that the road to Maastricht goes through Sarajevo. If Sarajevo dies, so does the idea of Europe embodied in the Maastricht Treaty.

NPQ

But it is not just the leaders who are betraying Europe by failing to act. The people also lack the courage of their convictions. As Milan Kundera, among others, has observed, Europeans have become too comfortable to wage war for moral reasons.

Henri-Levy

Yes, I agree. The idea of war has become inconceivable for the developed countries. War is unthinkable. Or rather, we are willing to make war on one condition: that no one of us dies. This idea is consistent with the general trend of the Diet Coke civilization: we want sugar without calories, butter without fat, birth without labor pains, dying without suffering. So why not war without dying?

The suppression of negativity; light without darkness — that is the strange new dream of our civilization. It is our fatal illusion.

NPQ

But isn't this a war among competing nationalisms, with each group trying to set up its exclusive nation-state? Isn't the conflict in the former Yugoslavia, as you have said, a war between "weak nationalism" and "strong nationalism?"

Henri-Levy

I think this is true between the Croats, the weaker nationalism, and the Serbs, the stronger. The situation in Sarajevo is different. Izetbegovic is not a nationalist. Sarajevo is a cosmopolitan city where different nations have lived together for five centuries.

NPQ

The Bosnian Serbs claim that Izetbegovic is trying to create a Muslim-dominated state in Bosnia.

Henri-Levy

No. There was one document from 1970, which the Serbs often cite, called "The Islamic Declaration." Izetbegovic has stated his disagreement with the document many times, and since he became president his policy has been demonstrably against the establishment of an Islamic state.

The government of Sarajevo is mixed, with a strict parity of the Muslim, Croat, and Serb ministers. There are six of each. The second in command of the Bosnian government's army is a Serb. Thirty percent of the population fighting to defend Sarajevo are Serbs. An ethnically mixed population is fighting against Serbian nationalism in Sarajevo, and in the western part of Bosnia-Herzegovina against Croatian nationalism. In Sarajevo, cosmopolitan and tolerant Europe is fighting the specter of the nationalist, populist, chauvinist idea of Europe.

NPQ

Throughout Paris one sees posters comparing Milosevic and Hitler. Are they the same?

Henri-Levy

I don't agree with this. God knows I hate Milosevic. He is a murderer. But all murderers are not Hitler. So far, Milosevic has not built gas chambers. He is not more criminal, in scale or intent, than Hitler. In any event, confusing specific phenomenan is not useful. Hitlerism was a very specific phenomena, and so is the Greater Serbia idea.

NPQ

On a broader subject, a number of theories have been concocted to give the post–Cold War experience a name. Some have called our emergent era "the end of history." Others have seen the opposite — the "return of history," with all its tribalism and ethnic strife, as a result of the "thawing of frozen worlds."

You see something different in the coming era — the construction of various alloys out of postmodern fragments, fusing together ideologically in as yet unknown combinations. Can you offer some more specific hint of what you see?

Henri-Levy

Those who believe in the end of history think that the triumph of democracy is certain. They believe it may take a while longer, but the spread of democracy is inexorable. This is the Hegelian point of view. Now that the worst enemy of democracy, communism, is finished, every day will be Sunday. Of course, this vision is contradicted every day by what happens in the Balkans, and Eastern and Central Europe.

As you said, then there are those who believe that history is returning, that old elements are resurfacing after being frozen in time by totalitarianism. One often has this impression when visiting someplace like Hungary. Some of the rising politicians there seem like phantoms, ghosts of the past.

This might be true, but it is not the whole truth. If it were so, we would remain in the realm of the end of history. It might take time to get rid of these remnants of the past, but in the end they will go. I think something else is happening.

Europe today is like it was in the 1920s. We exist in a huge laboratory where molecules are colliding. Some are destroying themselves. Others are splitting, and forming new and unforeseen combinations, new compounds.

In the Europe of the 1920s, we saw several currents such as nationalism or socialism. These movements splintered, some died, some took different paths, some combined with other movements. Who would have expected the emergence of that particular composition known as National Socialism?

We can see this phenomenon at work today in Russia. *Pamyat* is not just neo-Stalinism added to neo-Slavophilism added to anti-Semitism. The sum is an essence different than the parts. The mixture is something new and apart from anything before.

The same is true of Milosevic in Serbia. He is not just an old communist converted to nationalism. He represents something more for which we haven't yet found a name. One thing is certain, though. The red despotism and brown despotism of the past have been replaced by a new form of barbarity. It is not certain we will lose, of course, in this fight against the new barbarity. Who would have thought, after all, that Soviet communism would have fallen so quickly and so thoroughly? But it is also not certain we will win.

All we know is that some kind of chimera without a fully defined shape is staring at us from the future, haunting us.

NPQ

It is a paradox that in many European quarters, especially in France, anti-Americanism persists. Yet it may well be the Americans that saved the idea of Europe left to die by the Europeans themselves in Sarajevo.

Henri-Levy

That old French patient, anti-Americanism, is unfortunately still strong and well shared by both left and right. But it is wrong.

You might be right that the European idea will be saved by its American offspring. Especially under President Clinton, America seems more ready than anyone else to prevent the genocide of the Bosnian Muslims. In a way, America with its vast ethnic mix is the fullest realization of the European idea of cosmopolitanism and tolerance. Yet, after the Los Angeles riots, all of us have to wonder if the new face of barbarity may not be lurking around in America as well.

Hope and Horror in Africa

Wole Soyinka

Awarded the Nobel Prize for literature in 1986, Nigerian author Wole Soyinka's many books and plays include Death and the King's Horseman, Ake: The Years of Childhood *and* Isara. *He was interviewed in London by* NPQ *editor Nathan Gardels in the summer of 1994 as the massacre was taking place in Rwanda.*

NPQ

Africa today is living a moment of hope and horror. A young multiracial democracy has been proudly born in South Africa while countless corpses from tribal war clog the sad rivers of Rwanda. Which fate will win out?

Wole Soyinka

South Africa is our dream, Rwanda our nightmare. The dream can be our fate, but not tomorrow. Rwanda is clinically dead as a nation. The international community, in this case the Organization of African Unity (OAU) and the United Nations, should have had the courage to pronounce this fact. What we should concern ourselves with is the humanity that is trapped in this abattoir. We are not dealing with a nation, but a slaughterhouse.

When a nation is able to lose in a few days a quarter of a million of its people, when its so-called government lacks the means to protect its citizens from being slaughtered *en masse* by machetes, that government, whether by acts of omission or commission, dooms that space recognized by the world as sovereign.

I do not know an instance in our contemporary world where humanity has been so degraded, so nullified, so treated with total contempt, as it is today in Rwanda. Two years ago there was the Rio Summit on the environment. There have been global meetings in Japan to discuss threatened species of elephants, rhinoceros, or warthogs. Everyone is worried about the gorillas in Rwanda. A great stir has been made about the fact that poachers are killing a few thousand elephants a year, laws are made, commodities are banned. But we are talking here today about a human decimation. To talk about an endangered species is to talk about the Tutsis in Rwanda today.

NPQ

We've seen the Rwanda kind of unraveling before in Africa, in Liberia a couple of years ago, and more recently in Somalia. Now it threatens to engulf the entire horn of the continent. What is the underlying connection in this trend?

Soyinka

One hundred years ago at the Berlin Conference, the colonial powers that ruled Africa met to divvy up their interests into states, lumping various peoples and tribes together in some places, or slicing them apart in others like some demented tailor who paid no attention to the fabric, color, or pattern of the quilt he was patching together.

One of the biggest disappointments of the OAU when it came into being more than twenty years ago was that it failed to address this issue. Instead, one of its cardinal principles was noninterference and the sacrosanctity of the boundaries inherited from the colonial situation. That was a foreboding failure of political will. And now we see in Rwanda what that absence of African self-redefinition has wrought. If we fail to understand that all this stems from the colonial nation-state map imposed upon us, there will be little chance to correct the situation over the long term.

NPQ

But you can't blame it all on the colonial powers. You yourself wrote just a couple of years ago that Africans must accuse Africa's failed leadership for "the trail of skeletons along desiccated highways . . . the lassitude and hopelessness of emaciated survivors crowded into refugee camps . . . the mounds of corpses." Africa, you wrote, had been betrayed "from within."

Soyinka

You cannot, of course, dismiss the context for our failures. At the same time, you are right. So many decades of so-called independence have passed since the end of colonial rule. Unfortunately, African leaders have been so concerned with maintaining their power and authority within these artificial ponds created by colonialism, they have been so eager to preserve their status as king toad, that they've never really addressed the humanity that is entrapped within those ponds.

NPQ

Are you, then, proposing redesigning the "spaces" in Africa into a more harmonious quilt, or at least one less prone to tribal bloodletting?

Soyinka

Yes, we should sit down with square rule and compass and redesign the boundaries of African nations. If we thought we could get away without this redefinition of boundaries back when the OAU was formed, surely the instance of Rwanda lets us know in a very brutal way that we cannot evade this historical challenge any longer.

The horror of Rwanda is too high a price to pay for a very vaporous and whimsical notion of what constitutes inviolable territorial boundaries. How can we accept the brutal decimation of a quarter of a million people in a couple of weeks for the preservation of boundaries that aren't even ours?

NPQ

South Africa was the last nation in Africa to be liberated, but the only one in which liberation came through the ballot box, through democracy. Will this special quality enable South Africa under Nelson Mandela to provide the leadership role Africa's king toads are so sorely unable to offer?

Soyinka

It seems that a kind of political chemistry brewed by Mandela and (F. W.) de Klerk gives that nation a very good chance to make it. What has happened there through the democratic process is a rebuke to the rest of the African states for their failures. It should make Nigeria, the other African nation with great economic potential, ashamed at its betrayal of its people and the squandering of their promise. The tension and contradictions faced by South Africans were far more intractable than those in the rest of Africa. Yet, they were overcome and a democracy has been born. That gives the rest of Africa no excuse. No excuse whatever.

The Hindu Awakening

V. S. Naipaul

The Trinidad-born writer of Indian heritage, V. S. Naipaul's books include The Middle Passage *(1962),* In a Free State *(1971),* India: A Wounded Civilization *(1977),* A Bend in the River *(1979),* Among the Believers *(1981), and* India: A Million Mutinies Now *(1990).*

He was interviewed for NPQ *in New Delhi by Dileep Padgaonkar, editor of* Times of India.

NPQ

In today's India people tend to be either aggressive or apologetic about their cultural identity. They find it difficult to admit there are several layers in our culture — Hinduism in all its pluralistic splendor, the contribution made by Islam's long presence in the subcontinent, and the exposure to the West. Do you see it this way?

V. S. Naipaul

The alternatives — traditionalism versus Westernism — might be false. In reality there is no either/or. Literature, inquiry, and philosophy are a constant examination of oneself, one's world, and one's own culture. One hopes to leave the world with different ideas than those given when we entered the world. Alternatives proposed in today's India could lead to brutal clashes. Remember that India was trampled over, fought over. It had destroyed itself by its wars. It was almost at a standstill.

My book *India: A Wounded Civilization* is precisely about this. It is about a conquered people, a devastated people who felt smaller and smaller. You had the invasions and you had the absence of a response to them. There was an absence even of the idea of a people, of a nation defending itself. So, there is no reason really for people to be either aggressive or apologetic about all this.

NPQ

Unless, of course, the perception is that you have to contend with the "other." For the past ten or twelve years the feeling in India has burgeoned that Hinduism faces a threat from the mushrooming growth of Islamic fundamentalism, a threat that began with the Iranian revolution and Pakistani General Zia's "Islamization," and proceeded with the Salman Rushdie affair and attacks on liberal Muslim intellectuals. Such events have persuaded some forces in India to believe that a divided Hindu society cannot counteract Islamic fundamentalism.

Naipaul

I don't see it quite the same way. The things you mention are quite superficial. You cannot be a fundamentalist if you want to go and live in America. Yet, ask any Iranian where he wants to go: it is to America. If that is your goal, you cannot be a fundamentalist. I think fundamentalism is a passing phase even in Islam. It is a religion on the defensive.

What is happening in India is a new, historical awakening. Only now are people beginning to understand that there has been a great vandalizing of India. They understand now that the truth of their history can be found in the way invaders looked at their own actions. They were conquering; they were subjugating. Because of the nature of the conquest and the nature of Hindu society, such an understanding had eluded Indians before. In preindustrial India, people moved about in small areas unaware of the dimension of the country, without any notion of community or a nation. People seemed to say: We are all right here. The West may be disastrous, but we are not affected.

Now, however, things seem to be changing. What is happening in India is a mighty, creative process. Indian intellectuals, who want to be secure in their liberal beliefs, may not understand what is going on. But every other Indian knows precisely what is happening: deep down he knows that a larger response is emerging even if at times this response appears in his eyes to be threatening.

So, I don't see the Hindu reaction purely in terms of one fundamentalism pitted against another. The new Hindu attitude, the new sense of history being attained by Hindus, is not like Mohammedan fundamentalism, which is essentially a negative, last-ditch effort to fight against a world it desperately wishes to join.

Some Indians speak about a synthetic culture. This is what a defeated people always speak about. The synthesis may be culturally true. But to stress my point, it could also be a response to intense historical persecution. This is sometimes taken to absurd lengths, by the writer Nirad Chaudhuri, for instance, who talks about "Hindu aggressiveness" in the midst of massive cultural vandalism.

NPQ

All the same, my worry is that somewhere down the line this search for a sense of history might yet again turn into hostility toward something precious which came to India from the West: the notion of the individual.

Naipaul

This is where intellectuals have a duty to perform. The duty is the use of the mind. It is not enough for intellectuals to chant their liberal views or to merely condemn what is happening. To use the mind is to reject the grosser aspects of this vast emotional upsurge.

We all live in a universal civilization, some more than others. We have our individual particularities, but we are inhabited by universal civilization. It is very hard to go back.

NPQ

Where did your interest in Islamic societies come from?

Naipaul

There were Mohammedans among us in Trinidad. The Indian community there had strong bonds. But in Trinidad you had the Negro movement, a racial movement, headed by Eric Williams. This was in 1956. It brought us closer to the Mohammedans.

But, please understand that my interest is not in Arab Islam. It is in Islam outside the Arab world, in countries conquered by the Arabs or influenced by the Arab religion. When my book on these countries was published, it was not welcomed by the Arabs. But what do the Arabs know about Malaysia or Pakistan or Iran?

I think that the sense of injustice, the tragic sense of the world that you find in the countries I have mentioned, will transmute itself into something very creative.

NPQ

What about the Indian Muslims?

Naipaul

Those people are considerably lost. This is something that their fathers and grandfathers brought about; they had not thought their ideas through. When Iqbal [the Indian poet and philosopher, who lived from 1877–1938] spoke about the need for Islam to have its own society, he had not worked out the consequences. He had not considered the possibility of the "Bosniazation" of the subcontinent.

Iqbal maintained that Islam was not a matter of private conscience. What was needed was an Islamic society, an Islamic nation. But how do you create a society of believers? How about those who were going to be left behind? It is amazing that this thought never occurred to him. I attribute it to the fear of thinking things through.

NPQ

How did you react to the Ayodhya incident [where the Muslim mosque was desecrated by Hindu militants in 1993]?

Naipaul

Not as badly as others did, I am afraid. The people who say that there was no Hindu temple there are missing the point. Babar [founder of the Mughal Dynasty in India in 1526], you must understand, had contempt for the country he had conquered. And his building of that mosque at Ayodhya was an act of contempt for the country. In Turkey, they turned the church of Santa Sophia into a mosque. In Nicosia, churches were converted into mosques, too. The Spaniards spent many centuries reconquering their land from Muslim invaders. So, these things have happened before and elsewhere. In Ayodhya, the construction of a mosque on a spot regarded as sacred by the conquered population was meant as an insult to an ancient idea, the idea of Ram [the Hindu deity embodying chivalry and virtue], which was two or three thousand years old.

NPQ

The people who climbed on top of the domes of Ayodhya mosque and smashed them were not bearded people wearing saffron robes and with ash on their foreheads. They were young people clad in jeans and T-shirts.

Naipaul

One needs to understand the passion that took them on top of the domes. The jeans and T-shirts of the West are superficial. The passion alone is real. You can't dismiss it. You have to try to harness it.

That passion is linked to the new, bottom-up change taking place in India. I spoke earlier about the state of the country: destitute, trampled upon, crushed. You then had the Bengali renaissance, the thinkers of the nineteenth century. But all this came from the top. What is happening now is different.

The movement is now from below. It has to be dealt with. It is not enough to abuse these youths or use that fashionable word from Europe, "fascism."

There is a big, historical development going on in India. Wise men should understand it and ensure that it does not remain in the hands of fanatics. Rather, they should use it for the intellectual transformation of India.

NPQ

But the feeling now is that the individual will be subjugated if the basis of Indian nationhood is to be Hinduism alone. That is the potential danger.

Naipaul

There are too many people who think like you for that to be realized. Fortunately, this movement in favor of the individual has come as a result of education, of several generations of educated people. There are enough people who are educated to fight this. There is a self-regulatory thermostat that should take care of the problem.

NPQ

What are you thinking about, what are the issues that preoccupy you now?

Naipaul

There are two issues about black Africa I would like to go into. Why is there no Arab guilt about black Africa? The Arabs were importing slaves all along. African eunuchs were employed to guard harems. Castration of black Africans was common practice in Sudan and upper Egypt. And why is there no sense of guilt in Brazil, where slaves were imported until 1888? It probably has to do with the intellectual traditions of these countries. A sense of guilt or shock is doubtless linked to a tradition that fosters free thought and analytical abilities.

La Raza Cosmica in America

Ryzsard Kapuscinski

Ryzsard Kapuscinski has spent most of the post–World War II years reporting on war and revolution in Africa, the Middle East, and Latin America. He is the author of The Emperor, *on the fall of Haile Selassie of Ethiopia, and* The Shah of Shahs, *an account of the fall of the Shah and the Iranian Revolution. At present he is completing a book on Idi Amin of Uganda, the final book of a trilogy on dictators.*

In 1987, NPQ *asked Kapuscinski to turn both his talents of observation and his knowledge of disparate peoples and cultures toward the subject of America's future, as foretold in Los Angeles, now America's largest Third World city.*

The impressions that follow are excerpted from a conversation with NPQ *Editor Nathan Gardels at the New Seoul Hotel in L.A.'s Koreatown.*

LOS ANGELES

The mere fact that America still attracts millions of people is evidence that it is not in decline. People aren't attracted to a place of decline. Signs of decline are sure to be found in a place as complex as America: debt, crime, the homeless, drugs, dropouts. But the main characteristic of America, the first and most enduring impression, is dynamism, energy, aggressiveness, forward movement.

It is so hard to think of this nation in decline when you know that there are vast regions of the planet that are absolutely paralyzed, incapable of any improvement at all.

It is difficult for me to agree with Paul Kennedy's thesis in *The Rise and Fall of Great Powers* that America must inevitably follow historical precedent. That's the way history used to be — all-powerful nations declined and gave way to other empires. But maybe there is another way to look at what is happening. I have a sense that what is going on here concerns much more than the fate of a nation.

It may be that the Eurocentered American nation is declining as it gives way to a new Pacific civilization that will include, but not be limited to, America. Historically speaking, America may not decline, but instead fuse with the Pacific culture to create a kind of vast Pacific collage, a mix of Hispanic and Asian cultures linked through the most modern communication technologies.

Traditional history has been a history of nations. But here, for the first time since the Roman Empire, there is the possibility of creating the history of a civilization. Now is the first chance on a new basis with new technologies to create a civilization of unprecedented openness and pluralism. A civilization of the polycentric mind. A civilization that leaves behind forever the ethnocentric, tribal mentality, the mentality of destruction.

Los Angeles is a premonition of this new civilization. Linked more to the Third World and Asia than to the Europe of America's racial and cultural roots, Los Angeles and southern California will enter the twenty-first century as a multiracial and multicultural society.

This is absolutely new. There is no previous example of a civilization that is being simultaneously created by so many races, nationalities, and cultures. This new type of cultural pluralism is completely unknown in the history of mankind.

America is becoming more plural every day because of the unbelievable facility of the new Third World immigrants to put a piece of their original culture inside of American culture. The notion of a "dominant" American culture is changing every moment. It is incredible coming to America to find you are somewhere else — in Seoul, in Taipei, in Mexico City. You can travel inside Korean culture right on the streets of Los Angeles. Inhabitants of this vast city become internal tourists in the place of their own residence.

There are large communities of Laotians, Vietnamese, Cambodians, Mexicans, Salvadorans, Guatemalans, Iranians, Japanese, Koreans, Armenians, Chinese. We find here Little Taipei, Little Saigon, Little Tokyo, Koreatown, Little Central America, the Iranian neighborhood in Westwood, the Armenian community in Hollywood, and the vast Mexican-American areas of East Los Angeles. Eighty-one languages, few of them European, are spoken in the elementary school system of the city of Los Angeles.

This transformation of American culture anticipates the general trend in the composition of mankind. Ninety percent of the immigrants to this city are from the Third World. At the beginning of the twenty-first century, 90 percent of the world's population will be dark-skinned; the white race will be no more than 11 percent of all human beings living on our planet. Something that can only be seen in America:

In the manicured, landscaped, ultraclean high-technology parks of northern Orange County there is a personal computer company that seven years ago did not exist. There were only strawberry fields where the plant is. Now, there is a $500 million company with factories in Hong Kong and Taiwan as well. The company was founded by three young immigrants — a Pakistani Muslim, and two Chinese from Hong Kong. They only became citizens in 1984. Each individual is now probably worth $30 million. Walking through this company we see only young, dark faces —Vietnamese, Cambodians, Laotians, Mexicans — and the most ad-vanced technology. The culture of the workforce is a mix of Hispanic-Catholic family values and Asian-Confucian group loyalty. Employment notices are never posted; hiring is done through the network of families that live in southern California. Not infrequently, employees ask to work an extra twenty hours a week to earn enough money to help members of their extended family buy their first home.

In Los Angeles, traditional Third World cultures are, for the first time, fusing with the most modern mentalities and technologies. After decades of covering war and revolution in the Third World, I carry in my mind an image of crowds, tension, crisis. My experience has always been of social activity that leads to destruction, to trouble, to unhappiness. People are always trying to do something, but they are unable to. The intentions of people trying to make revolution are just and good, but suddenly, something goes wrong. There is disorganization, unending problems. The weight of the past. They cannot fulfill their objectives.

Usually, the contact between developed and underdeveloped worlds has the character of exploitation — just taking people's labor and resources and giving them nothing. And the border between races has usually been a border of tension, of crisis. Here we see a revolution that is constructive.

This Pacific Rim civilization being created is a new relationship between development and underdevelopment. Here, there is openness. There is hope. And a future. There is a multicultural crowd. But it is not fighting. It is cooperating, peacefully competing, building. For the first time in four hundred years of relations between the non-white Western world and the white Western world, the general character of the relationship is cooperation and construction, not exploitation, not destruction.

Unlike any other place on the planet, Los Angeles shows us the potential of development once the Third World mentality merges with an open sense of possibility, a culture of organization, a Western conception of time. For the destructive, paralyzed world where I have spent most of my life, it is important, simply, that such a possibility as Los Angeles exists. To adjust the concept of time is the most difficult thing. It is a key revolution of development.

Western culture is a culture of arithmetical time. Time is organized by the clock. In non-Western culture, time is a measure between events. We arrange a meeting at nine o'clock but the man doesn't show up. We become anxious, offended. He doesn't understand our anxiety, because for him, the moment he arrives is the measure of time. He is on time when he arrives.

In 1924, the Mexican philosopher Jose Vasconcellos wrote a book entitled *La Raza Cosmica*. He dreamt of the possibility that, in the future, mankind would create one human race, a mestizo race. All races on the planet would merge into one type of man. *La raza cosmica* is being born in Los Angeles, in the cultural sense if not the anthropological sense. A vast mosaic of different races, cultures, religions, and moral habits are working toward one common aim. From the perspective of a world submerged in religious, ethnic, and racial conflict, this harmonious cooperation is something unbelievable. It is truly striking.

What is the common aim that harmonizes competing cultures in one place? It is not only the better living standard. What attracts immigrants to America is the essential characteristic of American culture: the chance to try. There is a combination of two things that are important: culture and space. The culture allows you to try to be somebody — to find yourself, your place, your status. And there is space not only in a geographical sense, but in the sense of opportunity, of social mobility. In societies that are in crisis and in societies that are stagnant — or even in those that are stable — there is no chance to try. You are defined in advance. Destiny has already sentenced you.

Other countries, even if they are open like Great Britain or France, don't have this dynamic of development. There is no space for development. This is what unites the diverse races and cultures in

America. If the immigrant to America at first fails, he always thinks, "I will try again." If he had failed in the old society, he would be discouraged and pessimistic, accepting the place that was given to him. In America, he's thinking, "I will have another chance, I will try again." That keeps him going. He's full of hope.

NPQ

Unlike most nations on the planet, what ties us together in America is not our past, but our future. As Octavio Paz has remarked, America is "The Republic of the Future." In that sense, we are a nation divorced from the plural cultures that are all rooted in different pasts, and that now comprise us.

Kapuscinski

In America, a proper balance between past and future is possible. You can be attached to your culture, to language, to tradition, to habit, but the notion of the future is bright. The future occupies greater proportions in your imagination than the past. It is bigger. The openness of the culture allows you to revise the proportions — not to cut off your link with the past, but to give the past a proper place, a place that is less heavy, less important. You can verify your attitude toward your past.

In a society in crisis, in a society threatened by invasion or domination, the past plays a disproportionate role. It blocks the imagination. The past is the only thing the society can cling to in order to affirm itself. The main feature of a society in crisis is that you don't see the future. The future doesn't exist as a promising time. A man sees the future as a time more dangerous than the past. He sees that everything that is good has already taken place. He says, "Well, today, somehow, I got by." If he looks at the future, he sees a black hole. This lack of perspective is far more damaging, far more dangerous than economic or political troubles.

NPQ

As never before, for immigrants the American future and their past culture are tied together by new communication technologies and air travel. The proportions of their perspective can be balanced across time and space. I'm thinking of the *Korean Times* — a newspaper in Los Angeles that every day publishes sixteen pages of news sent directly by satellite from Seoul. I'm also thinking of Korean Air, which flies two nonstop 747s a day between L.A. and Seoul, of the Korean-language cable-TV channels, and the video movies from Asia.

Kapuscinski

Part of the civilization forming here is a new kind of fusion of time and space.

For an Eastern European, to come to America at the turn of the century was a very strong cultural shock. His connection to home was cut abruptly. For the rest of his life he was completely cut out of the place where he was born and where he worshipped. Many people never recovered from the shock. It damaged their ability to enter the new culture in a dynamic way.

The new immigrants don't need to live through this cultural shock. The world is much more open. You can be in America trying a new life, but still be closely connected with your past. Today, immigrants are living in one place physically, but they are sustained culturally from elsewhere. They can watch Mexican soap operas on TV, or regularly fly back and forth to Mexico on the cheap midnight flight out of Los Angeles International Airport. They can read Korean news at the same time it is being read in Seoul, and can take the daily jumbo jets to Korea. The freedom to have this sort of contact is culturally and psychologically very healthy. They don't feel completely cut off from their past the day after their departure from home.

Immigrants now have a higher level of education than in earlier times. The new immigrant tends to be a person with much broader ideas, with a flexible approach. Culturally, this person is much stronger in facing the difficulties of changing countries.

Ninety percent of Polish immigrants to America at the turn of the century were illiterate. The new wave of Polish immigration to the

U.S. after martial law includes some of our most educated people. A Polish immigrant to America in the nineteenth century was terrified. Now, the immigrant immediately adjusts himself to the new environment. Increasingly, he's able to participate in the new society from one day to the next.

Sixty percent of the Korean immigrants to the U.S. — some thirty thousand a year — have college educations. Even Mexican workers and peasants who come here largely benefit from the basic education provided by the Mexican government.

Emigrants would probably be willing to go to prosperous Japan. But Japan is small and dense. There is little space, geographically or culturally. Above all, there is the tremendous barrier of language. In America, by contrast, there is a complete freedom of language. To live here, you don't even need to speak English. And, however well or poorly you speak English, your speech is more or less accepted. You don't feel any stress. You can communicate easily. There is an ever growing sphere in Los Angeles where you don't even hear the English language. You don't see it on the commercial signs, in advertising, in the local newspapers. You don't hear it on the radio or on the cable-TV channels. As an immigrant, this gives you a relaxed feeling.

You can't find another country in which knowledge of the main language is not necessary for living. You can't find another country where speaking the dominant language in a poor, broken way is accepted as normal. If you go to a place like Japan, you are cut off. You can't communicate.

In America, nobody cares. Nobody asks.

NPQ

Disneyland is a metaphor of America as the land of dreams realizable. A place where the imaginable is attainable. You walk into this land of dreams through the reconstruction of a typical turn-of-the-century Main Street: an idyllic place from America's most idyllic time. Today, the new American Main Street is in the Southeast Asian community that now encircles Disneyland: Bolsa Avenue — a sparkling new sprawling shopping strip known as Little Saigon. The signs seen and the languages heard are Cambodian, Laotian, or Vietnamese. Here, in the shadow of the fake Matterhorn, the refugees from history's crises are rebuilding their dreams.

Kapuscinski

This kind of amazing settlement is not just a matter of the freedom of self-expression. It's the reconstruction of a whole town! They are putting, in Orange County, Vietnamese styles of architecture and design that have been developed over the centuries. And on such a tremendous scale! This scene is a potent symbol of the American future. These boat people have the possibility to recreate lost realities according to their image.

In America, immigrants find total tolerance to rebuild in the styles of their homelands. In Europe, if they tried to build whole areas into new cities of a foreign nature, the authorities would prohibit it. They would not allow immigrants to destroy the historical town that exists in that place. Here, having the open space physically and psychologically conducive to tolerance, everybody can recreate their past.

Nowhere else on the planet can you find this kind of multicultural space. A whole Asia, a whole Central America is being recreated here on a small scale. This is a completely new phenomenon in an already developed society.

NPQ

What's the appeal of American mass culture — Mickey Mouse, McDonald's, Madonna — to the rest of the world?

Kapuscinski

In the socialist bloc, at least, the appeal of American mass culture initially came from the taste of prohibition. I drank my first Coca-Cola when I was twenty-eight years old. Before that, I regarded it, as did my compatriots, as a tool of imperialist domination. It was poison. For those who didn't trust official propaganda, Coke was a symbol of freedom. It was the symbol of a dream, of the other world.

NPQ

In fast-food restaurants — like the McDonald's in Moscow or Kentucky Fried Chicken in Beijing — everything is made in a particular way by a particular formula. Everything is the same. The food is produced with automated efficiency. These convenience chains are themselves exports of conceptions of time and organization.

Kapuscinski

Yes, the idea of convenience is a cultural export related to the use of time.

And the culture of convenience, so well developed in America, appeals everywhere. In Warsaw, you can walk for miles with no place to buy a sandwich. That's the appeal of McDonald's.

If immigrants streaming to America are agents of world cultural fusion — the fusion of time and cultures — this fusion spills back out into the world through the exports of American mass culture: McDonald's are agents of the world cultural fusion.

Recently, I flew from Toronto to Philadelphia. It was late at night. My plane landed. Other planes were also just landing, from Miami, from Los Angeles. At this airport, Cubans and Puerto Ricans were coming to meet the planes with their whole families. Lots of children were playing, slipping down, crying. My luggage was lost. Nobody could find anything. It was hot, crowded, noisy. A mess. There I was in Philadelphia, the historical American town, and I hadn't seen one white face. There was terrible disorder, the lost luggage, the cry of the children, Spanish language only. I said to myself, "I'm at home. I'm in the Third World."

Features of Third World society are penetrating American life. Third World influences — dynamic disorganization, easygoing attitudes, a slower pace of life, a different measurement of time, and relations to family — are altering the once-dominant northern European ways of putting society together. The sphere of neat, well-organized white society is shrinking.

The wrong angle to approach the new multicultural reality from is the perspective of Western cultural values, including Greek philosophy. Each culture has something to bring to the new pluralistic culture being created. The Korean community in Los Angeles owes nothing to Greek culture. Their diligence, their dedication, their discipline, their familial loyalty and esteem of education know nothing of Plato.

The question is not value relativism. We can't say values are broken down. We are in a period of transition in which the notion of values is broader. We are departing from the time in which we accepted only one set of values as the truthful way of living. We are entering the period in which we will have to accept values that represent other cultures, that are not "worse" than our values, but different. This transition is very difficult because the nature of our minds is ethnocentric. The mind of the future man, however, will be polycentric.

NPQ

The value-relativism argument is often raised precisely because we are, for the first time, crossing a critical threshold where European values are colliding with positive values that are non-European.

Giambattista Vico, the Italian philosopher, believed that each successive human culture had its own vision of reality. That vision formed customs, modes of creation, forms of language. Each successive culture, Vico believed, was incommensurable with others. Each culture's virtues and values could only be understood in its own terms. Johann Gottfried Herder similarly believed that each society had its own center of gravity, a "lifestyle" that was equally valid but different from all others. These men concerned themselves with understanding the validity of all human cultures in different times, or of the same time in different places. Like Bronislaw Malinowski, the Polish anthropologist, they felt cultures could not be judged in a hierarchy.

Only in a place like Los Angeles — where different cultures exist in the same time and in the same place — is the philosophical task of intercultural communication confronted on a daily basis simply because disparate people live and work here, side by side. In the specific, practical situations of daily life, immigrants and non-immigrants make tradeoffs between rules, values, and visions of reality.

Is all this cultural diversity concentrated in one place the source of American dynamism? Karl Polanyi, the development theorist, has noted that throughout history the crucibles of development were always the places of greatest cultural diversity. Dynamism and creativity are born from the interaction of everybody challenging everyone else's assumptions.

Kapuscinski

Milan Kundera pointed out that at the beginning of the century, Vienna was a very colorful mosaic of different cultures — Austrians, Jews, Ukranians, Hungarians, and others all living in one place. The competition between cultures gave life to the times. The richness of different views, different beliefs, different races, different cultures created an immense capacity for development at the time of the Austro-Hungarian empire.

The Second World War established boundaries that impeded the natural interchange among peoples and, especially after the Jewish population was liquidated, the creativity of the culture collapsed in Central Europe. The dynamism faded away.

Vienna reveals an historical truth. Whenever there is a place where different cultures and values gather, a very dynamic situation is created. Development and progress explode.

Los Angeles is comparable to Vienna at the beginning of the twentieth century. But here, the basis of dynamism is vastly broader. It includes cultures, peoples, and beliefs from other continents and civilizations. Vienna's immigrants came from other regions in the same part of Europe.

NPQ

How can the rest of the world keep up with America? Immigrants coming here today are more educated and literate. Their home governments invested in their intellectual capital, and now America is the net beneficiary. There's a crisis in Poland; the educated leave for the United States. A net benefit for the U.S., a net loss for Poland. Political uncertainty looms over Hong Kong as it is reabsorbed by China; the capital flows here to the U.S., as well as the people. After the revolution in Iran, the educated middle class pulled up stakes and came to Los Angeles with their money. America gets all the goods; the rest of the world gets all the crises.

Kapuscinski

This trend will continue. It is an objective law of history. You cannot stop it. The danger for America, and the danger for the whole world, is that American development is so dynamic and creative that, by the beginning of the next century, America will be a different world on the same planet. The position and rule of dynamic America and the paralysis of historical societies — this is the big problem for the future of mankind.

Every day, America is producing more and more elements of a completely new civilization that is further and further from the civilization of the rest of the world. The world will enter the twenty-first century with a greater distance between developed and underdeveloped peoples than at the middle of the twentieth century. The differences are growing, not diminishing.

Two-thirds of our planet will not be able, in the foreseeable future, to come anywhere near matching American development. We know now that large parts of the planet will be left behind. This is a pessimistic statement, but it's true. Those who can, try to emigrate to America. They don't want to wait to participate in their own development. They know it won't be in their lifetime, or the lifetime of their children and grandchildren.

After all the upheavals of the twentieth century — the wars, the revolutions, the mass migrant movements, the birth of new states, the death of empires — the world that remains is plural, fragmented, a collage.

The collage is a strange structure. It is a structure that is a contradiction within itself. On the one hand, different pieces are put together that do not compose a coherent feature. On the other hand, these pieces exist together. They create a new structure. They coexist. They cooperate as a completely new entity. Collage started in art. Artists, having a great sensitivity and ability to see the future, created this form of reflecting reality. Now, the reality is evident for all to see. In Los Angeles, collage is the form of the new civilization. There is no Culture. There are plural cultures in the same place.

Los Angeles is a vast, sprawling, gigantic collage, a display of fragments: cars, roads, architecture, cultures, races, languages. All values, all structures have broken down. Everything has gone to pieces, thrown together in one place. We have a big table. On this table there are different things: papers, pictures, fragments of various goods. Everything is there. And when we try to reconstruct these things, to put them back in their original order, we are unable to do so. The result of this effort to reconstruct the broken reality is the collage.

But each piece of the collage has its aim. All these cars crisscrossing the freeways have their destination. They are going to a certain point — organized movement, going in one direction. So, there is an order in the chaos. Unity in disunity. Composition in decomposition. Although this new American reality is composed of many different historical roots, political systems, and geographic origins, everything is trying to compose into a new entity. Plurality is the defining feature of the new civilization. In this new world, values and cultures other than our own are demanding a place in our consciousness.

The world is growing up. And in the world we have more of everything — more people, more goods, more communications. This growth of everything demands more cultural space, and will destroy whatever does not accept this reality. That makes systems that don't accept plurality obsolete.

Every system that does not admit plurality as the new way of life is exploding.

Revolt of the Rich

Alvin and Heidi Toffler

Alvin and Heidi Toffler have collaborated on the best-selling books Future Shock, The Third Wave, *and* Powershift. *This article is adapted from a conversation* NPQ *editor Nathan Gardels held with the Tofflers at the Westwood Marquis Hotel in Los Angeles in October 1993.*

LOS ANGELES

For centuries, elites have feared and protected themselves against revolts of the poor. The history of both agricultural, or First Wave, and industrial, or Second Wave, societies is punctuated with blood-spattered slave, serf, and worker uprisings. But decentralized, knowledge-based, Third Wave societies are accompanied by a startling new development—an increasing risk of revolt by the rich.

When the USSR broke apart, the republics most eager to split away were the Baltic states and the Ukraine. Closest to western Europe, they were also the most affluent and the most industrially developed.

In these Second Wave smokestack republics, the elites — chiefly Communist Party bureaucrats and industrial managers — felt hamstrung and overtaxed by Moscow. Looking westward, they could see Germany, France, and other nations already moving beyond traditional industrialism toward a Third Wave information economy. They hoped to hitch their own economies to the West European rocket.

By contrast, the republics reluctant to leave the Union were the furthest from Europe, the poorest and most agrarian. In these heavily Muslim First Wave republics, the elites called themselves communist, but often resembled corrupt feudal barons operating through highly personal family and village networks. They looked to Moscow for protection and handouts. Second Wave and First Wave regions thus pulled in sharply opposed directions.

All sides masked their self-interest in flag-waving ethnic, linguistic, even ecological appeals. Behind the resultant clashes, however, lay sharply opposed economic and political ambitions. When the contrary pulls of the First and Second Wave regional elites became too strong for Gorbachev to reconcile, the great Soviet crackup ensued.

An X-ray of other large nations reveals similar fault lines based on First, Second, or Third Wave differences. Take, for example, China, the world's most populous country. Today, out of its 1.2 billion people, as many as 800 million are peasants in the interior, still scrabbling at the soil much as their grandparents did, under conditions of wretched poverty. In Guizhou the swollen bellies of hungry children are still all too visible amid shacks and other marks of misery. This is First Wave China.

By contrast, China's coastal provinces are among the most rapidly developing in the entire world. In factory-filled Guangdong, gleaming new high-rises pierce the sky, and entrepreneurs are plugged into the global economy. Looking nearby, they can see Hong Kong, Taiwan, Singapore swiftly transforming themselves from Second to Third Wave high-tech economies. The coastal provinces view these three so-called "Tigers" as models for their own development, and are linking their own local economies to them.

The new elites — some engaged in Second Wave enterprises based on cheap labor, others already installing leading-edge Third Wave technologies at a blistering pace — are optimistic, extremely commercial, and aggressively independent. Equipped with faxes, cellular phones, and luxury cars, speaking Cantonese rather than Mandarin, they are wired into ethnic Chinese communities from Vancouver and Los Angeles to Jakarta, Kuala Lumpur, and Manila. They share more in lifestyle and self-interest with the overseas Chinese than with First Wave Chinese on the mainland.

They are already thumbing their collective nose at economic edicts from Beijing's central government. How long before they decide they will no longer tolerate Beijing's political interference, and refuse to contribute the funds needed by the central government to improve rural conditions or to put down agrarian unrest? Unless Beijing grants them complete freedom of financial and political action, one can imagine the new elites insisting on independence or some facsimile of it — a step that could tear China apart and trigger civil war.

With enormous investments at stake, Japan, Korea, Taiwan, and other countries might be compelled to take sides — and thus find themselves sucked unwillingly into the conflagration that might follow. This scenario is admittedly speculative, but not impossible. History is dotted with wars and upheavals that looked highly improbable.

India, with a population of 835 million, is the world's second most populous state, and it is developing a similar split among its trisected elites. There, too, a vast peasantry still lives as in centuries past; there, too, we find a large, thriving industrial sector of roughly 100 to 150 million people; and there, too, we find a small but fast-growing Third Wave sector whose membership is plugged into the Internet and the world communication grid, working at home on their PCs, exporting software and high-tech products, and living a daily reality radically different from the rest of society.

A glance at MTV blaring out over Indian television screens, or a visit to the Lajpat-Rai market in South Delhi makes the cleavage between the sectors clear. There, customers haggle with hucksters over the price of satellite dishes, LEDS, signal splitters, videorecorders, and other gear needed to plug into the world's Third Wave infostream.

India is already torn by bloody separatist movements based on what appear to be ethno-religious differences. If we look beneath these, however, we may find, as in China and Russia, three opposed elites, each with its own economic and political agenda, tearing the nation apart under the guise of religion or ethnicity.

Brazil's population of 155 million is seething, too. Nearly 40 percent of the work force is still agricultural — much of it barely existing under the most abominable conditions. A large industrial sector and a tiny but growing Third Wave sector make up the rest of Brazil.

Even as masses of First Wave peasants from the Northeast starve, and out-of-control migrations overwhelm Second Wave São Paulo and Rio de Janeiro, Brazil already faces an organized separatist movement in Rio Grande do Sul, an affluent region in the South with an 89 percent literacy rate and a phone in four out of every five homes.

The South produces 76 percent of the country's GDP, and is routinely outrepresented in government by the North and Northeast, whose economic contribution, measured in these terms, is only 18 percent. The South, moreover, argues that it is subsidizing the North. Joking that Brazil would be rich if it simply ended just north of Rio, Southerners are no longer laughing. They claim they send 15 percent of their GDP to Brasilia and receive only 9 percent back. "Separatism," says a leader of a party committed to breaking Brazil apart, "is the only way for Brazil to shake off its backwardness." It may also be a path to civil conflict.

Even in Europe, just as thirty years of the process of integration was about to conclude, the wounds of separatism have become ever louder. Consider the electoral victory of the Northern League headed by Umberto Bossi. The League swept to a majority in Milan, the seat of the Italian corruption scandals, on a program calling for the more prosperous North to shed the burdens of the Roman bureaucracy and Italy's impoverished South.

Across the world, then, we are hearing a premonitory growl from the angry affluent in an environment of clashing civilizations. The rich want out. Many are thinking, if not saying aloud, "We can buy our needs and sell our goods abroad. Why saddle ourselves with an army of malnourished illiterates when our factories and offices might actually need fewer and higher-skilled workers in the future as the Third Wave advances?"

Combined with other splintering tendencies, notably rising protectionism and the kind of ethno-religious strife that has erupted from the Balkans to India, violent explosions are possible. These multiplying, fast-widening cleavages represent large-scale threats to peace in the decades ahead. They derive from the master conflict of our era — sparked by the rise of a revolutionary new civilization that cannot be contained within the bisected structure of world power that sprang up after the industrial revolution.

What we will see in the decades to come is a gradual trisection of the world system into First Wave states, still reliant on agriculture, Second Wave states built on smokestack industries, and Third Wave states, each with its own vital interests, its own feuding elites, its own crises and agendas. This is the grand historical context in which we today observe the civilianization of war, the proliferation of nuclear, chemical, and biological weapons, and of missiles; it is in this context that we witness the rise of completely unprecedented Third Wave war-forms, such as the World Trade Center bombing in New York, or the later poison gas attack in the Tokyo subway. Those incidents made it quite clear that the state has lost its monopoly on violence to small groups of often independent actors who possess lethal knowledge.

We are racing into a strange and novel period of future-history. Those who wish to prevent or limit war must take these new facts into account, see the hidden connections among them, and recognize the waves of change transforming our world.

In the period of extreme turbulence and danger to come, our survival will depend on our doing something no one has done for at least two centuries. Just as we have invented a new war-form, we will have to invent a new "peace-form" that uses the decentralization of power and knowledge to combat Third Wave forms of violence.

CULTURAL CURRENTS IN THE LAST MODERN CENTURY

Modernism was about trading in tradition for the future. It meant breaking with the past in pursuit of a promised land. Criticism was modernism's instrument in philosophy, revolution its instrument in politics, and the avant-garde in art. Progress was the modern faith that would see us through successive stages of development to Utopia at the end of history. Now, history may not have ended, but our belief in its preordained course has. Philosophy has deconstructed. Revolution has fizzled. And, having lost the foil of tradition in societies so flexible they accept any-thing, the avant-garde fails to shock. Without much of a past or a future, the postmodern Westerner finds himself abandoned in the permanently temporary present.

Diverse paths, not one Way; in the religious imagination the acceptance of plural truths, not monotheism; the con-vergence of times, not linear causality; the forfeit of utopias — these conditions of existence long accepted as reality in the East now characterize the West as well.

In this debris of crumbled certitudes, the West is, paradox-ically, discovering the founding assumptions of the East and other non-Western cultures. In a supreme irony of our unknowable existence, can it be that the trail blazed by the moderns has led to the doorstep of the ancients? Is a convergence of East and West in the works?

Octavio Paz, the Mexican poet awarded the Nobel Prize for literature in 1990, thinks so. In his contribution here he says "we in the West are only now discovering what the East discovered millennia ago." In a mirror image of this view, the Japanese philosopher Takeshi Umehara makes the argument that "ancient Japan shows postmodernism the way." Looking through a different prism, the Japanese literary critic Shuichi Kato criticizes here the same old Japanese ways that Umehara holds dear as the new path.

Jean Baudrillard, the French social critic known for his reflections on America, looks at life "after utopia." Oliver Stone, one of the more celebrated (if controversial) American filmmakers, talks about how the absence of any one truth about history figured in the way he filmed and edited JFK. Finally, Daniel J. Boorstin, the historian and Librarian of Congress Emeritus, looks at how the new media technologies of this century have "homogenized time and space," distorting our perception of reality.

West Turns East at the End of History

Octavio Paz

Awarded the Nobel Prize for literature in 1990, Octavio Paz is a poet, essayist, and art critic whose most recent volume of essays in English is entitled The Other Voice. *From 1962 to 1968 he was Mexico's ambassador to India. Paz spoke with* NPQ *Editor Nathan Gardels in the studio of his Mexico City apartment in late February of 1992.*

NPQ

In your essay "Breach and Convergence," you argue that rational skepticism, or the critical spirit that is the hallmark of modernism, has undermined faith in a unitary truth and led to the acceptance of plural truths. This spirit has led not only to other ways of seeing but to the discovery of other cultures. And, in a final negation, perhaps, it has demolished its own clock, the modern clock of progress, or linear time — History with a capital "H."

The "hours which have lost their clock," in the lament of the Chilean poet Vicente Huidobro, have now been liberated to march at their own tempo. As the world view of modernism recedes, the extraordinary diversity of times and cultures that had been hidden beneath the shadow of universality is reemerging.

Some have called this condition "postmodern." You reject that name. You call it "time without measure," or "pure time." Why?

Octavio Paz

Western civilization is experiencing a fundamental change in its temporal imagination. We have to reset our clocks. To call the present condition "postmodern" is still to refer to modernity; it is to fall into the trap of linear time, the narrative from which we have departed altogether.

Modernism, with its notion of progress, was really a kind of exaggeration of the linear time of Judeo-Christian civilization, moving forward from a moment of Creation and the Fall into sin toward Redemption and Paradise. It has always meant leaving the past behind in the name of something different or better in the time ahead.

Modernism started in the eighteenth century with criticism as a philosophical method. Then modernism emerged as a political method — revolution — that was critical of what existed in the name of the utopia that could be. . . . Finally, modernism became an artistic method — the avant-garde, which made a radical break with cultural tradition.

Modernism produced many good things. Above all, as you mentioned, the recognition of "other" civilizations. This opened the possibility of assimilating foreign traditions into Western culture, from Oriental poetry to the African masks and sculpture that stimulated cubism. Poets adopted the Japanese *haiku*, and Ezra Pound translated Chinese poetry. The Noh theater influenced Yeats and other playwrights.

Indeed, the first third of the twentieth century was the culmination of a long process of the discovery of other civilizations and their visions of reality. This process, begun in the sixteenth century with the exploration of the American continent, resulted in our time in the adoption of artistic forms that were not only different from, but contrary to, the mainstream tradition of the West.

The assimilation of the "other" into the Eurocentric imagination was the consequence of the aesthetic revolution that began with Romanticism. It also finally ended a tradition that had begun with the Renaissance, drawing its inspiration from Greco-Roman antiquity. By denying this tradition in the search for other forms of beauty, modern art ruptured the continuity of the West.

In the present moment we have a different vision of tradition, a way of assimilating the past but not breaking with it. An example of this today can be seen in architecture, which quotes both modern and neoclassical styles. This new vision is also a way of simultaneously assimilating other cultures with which we live in juxtaposition. And, as never before at the end of this century, there exist simultaneous forms of art. One moment neoexpressionism, minimalism the next.

The other important organizing principle of modern society has been the idea of the "future." Each civilization has a different idea of time. For medieval societies, the important thing was eternity — time outside time — and the past. They didn't believe in the future. They knew very well that the world would soon be condemned to extinction. The point was to save one's soul and not to try to save the world.

But modernity had a different conception: it was not the individual soul that could be saved, but the human race itself through "progress." The future on earth was the modern paradise that could be realized by all in the same march of "History." Under modernity, we sought collective, secular redemption — redemption inside time.

Now, we have lost our faith in "progress" and discovered the present, which, unlike the future, we know we can touch. The totalitarian attempt to reach the future has utterly collapsed. And even the great land of the open future, the United States, has become the land of "now." Some years ago this sensibility was simplistically formulated in the slogan "paradise now." Even crudely stated, this slogan nonetheless offers some idea of the temper of our societies.

In short, temporal succession no longer rules our imagination, which has retreated from the future to the present. We live instead in that conjunction of times and spaces, of synchronicity and confluence, which converge in the "pure time" of the instant.

One sees this, too, in the scientific developments of our day — with the new stress on chance and the random convergence of forces instead of logical causality. Coherence and equilibrium are the momentary exception, disequilibrium the rule. Linguistics has also discovered synchronicity.

This time without measure is not optimistic. It doesn't propose paradise now. It recognizes death, which the modern cult of the future denied, but also embraces the intensity of life. In the moment, the dark and the luminous side of human nature are reconciled.

The paradox of the instant is that it is simultaneously all time and no time. It is here, and it is gone. It is the point of equilibrium between being and becoming.

NPQ

Here you sound like Ilya Prigogine, the theoretical physicist known for his work in chaos theory, who looks to art to find a new model of nature in science.

Prigogine says that our role is not to lament the past. "What we have in mind," he says, "may be expressed best by a reference to sculpture — be it the dancing Shiva or in the miniature churches of Guerrero — in which there appears very clearly the search for a junction between stillness and motion, time arrested and time passing. It is this confrontation that will give our era its uniqueness."

Paz

I think Prigogine is right. The instant is a window to the other side of time — eternity. The other world can be glimpsed in the flash of its existence. In this sense, poets — muses of the moment — have always had something to show modern man.

The *haiku* of the Oriental tradition show this. In the West, our great poets, such as Czeslaw Milosz, have shared this perception of the instant, or the moment, as the reconciliation between three times — the past, the present, and eternity.

NPQ

The poetics of the instant you call "time without measure," Czeslaw Milosz calls "the eternal moment:"

> Whoever finds order
>
> Peace, and an eternal moment in what is
>
> Passes without trace. Do you agree then
>
> To abolish what is, and take from movement
>
> The eternal moment as a gleam
>
> On the current of a black river? Yes.

Milosz describes in verse his pursuit of the Truth but his discovery of the moment:

> I was running through room after room without
>
>   stopping . . . for I believed in a last door.
>
> But the shape of lips and an apple and a flower
>
>   pinned to a dress were all I was permitted to
>
>   know and to take away.

You mentioned the *haiku*. In the poet's embrace of the moment, one finds the same sensibility as in a typical Japanese *haiku*:

> Stillness
>
> Penetrating the rocks
>
> The sounds of cicada

Paz

These lines express very well what we have been talking about. Other poets and mystics in the Western tradition, such as William Blake and, although he was a Christian, St. John of the Cross, express the same sensibility. Wordsworth was the poet of great moments. What is the "Prelude" of Wordsworth, after all? It is the history of a man who has a few moments of illumination. And that, for him, was enough. It is not that all these poets or mystics East and West believe in the same thing. No. But at the same time they are saying something that is universal and touches the experience of all mankind.

NPQ

How is this aesthetic of the moment any different, really, than Nietzsche's idea of "art, and nothing but art" in the absence of any transcendent meaning?

Because God was a fiction, and there were thus no ethics, his idea was that aesthetics, the fiction of man, was the highest expression of existence, "the great ennobler of life."

Paz

Nietzsche was attractive in his belief that "art desires life." He wanted to dance in the abyss. But he also had a tragic vision of mankind without the possibility of redemption.

What we need to build now is not only an aesthetics and poetics of the convergent moment, but an ethics and a politics that follow from this perception of time and reality. In such a new civilization, the present would not be sacrificed for the future or for eternity. Nor would the present be lived, as consumer societies do, in the denial of death. Rather, we would live in the full freedom of our diversity and sensuality in the certain knowledge of death.

The ethical foundations of the new civilization would extol this freedom and creativity without illusion; it would seek to preserve the plurality of the present — the plurality of different times and the presence of the "other." Its politics would be a dialogue of cultures.

But plurality alone, as Nietzsche and Dostoyevsky understood, leads to nihilism. If there is no God, everything is permitted. Without such a higher unity, we only tolerate difference because we are equally indifferent to everything and everyone.

Relativism helped us discover different cultures and different moralities. It helped us discover that atheists as well as Buddhists or Christians can be saints. Each culture has a validity by itself. But how do we compare them and choose? In the case of Mexico, for example, how can we say that capitalism is better than human sacrifice? According to relativism, they are equal.

That is why we must seek to discover the unifying thread amid our extraordinary diversity. In the absence of a general perspective of mankind, and universal ethics, on what basis do we claim that one is morally superior to the other?

We must resist modern relativism and the deconstruction of reality into nothingness and moral indifference. Reason must be our guide in this resistance. Not the absolute, totalizing reason of Plato, but the limited reason of Immanuel Kant, reason that is able to criticize itself.

The instant, I believe, can be a point of departure for this new unity. In the moment, plurality can meet unity; the particular can be the universal. Out of the debris of the great narratives of our civilization — Christianity, Marxism, Liberalism — this new morality will be born.

NPQ

There is much talk these post–Cold War days about the "end of History" in the Hegelian sense — history that advanced through the temporal contradictions and conflicts of the unfolding world spirit, but that now reposes in the relative peace of the present. But aren't we really talking about something more profound? With the repeal of the future and the end of linear time, the end of the avant-garde. . .

Paz

. . . and the end of Hegel. . .

NPQ

. . . isn't the civilizational development we are witnessing really the end of the Judeo-Christian conception of time?

Paz

In a sense, we are undergoing a shift no less profound than the transition from the Greek idea of cyclical time to the Judeo-Christian idea of temporal succession.

The monotheistic Judeo-Christian idea was that each civilization had the same conception of time. With the relativism of modernity, however, we discovered that each civilization has its own clock. We found that the Greeks and the Romans, for instance, didn't believe in historical progress. And neither did the Chinese, the Hindus, or other polytheistic civilizations.

Since we now accept the plurality of civilizations, and thus of conceptions of time, the idea of one direction of time for all mankind has been demolished.

Yet I don't know if we can "end" a tradition as powerful and deep as Christianity. Christianity didn't abolish the pagan tradition; it assimilated it. After all, without Greek philosophy the church could not have built Christian philosophy. In our time it will be the same.

NPQ

Having discarded one truth in favor of plural truths, and having demolished the Western clock to trust only the moment, the critical tradition of modernism seems to have led us in the last decade of the twentieth century to where the East has long been.

Listen to Japanese literary critic Shuichi Kato:

> In the Japanese tradition, time has no beginning and no end. The whole continuous thread of existence is not broken into parts or periods. Consequently, the "here and now" has an autonomous importance without reference to the past or the future. No master story has been authored by a transcendent being, or traced in a grand comprehensive theory.
>
> There is also no conception that "history" is made by the human decision to move from the past to the promised land.
>
> The Japanese emphasis on the concrete here and now explains the paucity of utopian ideas in Japanese tradition. Japanese perceptions of time and space are clearly reflected in the arts. The *haiku*, which catches the impression of a single fleeting instant, illustrates the aesthetic of the moment.
>
> Similarly, Kabuki theater, which is composed of acts with independent meanings that were weakly related to each other, relies on immediate sensitivities to decipher the

meaning. Japanese music is not constructed as a single, continuous work, but arises from each separate note and the relationship between tones and pauses.

Other Japanese thinkers, like Takeshi Umehara, stress the polytheistic religious imagination dating back to the ancient forest civilization of Japan; and, of course, there is the "yin-yang" simultaneous presence of, as you put it, "the dark and the luminous."

Plural paths, not one Way. In the religious imagination, polytheism, not monotheism. The convergence of times, not linear causality. Synchronicity. The absence of utopias. The aesthetic of the moment. These are the new conditions of the West we have been discussing. It seems that, at the "end of History," East meets West.

Paz

This is very true. I have believed this now for many years. I am the son of Western civilization, not Oriental or pre-Columbian civilization. But I think we in the West are only now discovering what the East discovered millennia ago. But they too are discovering things the West first discovered — democracy, for example, and science.

In the Chinese classic *I Ching*, we can see the premonition of what we are now realizing. The *I Ching* depends on the simultaneous presence of a number of causes, on the confluence of influences, not singular causality.

When I was ambassador to India, I came to learn that all the great thinkers of the Oriental tradition came from India. The Chinese and Japanese took many of the metaphysical ideas of India and adapted them into Taoism, Zen Buddhism, and so on. What the Indians tried to do many centuries ago was to construct a critique of reality. They believed that reality was nothingness. The real — Brahma, Nirvana — was beyond apparent reality.

I have long felt that the West needed to make a similar critique of time. We have believed too much in time.

In a way, we are more prepared than others to make this critique of time because Christianity — even if it affirms the process of time as "history," as a sacred tragedy from the Creation to the Fall of Adam to the Redemption — knows that this reality we touch is not the real one. The true reality is outside time.

Modernity made a criticism of the time beyond, proposing that paradise was not there but here, in History and the future. Now we have learned that History and the future are illusions.

That is why we in the West are now prepared to accept a critique of time that leads us to a very similar perception as those civilizations that long ago undertook the critique of reality.

NPQ

Because the aesthetic of the moment in Japan cannot find its creative impulse in forward historical movement and conflict, the Japanese architect Arata Isozaki argues that it tends to exhaust itself over time in the endless refinement of ultimately empty forms, periodically requiring foreign influence to jump-start the creative process. How will the "aesthetic of the moment" avoid stasis in the West?

Paz

The avant-garde was driven by its escape from the past into the future. The new art will be built from the debris of the avant-garde. The new impulse will arise from the conflicts of confluence, from the frictions of diversity and plurality — and their reconciliation.

Japan itself is relatively ethnically homogeneous, which is why, standing alone, it tends toward paralysis and precisely requires the "other" for stimulus. In the West, as a result of modernist criticism, we have assimilated the "other" into our own imagination.

NPQ

East may be meeting West at the end of History, but Islam, in its confirmed monotheism and belief in the Absolute, seems the odd civilization out.

Paz

Islam today is the most obstinate form of monotheism. We owe to monotheism many marvelous things, from cathedrals to mosques. But we also owe to monotheism hatred and oppression. The roots of the worst sins of Western civilization — crusades, colonialism, totalitarianism, even ecological destruction — can be traced to monotheism.

For a pagan, it was rather absurd that one people and one faith could monopolize the truth. Outside Islam, the world again sees it that way. Islam stands alone. It is the most reactionary force in the world today.

The marvelous thing about Western civilization is that we could criticize religion with the weapon of philosophy and reason. And then we could criticize philosophy, or rationality, with the weapon of philosophy.

Even though Islam knew the Greek tradition before us — Islam translated Aristotle before us — it never rejected the belief that fate, the coherence of incoherence, was superior to reason. Thanks to Islam, whose scholars passed on to us knowledge of the Greeks, we have Thomist philosophy. But Islam doesn't have it. And without the reconciliation of faith with science in Islam, there will be great conflict with the vast relativist civilization that now stretches through most of Asia, across the Americas, to Europe.

The Civilization of the Forest:
Ancient Japan Shows Postmodernism the Way

Takeshi Umehara

*Director General of the International Research Center for
Japanese Studies in Kyoto, Takeshi Umehara is Japan's
most prominent — and most controversial — philosopher.*

*Formerly president of the Kyoto Municipal University of
the Arts, Professor Umehara is author of such books as*
The Concept of Hell, The Exiling of the Gods, *and* Japan's
Deep Strata. *Also a playwright, he is presently working on
a drama based on ecological themes.*

*In the following article and interview, he addresses, with a
fresh perspective rooted in Asian thought, the theme raised
by Western thinkers from Arnold Toynbee to Lewis
Mumford: the central role of the religious imagination in
the rise and fall of civilizations.*

KYOTO

The experience of losing the war in 1945 brought to Japan a sudden collapse of the value structure that had supported and guided it in the past. It was probably then, for the first time, that the Japanese were capable of understanding the nihilism of European existentialism.

In the immediate postwar period, young intellectuals like myself understood — on the basis of our personal experience — what this philosophical position meant. Having had the experience of the death of those around us, and having faced almost certain death ourselves — particularly with the horrifying specter of the nuclear holocaust at Hiroshima and Nagasaki — we simply could not place any faith in a secure life. I devoured the works of Friedrich Nietzsche and Martin Heidegger, and spent my youth filled with doubts and anxieties. Like so many others, consciously or unconsciously, I became an existentialist who could not place my faith in any claim to objective values, including those of the traditional Japanese moral code.

Yet, as I married and became established, and as Japan itself began to get back on its feet, I started to feel that I could not continue living by staring into the void. I began to feel that I could not survive by a philosophy that emphasized the uncertainties of existence. Since the latest thinking in the West offered only this emptiness, perhaps, I began to think, there were certitudes of great import for all of humanity to be found hidden in the culture and religious history of Japan that survived all around me.

First, I became interested in the teachings of the various sects of Japanese Buddhism — teachings that became part of our mental makeup without being part of our conscious thought.

Then I began to study Shinto, the indigenous religion of Japan. It was at this time that I came to believe there was something in the Shinto religious orientation of Japan, rooted in its ancient cultural origins, that could offer a philosophy of existence that fundamentally differed from the inevitable dead end of European thought. Further, through my research on the religions of native Japanese tribes, Ainu and Okinawan, I found common elements peculiar to both Japan and to Shinto.

For a variety of reasons, little was taught in our universities about Japan's cultural origins. Ever since the Meiji period, Japanese academic circles had regarded mastering the theories and scholarly disciplines of the advanced European countries as of the utmost importance. Additionally, during the nationalistic prewar days, fears that the sanctity of the national polity would be desecrated — a polity that consisted of chauvinistic State Shintoism linked to the notion of divine rule by the Emperor, or *tennō* — independent research into traditional Japanese topics was severely constrained.

Frankly, I had an allergic reaction to Shinto for many years, due to my bitter memories of chauvinistic State Shintoism linked to the war. And, precisely because of the close link between State Shintoism and the war, the American occupiers after the war harbored no enthusiasm for the recovery of Japan's cultural identity.

Even as Japan's economic recovery took on the sheen of world-class might, our cultural recovery lagged far behind. Although I have now been pursuing my research for years, it was not until the period of the Nakasone government in the mid-1980s that the first major institute — The International Research Center for Japanese Studies — was established in Kyoto to delve fully into the founding truths of Japanese culture.

My hope now is to discover in the cultural origins of Japan not only a new value orientation, which would benefit us as we forge the values our children can live by in the twenty-first century, but also to contribute to the whole of humanity a new value orientation that suits the postmodern age.

Japan's Pride

If Japan's civilization has any value, it rests in the fact that it retains the strong imprint of the forest civilization of its origins, the civilization of hunting and gathering. Two-thirds of Japan is covered by forests, and about 40 percent of the total area is growing in its natural state without human intervention. No other major industrial nation today can boast such a large share of forest land. This is a feature peculiar to Japan. I believe we should be more proud of our forests than of anything else, and that we must continue to treasure them.

There are two historical reasons why Japan has so much forest land left. One is that farming came to our country relatively late: only about 2,300 years ago. Japan basically became an agricultural nation during what we call the *Yayoi* period, which began about three centuries before Christ, and lasted for about six hundred years. Before the *Yayoi* period, the Japanese — like people in other countries in early times — were hunters and gatherers, or, it might be more accurate to say, fishers and gatherers. And it appears that the fishing and gathering culture was particularly highly developed in Japan. Evidence for this is found in the earthenware that has been excavated in Japan, some of which has been scientifically dated as twelve or thirteen thousand years old. Together with some earthenware that has recently been found in Siberia, this is the oldest anywhere in the world.

Japan's warm and humid climate produces luxuriant vegetation, which fostered the development of a fishing and gathering culture. This culture was probably at its apex about five or six thousand years ago, just when the farming culture of the Yellow River in neighboring China was rapidly developing.

This early Japanese civilization, which is represented by the earthenware found around the country (particularly in eastern Japan), is called *Jomon*. I believe that it can be considered a true forest culture, in contrast to the *Yayoi* civilization that followed it, which was a rice-growing culture. One reason for the persistence of forests in Japan is the fact that the *Jomon* civilization lasted so long and the introduction of agriculture came at a relatively late date.

Another reason for the survival of Japan's many forests is the fact that the agriculture that reached Japan's shores was from the rice-growing culture of China's Yangtze River basin. This form of agriculture made use only of the plains, leaving the mountains and hills mostly untouched. This is different from the practice of a wheat-growing culture, which also cultivates the slopes. Another point is that the form of agriculture introduction into Japan did not involve the raising of animals on pasture land, which could also have meant cutting down the trees on the hills and mountains.

In my view, Japan's culture is not unitary, as has traditionally been thought, but binary. It is analogous to Greek culture as viewed by Nietzsche, who analyzed two sorts of elements: the Apollonian and the Dionysian. In Japan's case, the two elements are the *Jomon* fishing and gathering, or forest civilization, and the *Yayoi* rice-growing, or paddy civilization. Recently, some physical anthropologists have been advancing the view that the races of people who were the principal carriers of these two civilizations were themselves distinct. They suggest that the forest culture was carried on by an early type of Mongoloid people living in Japan since ancient times, while the paddy culture was the product of a newer type of Mongoloid people who arrived during the *Yayoi* period. Various research supports this hypothesis, which destroys the traditional assumption that the Japanese come from an homogenous race of farmers.

Shinto: Religion of the Forest

This background has also had a major impact on the shaping of religious thought in Japan. Japan's major religions are Buddhism and Shinto. Buddhism is known to have come originally from India, passing through China on its way to Japan, but Shinto is generally thought of as an indigenous religion.

Shinto has come to the fore as Japan's national religion twice during the course of the nation's history. The second time this happened was in the latter part of the nineteenth century and the earlier part of the twentieth, when it was used as an ideological expression of Japan's nationalistic philosophy — influenced at that time by European thinking, particularly by the model of Prussia, and by Bonapartism.

The previous period of State Shinto, so to speak, was in the seventh and eighth centuries, when Japan first took shape as a nation-state. This was the period when the name Nippon was adopted for the country, and the title *tennō* was first applied to its monarchs; Shinto was the established religion of this new state. Two of its key rituals were *harai* and *misogi. Harai,* which may be translated as "purification," or "exorcism," represented the driving out of elements or persons harmful to the state. *Misogi,* or "ritual cleansing," was the forced correction or reform of such harmful persons.

I believe, however, that Shinto originated as a form of nature worship, rooted in the civilization of the forest, and had nothing to do with this sort of nationalism. It is hard to determine exactly what sort of world view was present in the original Shinto, but based on various forms of conjecture, I would suggest that it may have been something like this:

When people die, their souls depart from their bodies and go to the world of the dead. The old Japanese word for conducting a funeral is hofuru, which means to discard or throw away. And the word for corpse is nakigara, which might be translated as "empty remains." It is like the word nukegara that is used for the cast-off skin of a snake or shell of an insect. In other words, it is something that no longer has any use or meaning. And the ancient practice was simply to leave the remains exposed in the woods or fields, like any other item to be discarded.

The world of the dead in this original Shinto view is located somewhere in the sky. The spirits that go there live in families, just as on earth. Life in that world is similar to life in this world, with the exception that everything there is backwards. Here we walk with our feet down, but there they walk with their feet up. Here we dress with the right side of the kimono underneath and the left side on top; there the left side is underneath and the right side on top. When it is morning here, it is evening there; when it is summer here, it is winter there, and so forth.

What is particularly noteworthy about Shinto is that this view of the afterworld contains no vision of heaven or hell. Neither is there any figure who passes judgment on people after they die. In the Shinto view, almost everybody gets to go to the afterworld. In some cases, the soul may refuse to go because it remains too attached to the world of the living, and of course, if a person has been too evil while alive, the ancestral spirits may refuse to welcome that person's soul. In cases like these, the priest conducting the funeral must make doubly strong invocations to be sure that the soul actually makes it to the other world.

All the souls that reach the afterworld become *kami*. The word *kami* in this context is generally translated as "god" with a small g, but actually it refers to any being that is more powerful than normal humans. For example, snakes, wolves, foxes, and other animals that often harm people are also considered to be *kami*.

Thus, in the Shinto view, the souls of the dead go to the afterworld, where they live with their families more or less as they lived on earth. Furthermore, the two worlds — the world of the living and the world of the dead — are not cut off from each other. There are four Buddhist memorial days during which the spirits of the departed return to the world of the living: at New Year's, at midsummer, and at the equinoxes in spring and fall. They spend about three days with the families of their descendants, who wait on them and then send them off on their return journey to the afterworld. By waiting on the spirits of their ancestors during these four annual visits, the people of this world ensure that these spirits will look after them for the rest of the year.

After living in the other world for a time, the spirits of the dead are reborn in this world. When a child is conceived, the representatives of the ancestors on both sides of the family get together and decide whose turn it is to go back. The spirit of the person so selected then returns to the world of the living and slips into the womb of the mother, where it enters the unborn child.

Shinto Influence on Buddhism

What I have been describing are the beliefs of the Japanese before the arrival of Buddhism, but these beliefs continue to live among the Japanese of today. Most people in Japan are both Shintoists and Buddhists. To the Japanese mind, there is nothing contradictory about this. In general terms, rites relating to the dead are the province of Buddhism, while the rites of the living are the domain of Shinto. More specifically, Buddhist rituals are used for funerals, anniversary memorial services, and the services for the dead that are conducted at New Year's, midsummer, and the equinoxes. Shinto rituals are used for weddings, birth celebrations, and *shichigosan*, the special celebrations for boys at ages three and five, and for girls at ages three and seven.

Originally, of course, all these rites must have been Shinto, but when Buddhism appeared on the scene, it took over the central rites, namely, those relating to the passage from this world to the next. It is hard to trace the way Buddhism changed after being introduced to Japan, but it seems fair to state that the Buddhism that developed in Japan and won the belief of the Japanese people is a religion quite different from that originally created in India by Sakyamuni Buddha and his followers.

In the Buddhism of Gautama, the world is seen as a place of suffering. Human beings, and in fact all living creatures, are reborn each time they die, and thus they must face a perpetual cycle of pain. According to the teachings of this creed, the reason humans are trapped in this unending cycle is because of their passions. This requires a life of following the commandments, meditating, and learning. Through such a life, a person can hope to attain a state of quiet enlightenment, or *nirvana*, that will make it possible to leave the world of suffering forever. Buddhahood, in other words, means breaking free of the cycle of reincarnation.

In this form of Buddhism, only human beings are candidates for Buddhahood. And even for humans, the only way to become a Buddha is through religious training (including mortification of the senses), and study. But after being introduced into Japan, this religion changed dramatically. In contrast to the original teaching, which held that only a minority of people were eligible to become Buddhas, the religion as it developed in Japan gradually widened the scope of potential Buddhahood to encompass all human beings, and ultimately even nonhumans. Around the tenth century, an influential school of thought arose that proclaimed that "mountains and rivers, grasses and trees, all can become Buddhas." This school of thought has formed the basis for the various forms of Buddhism that have evolved in Japan since then, though the methods that are prescribed for attaining Buddhahood — such as chanting and meditation — differ from one sect to another.

Another feature of Buddhism in Japan is the common practice of giving posthumous religious names to dead people. This, in effect, certifies that the deceased person has become a Buddha. Even in today's Japan, people often refer to the dead as *hotoke-sama*, or Buddhas. In other words, the Buddhism that has taken root in Japan seems to have been influenced by the traditional Shinto belief that all people become *kami* (gods) when they die.

Another interesting parallel between Buddhism in Japan and the original Shinto beliefs is to be found in *Jodo Shinshu*, or the True Sect of the Pure Land, which was founded by Shinran in the thirteenth century, and continues to be one of the main sects. Shinran preached the value of two types of *eko*, or transferences of one's virtue to others for the attainment of Buddhahood. One, called *oso-eko*, means that a Buddhist devotee calling Amitabha's name at the deathbed could attain Buddhahood by being reborn in the Pure Land, or Amitabha's paradise, after his or her death. This was preached by Honen, Shinran's teacher, in the twelfth century. In addition to this, Shinran stressed the other type of *eko* called *genso-eko*, which refers to the return of a dead person to this world from the Pure Land in order to save others.

According to Shinran, this is the sort of act performed by a *Bodhisattva*, who is a person who seeks to relieve the sufferings of others and save their souls. In other words, through the practice of *nenbutsu,* or chanting the praises of Amitabha Buddha, a person can go to paradise; being *Bodhisattva,* however, such a person will not be content to remain there forever but will return to this world to relieve the living of their pain.

Shinran maintained that the true practitioners of *nenbutsu* were those who would keep returning to the world of the living time after time for the salvation of other humans. This seems quite similar indeed to the Shinto belief in reincarnation. Over the centuries of its evolution in Japan, culminating with the teaching of Shinran, Buddhism developed thinking that was amazingly similar to that of the indigenous religion.

The Eternal Cycle

To sum up, it seems clear that the belief in an eternal cycle of life and death is a basic element not only of Shinto, but also of Japanese Buddhism. This is a belief that is surely not just Japanese; it was probably held in common by all human beings during the Stone Age. People who lived in the forest probably developed similar philosophies. The difference in Japan's case is that this primitive thinking has shown a stronger ability to survive here than elsewhere.

It may be a primitive philosophy, but I believe that the time has come to reexamine its merits. Modern science has demonstrated that all life is basically one, and it has shown that living things and their physical surroundings are all part of a single ecosystem. Further, we have learned that even though the individual dies, his or her genes are carried on by future generations in a lasting cycle of rebirth. Even more important, the human race has finally realized that it can survive only in "peaceful coexistence" with the other life forms of the animal and plant worlds.

Ever since human beings learned how to raise crops and livestock, they have been attempting to control, or conquer, nature. And in the process of this conquest, they have come to see themselves as somehow superior to other living things. We must now reconsider this feeling of human superiority. In order to do so, we need to refer back to the wisdom of the people of the hunting and gathering age that preceded the age of farming and livestock raising.

The Rhythms of History

Arnold Toynbee understood world history as the rise and fall of various civilizations. He placed religion at the center of civilization, because he believed that it is religion that supports civilization. From this standpoint, it seemed to Toynbee that modern Western civilization, which had arisen from Christian civilization but had now weakened, was in grave danger.

I hold a pluralistic view of history, according to which any individual civilization or nation inevitably and repeatedly rises and falls. Any individual civilization necessarily has certain central ideas. When these ideas are valid and effective at a certain stage of history, then that civilization and the nation founded upon its principles are strong and prosperous. When, at another stage, the principles of that civilization go against the movement of history, then that civilization faces a decline. The principles of a single civilization can never be equally valid in all historical situations.

No doubt the nations of Europe, led by the principles of their civilization, have indeed played an overwhelmingly important role in history between the sixteenth century and the present. However, the times have now clearly changed. Nations based consciously or unconsciously on principles other than those of European culture have arisen, and are now proclaiming principles that are unique to themselves. Moreover, the times are now such that the U.S. and the countries of western Europe are having difficulty forcing the principles of their own civilization upon other nations. What the people of the world need to do under these circumstances is to form a clear idea of what the principles of European civilization really are: to determine what it is about those principles that no longer work in the present and, if civilizations other than that of Europe do indeed have some significance, to judge coolly just which aspects of those non-European civilizations may serve as a medicine to remedy the defects in the civilization of Europe.

West Meets East

Modernism, born in Europe, has already played itself out in principle. Accordingly, societies that have been built on modernism are destined to collapse.

Indeed, the total failure of marxism — a side current of modernist society built on warped principles — and the dramatic break-up of the Soviet Union are only precursors to the collapse of Western liberalism, the main current of modernity. Far from being the alternative to failed marxism and the reigning ideology "at the end of history," liberalism will be the next domino to fall.

Since modernism as a world view is exhausted, and now even constitutes a danger to mankind, the new principles of the coming postmodern era will need to be drawn primarily from the experiences of non-Western cultures, especially Japanese civilization.

Hegel regarded Descartes as the founder of modern philosophy with his famous principle *cogito, ergo sum* — I think, therefore I am. This idea placed man at the center of the universe. Descartes divided the world into two diametrically opposed realms — the realm of the thinking mind and the realm of inert matter. He believed that the mind could better control matter through knowledge of the physical principles, or mechanical laws, of the material world. Natural science and technology are the expressions of this world view.

The rational liberalism of the West wholly embraces the Cartesian world view that made the individual — the thinking self — absolute, endorsed man's total mastery over nature, and recognized only the existence of mind and matter. Nonhuman life was left entirely out of the picture.

Marxism adopted Descartes's idea of the relationship between man and nature in a more exaggerated and crude way, seeking only to increase productive capacity by ruthlessly exploiting nature, extolling class hatred, and harnessing man.

Guided by Cartesian philosophy, the modern world is wiping out nonhuman life, and threatens to bring death to the human species as well. Is it so hard today to see that modernity, having lost its relationship to nature and the spirit, is nothing other than a philosophy of death?

Nietzsche and Dostoyevsky very seriously considered the Europe of their time to be in the "age of the death of God," and lamented that Europe was surely courting grave danger. I believe that their concern is now realized. No matter how tenaciously humans cling as individuals to the "self," in the end this "self" is limited and destined to die. And if there is nothing beyond death, then what is wrong with giving oneself wholly to pleasure in the short time one has left to live? The loss of faith in the "other world" has saddled modern Western society with a fatal moral problem.

Modern Western civilization arose from Christian civilization. In Catholic Christianity, human beings go after death to purgatory where they await the Second Coming of Christ. At the end of time, Christ presides over the Last Judgment and decides the fate of each person: either to fall into everlasting Hell or to receive eternal bliss in Heaven. In other words, the soul of a person lives on even after death until the Last Judgment, when it is consigned either to Heaven or to Hell.

Modern European civilization rejected this concept of life after death as an unscientific delusion. Thus, people ceased to believe in the afterlife, and took it that victory is possible in this present life only. It is thanks to so powerfully realistic an outlook that Westerners have conquered the world in modern times.

Because it successfully modernized without losing its soul, Japan is perhaps better positioned than other non-Western cultures, such as the Indians who benignly dwell in the forests of South America, to offer guidance to postmodern man. In a sense, we have modernized while still preserving old principles, just as we became a *ritsuryo* society — a society of laws — through the Chinese influence in the seventh and eighth centuries.

Japan's ancient, non-modern societal principles apply to art and culture as well. It is these ancient principles that I propose as Japan's postmodern contribution. The first principle is a horizontal one — "mutualism," or the ethics of interpersonal responsibility.

The second is a principle of vertical, or generational, responsibility born of the concept of "cyclicity" in time. This means that human society does not progress, as modernity would have it, or regress. Rather, the same spirit repeats itself in a continuous cycle of life, death, and rebirth.

Such a view implies a responsibility to all the inhabitants of eternity because the other world is a living reality. It implies an ethic of being the custodian of the continuity of life instead of a one-shot plunderer during a brief episode of mortal splendor. In the Japanese imagination, the other world is present in every moment.

Mutualism

Tetsuro Watsuji, the Japanese philosopher, does not see ethics from the standpoint of the individual as modernism does, but rather from an interpersonal standpoint. His views reflect the mainstream beliefs of contemporary Japanese culture.

Watsuji has formulated a philosophical system that centers on the relationships of family, nation, and society. In Japan, the word *ningen*, which means "person," originally meant "between people." Watsuji's fundamental belief is that ethics do not originate in individuals, but between people. Of course, this way of thinking comes from Confucianism; *ningen* is actually a Confucian word. The ethical foundations of Confucianism concern "devotion to one's master, and dutifulness to one's parents."

Quite obviously, such an ethics would support a feudal structure. Watsuji, who was strongly influenced by Immanuel Kant's modernistic concepts of personality, thus does not place the ideas of loyalty and learning at the center of ethics. He gives more weight to horizontal rather than vertical relationships, proceeding from couples and families to the nation and society. Relationships are emphasized more than anything else. "Harmony," first identified as the principle behind Japanese society by the great thinker and politician of the tenth century, Shotoku Taishi, is still today considered to be of supreme importance. In effect, whoever breaks ranks is censored by the silent majority in the name of equilibrium in the community.

Neither modern nor feudal, and far from individualistic, the Japanese ethos is a modernistic transfiguration of Confucianism. Or rather, it is modernism that has undergone a great transformation on Japanese soil.

Modern ethics, which make individualism the absolute value, have now reached their limit, causing us to forget that our essential responsibility is not self-expression or personal freedom, but passing on life to posterity.

Certainly what is needed today is an ethics in which the highest value is placed not on the absolute rights of the individual, but on the continuity of life, the continuation of civilization, of the species, and the ecological system of the planet itself.

During the past three hundred years, the West has built an abundant world based on the domination of nature by thinking man. For most of that period, non-Western man — "the other" — was also subjugated. But the West's abundance is now threatened by the limits of nature to absorb the consequences of its plunder, and by the resurgence, particularly in Asia, of prosperous and competitive non-Westerners.

In these tribal times of postmodern pluralism, we need new principles for the coexistence of all races, North and South. One such principle, which offers an alternative to dominance and submission among human beings, is "mutualism." In this moment, what principle could be more necessary?

The principle of mutualism is also a necessary ethic between human beings and other living things. The world of the twenty-first century would do well to adopt the natural mutualism deeply embedded in Japanese civilization. It is expressed in the saying "Mountains, rivers, grass, and trees all attain *Nirvana* (Buddha-hood)." This means that all natural phenomena can become Buddhas because all living things — plants, rivers, trees, animals, and man — are regarded equally.

Cyclicity

Cyclicity, the principle latent in Japanese religion and art, is a concept also shared by the Indians of America. It rejects the idea of breaks in the continuity of time, as with the modernist notion of the avant-garde. Finality is not a dimension of cyclical time.

Time does not begin with creation and end with death. Rather, the structure of time is seamless and recurrent. Life, death, and rebirth are part of the same whole, continuous aspects of each other. There is thus a simultaneous sense of temporariness and eternity in Japanese religion and art. Life does not die, it goes on in renewable cycles. Life must be made anew before it becomes old.

For example, the Ise Shrine in Japan is rebuilt once every twenty years. This is the exact opposite of the Western idea of building eternal stone monuments. The renovation of the shrine represents the Japanese belief in renewable cycles: if God's dwelling is not made new every twenty years, its spiritual power will wither.

The coronation ceremony for Emperor Akihit in 1991 was based on this same idea. The previous emperor's life had grown old and died. The coronation is a ceremony in which the previous emperor's spirit is received in the body of the new emperor, giving him spiritual strength.

Haiku is an art that links the passing moment, the temporariness of form, to the eternal cycle of the spirit. The four seasons always play significantly in *haiku,* sharply portraying the passages and recurrences of an existence that is continually withering and regenerating.

The principle of cyclicity is also related to the ethic that the continuation of the family is more important than the individual, and the continuation of society and mankind more important than the family. In other words, the ethic of cyclicity is the custodianship of existence.

In Japanese culture, as in Indian cultures, there was the belief that the souls of descendants are the returned souls of dead ancestors, the same lives passing through different earthly forms. The other world was not divided into heaven or hell. All who died lived together, even in the same family units as in this world. This belief appears to have been widely shared across the world well before the foundation of world religions such as Christianity or Buddhism.

Though this belief in a direct ancestor-descendant relationship no longer remains in Japanese culture, relics of it do. For example, the fact that Japanese soldiers in World War II didn't seem to fear death as much as Westerners and recovered more quickly from the shock of defeat seems to have originated from their belief in the cyclical recurrence of life. Even today, most Japanese subscribe to the optimistic view that after the darkest hour, the dawn is sure to follow.

The immortality of the soul, or the recurrence of life in new forms, has, as I noted earlier, also been confirmed by genetics. Even though an individual dies, his or her genes are carried on by future generations in a lasting cycle of rebirth.

Cyclicity, I believe, is the new clock of postmodern time. French structuralists always cite Friedrich Nietzsche as the first postmodern thinker of the West. He discerned for Western philosophy — and aesthetics — the existential rhythm of "eternal recurrence" that Japanese civilization has long held as a fact of nature. But, imprisoned in the absolute subjectivity of the thinking man, Nietzsche could see only the death of God, not the continual rebirth of life. He couldn't, so to speak, see the forest for the void, or the grass, animals, and other living organisms of the ecosystem.

The central principles of the postmodernist world view, then, are mutualism and cyclicity: mutualism — ethics born out of relationship with the "other" and nature instead of by the self-interest of the absolute individual; and cyclicity — an ethics of generational responsibility born of the belief in continuous rebirth, a belief in the fusion of being and becoming into a time of eternal recurrence. With the scales pulled from its eyes by the dead end of modern philosophy, the West is just arriving at the realization of these truths lodged deep in the recesses of Japanese civilization.

NPQ

How much of the harmonious quality of the Japanese religious practice results from a polytheistic belief in many gods, as opposed to the Western belief, rooted in Judaism, of one God? Is monotheism the cultural root of disharmony?

Isn't a polytheistic religious orientation better suited to what in the West has been called a postmodern world — a world with plural centers of power, a world of plural truths?

Umehara

I think monotheism has served to justify the exploitation and conquest of nature. While the polytheist sees mountains and rivers as gods, the monotheist believes in a single transcendent God and denies the reality of the gods of mountains and rivers, and so is free to exploit nature. I also think monotheism is a powerful spur to the conquest of other human beings.

Historically speaking, after its emergence during the transition from the Bronze Age to the Iron Age, Christian monotheism became the dominant form of religion, the form of religion of the peoples who conquered the world. But as we enter a new age, both Christianity and European society are changing. The Catholic Church, for example, has recently come to value the opinion of Nicolaus Cusanus, who advocates the tolerance of contradiction. The Catholic Church has begun to recognize the existence of other religions. Because they have embraced freedom of religion, modern Westerners are inevitably becoming polytheistic.

NPQ

Obviously, the ideal of the civilization of the forest is at odds with rapid economic growth in Japan and the environmental destruction that growth entails. Even so, Japan is the most energy-efficient and least polluting of all advanced nations. But isn't there a double standard with respect to the outside world? While 70 percent of Japan remains forested, Japanese timber companies are destroying the Malaysian forests.

Umehara

There is no question that the modern Japanese reality contradicts the ideal I put forward. Unfortunately, my opinion is a minority view in Japan. I ask you to wait ten years. By then, I believe my opinion will be the majority view. Until that time, I will repeat my ideas again and again, whenever and wherever I have the opportunity to do so.

Civilization began with destroying the forest. King Gilgamesh, a hero of the Epic of Gilgamesh in ancient Sumer (present-day Iraq), had to kill the gods of the forest when he established the first urban civilization 5,000 years ago. It is hard to imagine that the now desolate Cradle of Civilization was once covered with forests.

While searching for economic prosperity, the Japanese have done the same thing, forgetting the value of their own country's traditional culture. However, I have faith that when this aim has been achieved, the Japanese will gradually reflect upon their conduct, and begin to understand how necessary and important it is to preserve the forest, not only in Japan, but all over the world.

As I mentioned earlier, rice cultivation is less destructive to nature than wheat cultivation, which is mostly accompanied by cattle farming. In Japan, where the introduction of rice cultivation was comparatively late, its blending with the native forest culture and the hunting and gathering culture created an amalgamation unique to Japan.

Today, Japan's goal should be to create another amalgamation — a new civilization — that blends the civilization introduced from Europe with the Japanese native culture of the forest.

NPQ

The journalist Ian Buruma has argued that your call for a return to the roots and origins of Japanese culture is little more than a racist belief in the blood superiority of the Japanese people, similar to the Nazi belief in the *Volk*.

Umehara

I have never advocated blood purity nor the racial superiority of the Japanese people. Habitually, I take a multiracial viewpoint in considering the history and makeup of the Japanese people. I always address issues related to Japanese culture, never blood. In short, I am not a Yamatoist — the national racialists associated with Japan's World War II chauvinism.

As we've discussed, I trace the tradition of Japanese culture to the *Jomon* culture of some 12,000 years ago among the Ainu and Okinawan peoples. As a matter of fact, Japanese "supernationalists" who have strongly claimed the prewar concept of "blood purity" do not consider the Ainu to be Japanese from the ethnological standpoint. But I, almost alone among Japanese thinkers, say "learn from Ainu culture." I have advocated and continue to advocate that we learn from the "wisdom" developed in the cultures not only of the Ainu, but also the American Indians, the tribes of Africa, and, indeed, many of the peoples who are today considered "undeveloped." Hidden in all of their cultures is a deep wisdom that mankind cannot live without coexisting with nature.

I do not, however, advocate giving up modern life and its technologies in favor of a return to a "primitive life." Indeed, I am saying that we are approaching a point where it will no longer be possible for mankind to live in opposition to nature. By learning more about early civilizations, I believe we can better transform ours from one that uses technology to conquer nature to one that employs technology to coexist with nature.

It is from this point of view — not from the standpoint of racial superiority — that I criticize the man-centered philosophies of modern European civilization.

Japan's Empty Core

Shuichi Kato

Japan's leading social critic, Shuichi Kato is the author of the definitive three-volume study, A History of Japanese Literature *and* Form, Style and Tradition. NPQ *spoke with Kato in July 1987.*

NPQ

The U.S. and Japanese economies may be the most intertwined of any in history. We drive the same cars, watch the same VCRs, and fly in the same airplanes. Yet, our conceptions of time and space differ radically. How do you see these differences between our two cultures?

Shuichi Kato

The American conception of time comes from the Judeo-Christian heritage of the West, in particular the Old Testament. Time is structured with a beginning — Genesis — and an end. It is an unfolding story given meaning by a transcendent God, progressing along a straight line from the past into the future without repetition. Time advances from the familiar past to a new and unfamiliar moment. In Exodus, a choice is made to leave slavery behind and continue forward to a new, clearly defined goal, "the Promised Land." Once the choice is taken, "history" is made. The moment of decision doesn't come again.

In the Japanese tradition, time has no beginning and no end, only infinity and repetition. Time is a succession of events extending from the present. The whole continuous thread of history is not broken down into parts and periods. Consequently, the "here and now" has an autonomous importance without reference to the past or the future.

Defined only by the present moment and the vague mists of infinity, time does not lend itself to structure. No master story has been authored by a transcendent being, or traced in a grand, comprehensive theory. Eschatology — a theological doctrine about death, judgment, and resurrection — doesn't exist. There is also no conception that "history" is made by the human decision to move from the past to a promised land. "The flow of events is beyond influence" goes one Japanese saying. "The past is past" and "tomorrow blows tomorrow's winds" are others.

These differences between Japan and America in the perception of time are reinforced by the conceptions of space. In America, the basic cultural pattern is individualism. America is the initiative of individuals from many cultural backgrounds, building a nation in a vast and open continent. This initiative in a vast space accounts for the aggressive personal style of Americans, as well as their openness to others. The American quality of initiative also carries further the Western notion of history-making. Rather than adapt to the environment, Americans try to change the environment.

In Japan, individuals don't exist. They are absorbed by the group. The basic cultural pattern of "groupism" originated in the enclosed village communities of this ancient, crowded island. The group is insular and closed to the outside. There are sharply different attitudes toward insiders and outsiders, and little openness between them. Personal style is reserved and adaptive. When an individual conflicts with the group, the resolution is for the individual to adapt, not for the group to change. That's the famous Japanese consensus. And by extension, the group adapts to the environment and doesn't take the initiative to change it.

The Japanese emphasis on groupism and the concrete here and now, so unlike the Western emphasis on the individual and on abstract and comprehensive systems of thought, explains the paucity of utopian ideas in the Japanese tradition. Thus, a belief in religious or ideological systems that transcend the concrete reality of the group has not been widespread in Japan.

Japanese perceptions of time and space are clearly reflected in the arts. A typical seventeenth-century Japanese *haiku*, which catches the impression of a single instant, illustrates this aesthetic of the present moment:

> Stillness
>
> Penetrating the rocks
>
> The sounds of cicada.

Similarly, Kabuki theater, which is composed of acts with independent meanings that are only weakly related to each other, relies on immediate sensitivities. Japanese music is not constructed as a single, continuous work, but arises from each separate moment and the relationship between tones and pauses.

The qualities of the concrete here and now and groupism can also be seen in the Japanese language. Sentence structure begins with a phrase that modifies the noun, and then ends with a verb; it begins with the details and builds into the whole. Almost all Japanese prose is broken into small, limited sections without consideration for the whole structure.

In everyday speech, personal pronouns are frequently omitted from conversation. Whether the subject of the sentence is mentioned or not depends entirely on the situation in which the speaker and listener find themselves, revealing the limited ability of the Japanese language to transcend particular, concrete situations. Consequently, more emphasis is placed on the spoken word than the written word. The universal validity of written statements is not trusted.

NPQ

The Japanese world view from ancient times seems like postmodernism, the latest evolution of Western thought. Postmodern style is disconnected from the coherent structure offered by the past. Postmodernism means "deconstruction" from a grand narrative or the comprehensive interpretation of history. Postmodern man exists without a center or a transcendent meaning.

From this perspective, the Japanese conception of time and space has always been "postmodern."

Kato

That is completely true. That's why I am against the imported postmodernism in Japan. I consider it very superficial. Postmodernism is a reaction against the rational system of Western modernity. It is a form of confrontation with the past. But the past doesn't exist in the same way in Japan as in the West. And without a confrontation with the past, postmodernism is a rather hollow revolt.

NPQ

This Japanese way of seeing reality and organizing behavior fundamentally differs from the West. Karel van Wolferen, the author of *The Enigma of Japanese Power*, has labeled this difference "the crucial factor," by which he means the absence of universally valid principles that apply across all circumstances. Therefore, Japan is a nation that can't be trusted to play by the rules in an interdependent world.

Others have seen the same phenomenon not as a problem but Japan's positive strength, as the genius of reconciliation — an admirable flexibility and pragmatism that allows accommodation to all circumstances, including interdependence. What's the truth?

Kato

Well, these things are two sides of the same coin. The Japanese are flexible and always prepared to compromise and adapt. This is the positive side. Negatively, they act without principle or adherence to any absolute standard. They are fundamentally opportunistic, and the value system, especially with respect to outsiders, is completely relativistic.

In practical terms, one cannot separate the positive from the negative. They are part of an inseparable phenomenon rooted in the groupism that emerged from the long history of Japanese isolation and essentially monoracial village life. Additionally, while the West stresses the absolute value of the individual, the Confucian influence in Japan stresses the value of inter-human relationships.

With such vastly different takes on reality, it is not surprising that the problem of cultural communication is so great that someone like van Wolferen could consider Japan incompatible with the international community. However, it is not often considered by Western observers that this communication problem also exists among different groups of insiders in Japan as well.

Even in Japan, real communication is confined to restricted areas:

one's own family, group of contacts, or immediate work place. Outside these restricted areas there is a refusal to communicate.

Politeness is one form of refusal. The famous Japanese politeness is actually a very sophisticated psychological barrier: it admits no emotion, no conflict, no debate — and, though very polite, it is just empty, pointless words; voices signifying nothing. It is a mask of communication.

NPQ

In the West, of course, both in personal and public discourse, there is plenty of conflict, impoliteness, divisiveness, and debate — at the extreme, even religious wars and Cold Wars based on ideological principles. We are individuals who profess belief in absolute values. The kind of compromise, adaptability, or flexibility one sees in Japan would carry with it in the individualistic West a strong scent of humiliation and defeat. What are the cultural roots of these attitudes?

In the West, ethnically diverse individuals are linked by absolute values that apply universally. In Japan, the monoracial group is linked by blood to the Emperor, while the polytheistic Shinto roots temper conflict among "gods" or contradictory ideas.

Kato

I don't know if I would call it polytheism; I rather prefer to see it as an absence of absolute authority. I know that Professor Takeshi Umehara and others have looked to monotheism, rooted in the Judaic tradition of belief in a single angry God, as the basis for aggression and conflict in the West. By contrast, polytheism is supposed to be relatively pacific. The historical facts just don't bear this out.

In practical terms, some monotheistic nations, such as Sweden or Switzerland, have been pacific, while polytheistic societies, such as ancient Greece, ancient Egypt, ancient Rome — not to speak of polytheistic Mongolia under Genghis Khan — have been extraordinarily aggressive.

So, therefore four possibilities: monotheistic aggressive, monotheistic nonaggressive, polytheistic aggressive, and polytheistic nonaggressive. From what we know, in ancient times Japan was not particularly aggressive. However, by the beginning of the fifth century, before the Nara period, it was quite expansive. In the late sixteenth century, during the Hideyoshi period, again Japan was quite aggressive. And, of course, everyone knows about the Japanese aggression earlier in this century. So, I am not sure the polytheism versus monotheism dichotomy explains much.

There is another dimension of the so-called pacific polytheism that must be considered, namely, the tolerance of different religious beliefs within Japan. While there is tolerance among the Shinto gods — in fact, the Shinto god of fire has the role of mediating between the other gods associated with the forest, sun, different animals, and so on — there was little tolerance for Christianity when it was introduced in the sixteenth century. In fact, the large-scale extermination of foreign and Japanese Christians in the sixteenth and seventeenth centuries would be hard to distinguish in empirical terms from a religious war. So, it is nonsense to suggest that Shinto polytheistic acceptance of many gods is equivalent to a mentality of peace and tolerance.

Moreover, Christianity is not merely a matter of an absolute God intolerant of others. What about the internal ideals of Christianity — love and compassion, a merciful God, the sin of selfishness? Those are hardly negative values leading to aggressiveness and war.

NPQ

Yet, polytheism is linked to the pragmatic flexibility in the Japanese way, isn't it?

Kato

I agree — the Shinto belief system, which emphasized adaptation to nature, has molded the Japanese mentality into a pragmatic one. Significantly, the this-worldly nature of Shinto enables the absorption of new elements into the belief system without soiling the purity of a transcendent truth.

At least in the State Shintoism developed after the eighth century, the central god is present in the form of the emperor, but he is inside the group, not beyond it. He is not transcendent like the Islamic or Christian God.

Amaterasu, the Sun Goddess, is the major god with which each new emperor must commune in order to carry on as a descendant of the divine lineage. But *Amaterasu* encompasses everything, and thus has no particular principles and imparts no ethical codes. There are no Ten Commandments and no laws that she lays down. There are only loosely organized rites, sometimes animistic, sometimes shamanistic, sometimes having to do with the cult of ancestors.

In State Shintoism, *Amaterasu* only authorizes the enthronement of a new emperor who is the symbol of the community of Japan. But there is no substance at the center, only a void. The core is empty. And, if the core is empty, one can do anything.

NPQ

Thus, all truths are socially constituted "positive right," as they used to say in the debates about natural law.

Kato

Very much so. Adding the Buddhist influence into all of this, there is also a certain sense in Japan that the West is naive, even foolish, in its fixation on absolutes and individual differences, which are regarded as ultimately illusory.

NPQ

The spirit of adaptation to nature, rather than its domination, is something else that emerges from the polytheistic disposition of Shinto. Professor Umehara, for example, has argued that Christian monotheism "served to justify the exploitation of nature" because the spirit of domination is inherent in such a belief. While the Shinto polytheist sees mountains and rivers as gods, the monotheist denies this reality and believes in a single transcendent God. He is thus free to exploit nature.

Kato

I think Umehara confuses the destruction of nature with Christian monotheism when it is really a matter of the Scientific and Industrial Revolutions, which put man at the center of the universe.

NPQ

As Ivan Illich has pointed out, the "death of nature" — the reduction of nature to dead material for manipulation by the will of man — only emerged with the Scientific Revolution in the seventeenth century. From Anaxagoras around 400 B.C. up through the sixteenth century, an organic and whole conception of nature in which man was only a part was a constant theme in the West.

Kato

Not only this. The secular, man-centered mentality that accompanied the Scientific and Industrial Revolutions has not, after all, penetrated monotheistic Islam.

NPQ

Nevertheless, is there some remnant from the cultural heritage of Shinto that infuses an ecological consciousness among Japanese? While Japan may be something of an eco-bandit in destroying Malaysian forests, 70 percent of its own forests are intact; it is the most energy efficient, and it has the strictest auto emission standards of any advanced industrial nation.

Kato

No, I don't think so. Much of our forests are in very high mountains, and it is uneconomical to go logging there. As a source of wood, it is much cheaper to log in Malaysia or the Amazon. Our flatlands, however, are bereft of forests. In Saitama Prefecture, for example, which is some eighty kilometers outside Tokyo, a new national "park" has been designated. Even though it is a very tiny forest, a fraction of the size of Germany's Black Forest, so little forest remains on accessible land that we are making these scarce woods into tourist attractions.

Where we do cut trees down in the mountains, it is true, there is always reforesting. But Japan's flatlands are a disaster, and the sea is very polluted. Generally speaking, Japanese destruction of nature is extraordinary. How can we pretend to love nature? Who loves it? Very few in present-day Japan. Japanese today don't love trees, they love money!

Saving the environment is one thing upon which both Umehara and I agree, though. We both signed a protest against the construction of a new golf course in Kyoto. The very beauty of Kyoto is linked to its surrounding mountains. They have inspired cultural and religious life in Japan for ages. These wooded mountains are the very core of artistic expression of the Japanese. And some company wants to build a golf course there!

NPQ

Is Japan incompatible with the world, or is it capable of joining the world?

Kato

I think Japan can become internationalized, as it is doing every passing day. But it will not become cosmopolitan for a long time to come, not before the end of the twenty-first century.

Japan will remain the most insular of all the advanced nations; its insularity is deeply rooted. But this expression of difference should be, and can be, peaceful and cooperative. I don't think Japan is dangerous, nor a threat. I also don't think it is a model for the future.

NPQ

Just as there is anxiety in the world over the reunification of Germany, is there cause for anxiety over the reunification of Japan? By this I mean the reuniting of Japanese nationalism with its financial and technological might.

Kato

I hope not. Yet there has emerged, over the past few years, widespread Japanese nationalistic sentiment. It is more than pride, probably less than chauvinism. Because Japanese cars are good, everything Japanese is good. That's the logic. Extolling Japan's cultural roots as superior to those of the dying West, as Professor Umehara does, for example, with his arguments about polytheism and Shinto and the forests, plays into the neo-nationalist sentiments.

And because everything Japanese is good, a blind eye is turned to the war crimes and oppression of Japan's past. We speak about the past in vague ways with sophisticated words — the real point being to attenuate our unspeakable wartime ways. For the moment, the neonationalist sentiment has not crystallized into any political platform, despite the goings-on of the likes of Shintaro Ishihara. So far, it remains a diffuse feeling and nothing more.

NPQ

Among the youth as well?

Kato

Well, among the youth, Asia is the fashion. In languages, they are interested in Chinese and Korean, not just English as was true only recently. More and more, they take their travel vacations not to Paris or California, but to Burma and Thailand. It's à *la mode.*

NPQ

Do you see parallels between the anti-Western vaunting of Japanese and Asian values by intellectuals such as Umehara now, and a similar intellectual current in the prewar days?

Kato

As a matter of fact, yes. In 1942, when we were already in the Pacific War, a very famous symposium of philosophers and intellectuals was organized entitled "Overcoming the Modern Age." The "Modern Age," of course, meant Europe and European ways.

The argument then — as the Asian postmodern argument goes now — was that the individualistic West was decadent and in collapse. Thus, the world needed the help of Asia. And what would be the new model for all of humanity? Japan, of course.

NPQ

Unlike most societies that have a very long past, Japan does not seem weighed down by its history. What is the secret of this genius of reconciliation between the past and the future?

Kato

A world view that centers on the group and does not include transcendental values implies that accepting the new does not require discarding the old. The confrontation between past and future involves changing an abstract conception of reality and ethical codes to conform with the new realities of the concrete situation. In the absence of such abstraction, there is no change in principle, only continuous adaptation without confrontation. For this reason, Japan has never had the religious wars of Christian and Islamic civilizations. In China, too, they have tended to destroy the old when they chose the new.

The Japanese world view has also enabled us to adapt foreign ideas and methods to indigenous ways, from Sung Confucianism at the time of Tokugawa to American mass-manufacturing methods in the twentieth century. This practical flexibility has been the secret of Japan's ability to modernize without a crisis of cultural integrity. Today, we produce futuristic high-tech products and still have an emperor.

Group Existentialism

NPQ

It is tempting to suggest that the Japanese world view amounts to a kind of group existentialism, characterized by situational ethics and moral relativism. Where is the center? What are the absolute values? In the words of Fukian Fabian's sixteenth-century polemic against secularized Buddhism, where is the "lord who punishes evil and thus preserves morality?"

Kato

There is no absolute value relating to outsiders. Inside the group, there is very much a certain state of mind where it is considered morally good to be honest, pure-minded, or sincere, and not egoistic in one's actions. Ethical behavior toward outsiders is based on a different criterion. For Japanese, the largest insider group is the nation of Japan. For us, the whole human race is divided into two subcategories — the Japanese and the non-Japanese. Unfortunately, most Japanese don't have much sympathy for non-Japanese. Hiroshima evoked deep sympathy because it was the Japanese who were hurt. But, to take only one example, the lack of reaction to the Vietnamese boat people that drifted in the seas around Japan during the late 1970s was appalling. The Japanese aren't much interested in any country that doesn't produce oil or buy Japanese cars.

The Export Surplus of American Culture

NPQ

Although America has a large trade deficit with Japan, we have a massive surplus in the export of popular culture, from Mickey Mouse to Madonna. What accounts for the powerful appeal of our mass culture as it is globally diffused through Japanese TVs, stereos, and the Walkman?

Kato

American culture is the first mass culture in human history that has crossed beyond its national boundaries. In the past, high culture has of course been exported by Germany, France, or England. Shakespeare crossed the English Channel, but British popular culture, perhaps with the exception of the Beatles, who played an American form of music, has never even crossed the Dover Strait.

There are three reasons for the appeal of American mass culture in the world. First, America has been a world empire for the last forty years. The cultural influence of the Soviet Union, by contrast, has been limited. Outside Eastern Europe it is practically zero. But the whole world is concerned with the United States.

Second, as distinct from the British empire that preceded it, America dominated the world in the first age of mass media, particularly with television.

Third, American popular culture is the only culture that has been created and accepted by a multiethnic population. Within its own boundaries, the U.S. is already a world culture. To the extent that popular culture has been exported from anywhere, it has come to America in the physical embodiment of the immigrant masses. If all of these ethnic groups can inhabit the symbolic realm of the "American Way of Life" — baseball, supermarkets, shopping malls, rock or country music, the car culture, and Disneyland — why not the rest of the world?

The rest of the world sees the extraordinary originality and creative genius of the American people. In this century, the Americans have created things that never before existed! American films created a whole new artistic expression that imitated nothing which had existed in previous cultural achievements. While old culture struggled with stagnation, America invented jazz and rock 'n' roll. The popular cultures in most of the world are not at all creative, but longstanding and heavy with tradition. In America, two individuals can meet and create something. Nothing stands in the way of a new departure.

NPQ

Will the appeal of American mass culture outlive the end of empire?

Kato

As long as the creativity of America continues, then I think its mass culture will dominate. On this planet, it is hard to see where else the "culture of the new" that so appeals to the world could arise.

Japan, meanwhile, is bounding along, wresting economic leadership from the United States. Yet, critics charge that artistically it has become a leveled wasteland. Do you agree?

Kato

In the postwar period, Japan produced good literature up until the 1960s. Especially in the 1950s as we rebuilt, there was a sense of openness and possibility. Individual writers explored alternative paths for Japan's future. But in the 1960s, the whole society became geared to technology and money. GNP became our sole purpose. The new writers only talk about trifles; everyone knows the only important thing is the stock market. Now, the future of Japan is closed, fixed like a slab of concrete in boringly unanimous consensus. The imagination dulls because there are no alternatives.

The Pathos of Autumn

NPQ

In his book *The Nobility of Failure*, the British scholar Ivan Morris evokes Japanese heroes of the past who die a "splendid death" by suicide, and thereby display the quality of absolute sincerity that can only be demonstrated on behalf of a lost cause. How does the nobility of failure cope with Japan's economic success?

Kato

The Japanese deeply admire people who have tremendous ability and enormous possibility, but who have been forced to fail by an unfortunate environment. There is great sympathy for the person who fails not because of his own fault or weakness, but because of fate. One such tragic hero, the military commander Nogi Maresuke, won a brilliant victory at Port Arthur in the Russo-Japanese War, but failed in later battles and finally committed suicide on the day the Emperor Meiji died in 1912.

NPQ

Is the admiration of noble failure linked to an expectation of failure, a belief that success can't go on? Once before in this century Japan was strong and successful, but it all came to ashes.

Kato

A popular interpretation of history, appearing in much of our literature, is that decline always follows the height of success. Rise and fall are always repeated. The four seasons are central to the Japanese imagination, but autumn is particularly important. In the West, it is the symbol of harvest as well as decay. In Japan, autumn only symbolizes decay. After the vitality and exuberance of summer, autumn is a sad season in which all the leaves fall. As long ago as the tenth century, we can find Japanese poets lamenting the "pathos of the autumn moon."

After Utopia:
The Primitive Society of the Future

Jean Baudrillard

The French social critic and lapsed sociologist Jean Baudrillard is author of the highly acclaimed America *and* Cool Memories. *One of the more poignant foreign observers of America since his compatriot Alexis de Tocqueville roamed these lands, Baudrillard's insights, in the manner of the parochial universalism of Parisian post-Marxist intellectuals, dazzle somewhere between the brilliant and the impenetrable.* NPQ *Editor Nathan Gardels talked with Professor Baudrillard in a haute-tacky Los Angeles hotel called the Royal Palace in 1990. Baudrillard regards Los Angeles as his favorite city. For him, L.A. is the closest thing to a center in this heterogeneous, ex-centric world.*

NPQ

You have called America the "primitive society of the future."

What do you mean?

Jean Baudrillard

Like primitive societies of the past, America doesn't have a past. It has no "ancestral territory" — speaking not of land but of symbolic terrain — that has accumulated centuries of meaning and cultivated principles of truth. In short, America has no roots except in the future, and is, therefore, nothing but what it imagines. It is perpetual simulation. America has no context other than what it, concretely, is. From a historical standpoint, America is weightless. . . .

NPQ

. . . the "lightness of being" on a grand scale!

Baudrillard

Exactly. Like primitive societies, America lives primarily in nature and the unconscious realm of myths and symbols. America is only nature and artificiality, space plus a spirit of fiction. There is no self-reflexive, self-mirroring level, the civilizing level of unhappy consciousness, which comes with history and which places a distance between the symbolic and the real. It is this lack of distance and incapacity for ironic reflection that accounts for America's naive and primitive qualities. Without knowledge of irony, the imaginary and the real are fused and indistinguishable. Disneyland is authentic! Television and movies are real! America has created an ideal world from nothing, and consecrated it in the cinema.

NPQ

This absence of critical distance is also reflected, wouldn't you say, in the aesthetic nausea of the built environment in Los Angeles — the freeways, the commercial strips with their revolting signs competing for the attention of mobile consumers, with each building architecturally unrelated to the others?

Baudrillard

America is beyond aesthetics. It is transaesthetical, like a desert. Culture exists in a wild state where all aesthetics are sacrificed in a process of literal transcription of dreams into reality. In the car ads, for example, there is no difference between the car and happiness. In the mind of the consumer, the material reality of the car and the metaphysical concept of happiness and contentment are identical. A car is happiness. Who could ask for anything more than a new Toyota? Aesthetics requires context, and in America, the only context is its own mythic banality.

In Europe, we philosophize on the end of lots of things. It is in America, though, that we should look for the ideal type of the end of our culture.

NPQ

The medium is the myth, so to speak. How, then, is America "utopia achieved," as you have put it?

Baudrillard

Well, what did the European philosophers expect utopia to look like? America is, in concrete form, the traumatic consequence of European dreams. America is the original version of modernity, the weightless paradise of liberation from the past. Europe is the dubbed or subtitled version. What is only thought in Europe, becomes reality in America. It is we who imagine that everything culminates in transcendence, and that nothing exists that hasn't been conceptualized. Americans are not interested in conceptualizing reality but in materializing ideas.

NPQ

"Don't let us get too deep," as Edie Brickell sings.

Baudrillard

Americans inhabit true fiction by giving it the form of reality, while we are condemned to the imaginary and to nostalgia for the future.

We anticipate reality by imagining it, or flee from it by idealizing it. Americans merely radically implement everything we think about, from mass egalitarianism to individualism to freedom to fantasy. In so doing, "utopia achieved" has transformed into the anti-utopia of unreason, of weightlessness, value neutralism, and indifference, the indeterminacy of language, and the death of culture. Having hyper-realized modernity, the hyperreality turns against modernity.

America was "de-constructed" from the outset because of its original inauthenticity — the utopian moral sphere has always been your primal scene, while history and politics remain ours. California, in particular, is the world center of the inauthentic. As the scene of anti-utopia, its vitality is the mirror of our decadence.

NPQ

The vitality of Los Angeles springs from the weightlessness. The cultural indifference is precisely what enables the new wave of Third World immigrants, who have left their ancestral territory, to build their own particular utopia inside the anti-utopia. I'm thinking here not only of the Mexican and Korean immigrants, but especially of the Vietnamese boat people who have reconstructed a mini-Saigon in the shadow of Disneyland's fake Matterhorn.

Baudrillard

These emigrants from real space to hyperreality reinforce the American model. They are complex hybrids of origin and artificiality. In this powerful simulacrum of California, they are giving the form of reality to their fiction.

NPQ

In Los Angeles, it is possible to touch the living, breathing hybridity and fragmentation of cultural life, the deconstructed and decentered diaspora so eloquently theorized upon in Parisian salons. But tell me this. What accounts for Europe's craving for American inauthenticity? We export it by the boatload. Our consecrated fictional realism plays in most Parisian movie theaters, McDonald's graces the Champs Elysée, and Disneyland has opened just outside Paris. How can simulated inauthenticity be so appealing?

Baudrillard

We are both attracted to American mass culture and repelled by it. We still have enough distance to be fascinated by, rather than inhabit, its factitiousness.

But the resistance is fragile. We don't have anything to oppose to this cultural contamination. Culturally and philosophically exhausted, we remain unable to transform our past into living values for the present. Our cultural antibodies have acquired an immune deficiency, and can't resist the virus.

NPQ

Isn't the name of that immune deficiency syndrome "indifference?" Marcel Duchamp noted long ago that the ultimate face of modernity was this "freedom of indifference."

Baudrillard

In Europe, at least, a sense of loss still accompanies indifference. But in America, indifference is already anachronistic. The strategy of indifference was there from the start. In fact, America's genius, as Alexis de Tocqueville noted in both horror and admiration, was the irrepressible abolition of difference. Sheltered from the vicissitudes of history far from its shores, America was indifferent to the world. Inside its boundaries, the radical form of its indifference became the toleration of any and all differences.

In the end, this is what the universal cultural problematic of deconstruction is all about. Without a center, without a transcendent context, how do you value differences?

Thanks to the hegemony of the West, indifference has become a universal fact. In the future, power will belong to those peoples with no origins and no authenticity. It will belong to those who, like America from the beginning, can achieve "deterritorialization" and weightlessness and figure out how to exploit the situation to the full extent. Whether we like it or not, the future has shifted away from any historical center toward artificial satellites.

The unintelligible paradox of Japan is a powerful example of this. Having freed itself from the ancestral terrain, it floats, culturally weightless, as an economic powerhouse on the world scene.

NPQ

Your vision of the world sounds like Salman Rushdie's: a world of uprooted migrants, fragments, debris of the soul, bits and pieces from here and there — all with a hole inside, "a vacancy in the vital inner chamber." In your terms, weightless, indifferent satellites floating unattached about the planet. Rushdie's vision, however, was challenged from the quarters of the centered absolute, the ultimate face of the antimodern: Khomeini.

Baudrillard

I agree with Rushdie that the whole world is implicated in this fragmentation and uprootedness, including China and Russia. There is one exception: Islam. It stands as a challenge to the radical indifference sweeping the world.

NPQ

It seems that all these weightless fragments are juxtaposed, living side by side in ontological uncertainty without mixing. . . .

Baudrillard

. . . and that is unstable. Perhaps that is why the West is so weak and vulnerable in the face of the certitudes of radical Islam.

In a way, radical Islam is the revenge of modern history. The West inoculated them with our virus, and now they are immune to us. So now, people like Ayatollah Khomeini can contaminate the whole Western world with terrorism and death threats.

Khomeini's question about the West is perhaps also ours. What happens after the great orgy of freedom that has left us all indifferent?

NPQ

In effect, what comes after utopia?

Baudrillard

Perhaps reversibility. The march of history has broken from its forward path. It seems anything can happen beyond this point, good or bad. We can't live with the past, but neither do we have a project. Every day is rich with unpredictable happenings: terrorism, AIDS, electronic viruses. . . . The course is uncharted.

NPQ

Man's fate has checked into purgatory.

Baudrillard

Well, Europe, at least, still survives in the purgatory of simulation. We still harbor a vague regret over the loss of origins and are wary of the inauthentic. Americans are in the paradise of simulation, long comfortable with weightlessness as a way of life.

For Europe, there may be no way from purgatory to paradise. And that could be our salvation.

Splinters to the Brain

Oliver Stone

The director of films such as Platoon, Born on the Fourth of July, The Doors, JFK, *and* Natural Born Killers, *Oliver Stone's most recent film is* Nixon. *He spoke with* NPQ *Editors Nathan Gardels and Leila Conners in Los Angeles about truth and the image.*

NPQ

Your film *JFK* has been roundly trashed by most of the print media, the domain of the typographical mind. Before the advent of the image media, they were the sole owners of history, the chief custodians of reality. Behind the various criticisms of *JFK* seems to stand a profound suspicion of the image media itself, especially of the rapid-splice editing common to MTV rock videos that you used in the film. Indeed, doesn't the MTV technique constitute a kind of cerebral bypass in which surface appearances are transported directly into the depths — the subconscious realm of myths and symbols? What about that critical pause for reflection that distinguishes our civilized condition from that of the primitive state of the pure unreflective subconscious? What about the reasoning mind that allows us to distinguish fact from fiction, truth from falsity?

Oliver Stone

To start with, the killing of JFK was a primitive act. The president's head was blown off at high noon in Dealy Plaza by assassins. I want you, the viewer, to be in the skin of the event, inside the surface. I want you to be subjective in your reaction. I want you to feel the sorrow, the pity, the pain, fear and horror. So I went at it with every tool I had. Sixteen and eight millimeter cameras. I blew up frames. I used black and white. I used color. The camera zooms in; it zooms out.

JFK is one of the fastest movies made. It is like splinters to the brain. We had 2,500 cuts, maybe 2,200 set-ups. We were assaulting the senses in a kind of new-wave technique. We wanted to get to the subconscious.

The idea of the film was not so much to solve the mystery of who killed the president. The idea was to present an overarching paradigm of all the possibilities of the assassination. I would tap one perspective, then another and another. I was digging up evidence from all sorts of different places, buried like Schliemann's Trojan walls in several different layers. As a film, *JFK* can be seen as an archaeological investigation, a deconstruction, of one of the central events of American life. *JFK* is really akin to the Japanese film *Rashomon*, Akira Kurosawa's fable about the impossibility of ever arriving at a single truth.

In my film, the camera reflected the search for truth. Its various angles captured the simultaneous points of view of an array of witnesses, and their own fragments of apprehension. The camera itself was the critical instrument. It should be self-reflexive. What you see represented over and over again in the film are fractals of consciousness that, altogether, add up to the reality of a moment. They are shards of an event about which the whole truth is perhaps unknowable. *JFK* is a three-hour avalanche of fragments of the truth.

Ultimately, *JFK* is not really a political film. The ultimate questions are philosophical: Who owns reality? Who owns your mind? Isn't history a distorted hall of mirrors that depends on the kind of surface that reflects its essence and its events? Unlike many of my critics, I don't think that reality belongs to the *New York Times* and the *Washington Post*.

NPQ

So, the one-shot theory of history is dead. Singular causality and singular perspective are as dead in truth-telling as in science, where the stress now is on the confluence of forces, on synchronicity and simultanaeity.

Stone

What form of representation best grasps reality is really the question you are asking. As in some historical literature, do you pile fact upon fact and call it history? Or, in looking at Julius Caesar, for example, do you look at the vision of a man's life? A life, you see, is not based on the accumulation of facts, but on flashes of insight, on moments of the spirit.

So, do these flashes blind or illuminate? In this sense, I like the MTV-style flashes of imagery because they have circumvented conventional narrative in the same way James Joyce in *Ulysses* circumvented Charles Dickens. Joyce was just pushing the envelope a little further in creating a form that represented the multiple perspectives of reality. After Joyce, it is almost impossible for me to go back and read *Great Expectations* by Dickens.

NPQ

But does the MTV-*JFK* style touch truth, or can the image lie better than the word?

Stone

What tells you more about what happened that day in Dallas, image or "historical fact?" The volumes of Warren Commission testimony concluded, through the "cold light of reason," that one magic bullet fired from the Book Depository by Oswald killed both President Kennedy and, after hanging in the air for seemingly eternal seconds (which seems plausible on paper, but highly improbable in the real time of the image) wounded John Connally.

The core of my film — the Zapruder frames — reveals the blunt truth that JFK's head was jerked backward from a shot that came from another direction. In the film, that scene of the Zapruder film is magnified. It is shown frame by frame, detail by detail, again and again. To see the president's head blown off in this way hits you in the gut, at the subconscious level. It is the moment in every movie theater where there is a collective gasp by the audience.

That instant in Dealy Plaza — which looks like a Greek proscenium — was a bold signal to the world. It was meant to be symbolic. It had a Greek mythological resonance to it. What *JFK* did was to use that moment on film to establish a counter-myth to the official myth of the U.S. government.

As a filmmaker, I do believe in what might be called "Dionysian politics." I believe in unleashing the pure wash of emotion across the mind to let you see the inner myth, the spirit of the thing. Then, when the cold light of reason hits you as you walk out of the theater, the sense of truth will remain lodged beyond reason in the depths of your being, or it will be killed by the superego of the critics.

NPQ

Newt Gingrich's revolution is not just about overthrowing the welfare state, but the media class as well, which the neo-conservatives regard as having been captured by counterculture types like yourself. This cultural elite is said by them to be remorselessly secular, nihilistic, hedonistic, and anti-family. Is there such a media class; is it as they describe?

Stone

Unquestionably, movies and television programs have played an important role in setting the tone for the times. American television during the 1940s and 1950s, when I grew up, was commercial propaganda for a certain idea of the good life, the life seen in *Leave It to Beaver* or *Donna Reed*. Get a wife, have children, make money, spend money, get a toaster and two cars in the garage. That was promoted as normal. Newt Gingrich may not be as aware, say, as his lesbian sister or his first wife, that he is a victim of this propaganda about what is normal America. If my films do not portray normal America in his view, it doesn't mean they are counterculture, but counter to the tone of the times set by TV in the 1950s.

In my view, there is no conformity to reality. The idea of conformity or normality is merely the fashion of the times, but that has nothing to do with real life. Even in the days of Donna Reed there was a lot of suicide, anguish, and divorce in America; many families were silently — that is not on the screen — torn apart over issues of homosexuality and race.

I know my films are thought to be subversive to mainstream values, but these TV shows of the 1950s were subversive to reality. Though they bought the toasters and two cars, lots of people just couldn't live up to the image and cracked. There are a lot of walking wounded around today as a result of the tone of the 1950s.

So, what is the function of art, of films? It is to question values, to subvert conformity. You see this even in science fiction. *Invasion of the Body Snatchers* ridiculed the conformity of the 1950s. The *Godzilla* films ridiculed the conformity in Japan that allowed the monster to take over. Even the most commercial movies are performing a deadly social purpose. *Jaws* was about how an unexpected evil arose from the sea and upset the complacency and conformity of a community.

I suppose to some, I also appear like a monster, with *Scarface* and *Natural Born Killers*, spreading fear and havoc in the community. That is the point of art and films: to subvert.

NPQ

Barbra Streisand has defended Hollywood by saying something similar — that artists have always thrown bombs at the boundaries of the mainstream, and for that they have long been chastised.

But isn't it different now? The avant-garde is not pushing the limits from the outside, like some marginal poet or cubist painter, but from inside; the subversive ethos inhabits the mass culture through the mass media. It is the consciousness of the mainstream. As Madonna demonstrates, assaulting norms is big business.

And since images rule dreams, and dreams rule actions, this is a whole other ballgame. The propaganda today is to subvert and ridicule all authority, from mom to Imam; to regard everything with a cynical eye and trust no faith.

Stone

That is true, not just in film but across the board in the mass media. In this sense, David Letterman is far more dangerous to values than I am. He doesn't have values; he makes fun of values. For Letterman, everything is an object of ridicule — it almost doesn't matter who is on his show. There is no discussion of issues or values, just constant, remorseless ridicule of everything and anything. To the extent that kind of show sets the tenor of discourse, I think we have a real problem.

You can also see this in the advertising for grunge clothing. The kids are rebellious, snotty, sticking their butts in the air. The "fuck you" attitude reigns in advertising. That is very deeply antisocial.

Good art restores values. It aims to destroy the false — not all values, not all authority — and create the good and virtuous. As a director, I've had different functions at different times. *Heaven and Earth*, about a Vietnamese woman who married an American soldier and emigrated to the United States, was meant to be restorative and healing, looking for the construction of new values in terms of the consensus about immigrants coming into America. *Natural Born Killers* was a wholly destructive film, aimed at destroying what I believe is the hypocrisy of the 1990s, of idolizing the image and not coping with the shadow of violence and aggression in American life. "Love overcomes the demon" was another message, though that was seen by many to be what I was destroying.

So, at times the artist works to create and at other times to destroy, sometimes unwittingly. But I would separate that from the drumbeat of cynicism and irreverence of the mass media in general.

NPQ

Are you agreeing, then, with the thrust of the critiques from people — ranging from Newt Gingrich to some Muslim clerics — that the main meme, or ideological message, of the Western-dominated mass media is anti-authoritarian and cynical?

Stone

Yes, I think that is true.

NPQ

Isn't that a problem now? No doubt such a message was powerfully important when the Soviet Union existed, and, to be sure, it still undermines the Chinese communist system, but isn't the real issue in free societies not the oppression of authority, but where to draw the limits on freedom?

Stone

This is the same point Francis Fukuyama has made, that the anti-authoritarian impulse had gone too far, that it was breaking down the basis of shared social norms. He has said that when "question authority" becomes the chief slogan of a culture, that culture is doomed because it won't be able to hang together.

I think there may some truth to that. The pendulum has probably swung too far. You know the Buddhists talk about the middle way, about moderation in all things to keep an equilibrium.

We are out of balance on this, the cynicism has gone too far. We are becoming what the history books tell us late Rome was like: mired in decadent self-absorption and lacking virtue.

You can see how this comes about through the media when there is such scant portrayal of strong father figures. Even back in the 1950s, the father figures were ridiculous on the TV shows; mothers have been stronger. As a result, it is harder for men to establish authority.

I notice with my own two children, that, because of television, my authority is very limited. The Oedipus complex is on the TV. My authority was undermined in the house. Kids today are exposed only to violence, even in cartoons, and not to wisdom. Being aggressive and kicking ass — not using your wits or solving things in an indirect way — is the answer to all problems. On these points I think Gingrich and company are probably right.

NPQ

Hollywood and the American mass media have global reach. You can imagine how the impious message of this medium is received in many Islamic societies still struggling to be pious. The Islamic writer Akbar Ahmed talks about how the postmodern cynicism and irony of the Western media is a challenge to the faith and piety that lies at the core of the Islamic world view; that it is a far greater threat to Islam than guns or missiles or Mongol armies ever were.

Stone

I got a sense of this recently when I went to show *Natural Born Killers* at the Cairo Film Festival. The idea I was critiquing in that film was that the new god is image. The film is cut so that the image deconstructs itself as it goes. . . .

NPQ

Islam, of course, has always been suspicious of the image and even banished it in art. The image of God conceived by man could lead to idolatry of the image, not piety toward God. . . .

Stone

And this is why I think they understand, perhaps better than we do in the West, the power of the image. The religions of the East — Buddhism, Hinduism — handle the image differently. They know the image is only an illusion; it doesn't penetrate the spirit, but rolls off the shoulders.

A History of the Image:
From Pseudo-Events to Virtual Reality

Daniel J. Boorstin

The Librarian of Congress Emeritus, Daniel J. Boorstin is one of America's most enduring and insightful thinkers. He is author of the acclaimed series The Americans *(three volumes: 1958; 1965; 1973) as well as* The Creators *(1992), and* The Discoverers *(1983). His newest work,* Cleopatra's Nose: Essays on the Unexpected, *was published by Random House in 1994.*

Dr. Boorstin has also been director of the National Museum of History and Technology, and senior historian of the Smithsonian Institution. He was interviewed by Nathan Gardels in the booklined study of his home in Washington, D.C.

NPQ

In your 1961 book *The Image: A Guide to Pseudo-Events in America,* you were the first to alert us to the coming dominance of the image, of presidents elected and governing by PR, of the creation of a "thicket of unreality" that "befogs our experience" and stands between us and the facts of life. On the frontispiece of *The Image*, you even cited Max Frisch saying "Technology [is] the knack of arranging the world so that we don't have to experience it."

In 1994, young media theorists of Generation X like Douglas Rushkoff have fulfilled your worry, writing that the televised experience that media technology has created is the real thing. Others, like Carl Bernstein, the journalist of Watergate fame, are saying that America has become the Talk Show Nation drowning in the trivia of an "idiot culture." Perhaps technological revolutions, too, have their Thermidor. Has the Information Revolution that was supposed to bring us an enlightened global village produced instead an "idiot culture?"

Daniel J. Boorstin

Let's leave aside disparaging and eulogistic clichés like "idiot culture" so that we can focus on what is important: the broader implications of technology for human experience.

The first important thing is that media technology has a tendency to homogenize time and space. What is there is also here — at the same time. Or what was there can be here again on the screen if it was filmed. What we must consider when we are talking about the effect of technology on experience is what happens when the distinctions of time and space are erased.

One consequence of television is thus what I call *diplopia*, the double image: not knowing whether it is real or not, whether it is happening or not happening. That gives a kind of iridescence to experience. I am less willing to lament it than you are. The question is how to come to terms with it and make something of it if we can.

When people share experiences so broadly this can change, for example, the nature of discovery. When the American astronauts landed on the moon we were there, right there! We were there. It gave us all a sense of discovery that no one but Columbus himself and his crew had when he landed in the New World.

Another consequence of television has been to offer us new avenues to community. Democracies are very weak in ritual. Ritual is something that brings people together in community; it is a symbol of community, of everyone being in it together, of having the same experience. Of course, there is always religious ritual, but that is on the wane in our society. The low churches and the evangelical churches don't even pay attention to ritual.

So, there is a tendency for the media to fill in the gap. The poverty of ritual in a democracy creates a lacuna into which technology can flow with its miniseries, talk shows, and other vapidities. This ritualistic role of media was also evident in recent public events: the death and funeral of Richard Nixon, the death and funeral of Jackie Onassis, and the anniversary of D-Day. Americans in recent times have seldom felt so drawn together by the death of a president as they did by Richard Nixon's death. On TV, they watched all the other living presidents attending the funeral together, they saw the expressions on their faces. It was a moment of community that the media created.

The ability to enjoy with our fellow countrymen the special qualities of Jackie Onassis was made possible through the reproduction of memorable television footage and photographs from decades past. In such events you are more there when you are here; in your own home you have a better seat at the funerals or the D-Day reenactments than if you were actually present. Yet at the same time you are part of something bigger shared by the whole country.

A third consequence of television is what could be called "chronological myopia," the tendency to focus on the more recent. The 50th anniversary of D-Day was made into a commemorative super-event by the reenactment of the invasion; yet the 250th anniversary of Thomas Jefferson's birthday, which was also supposed to be celebrated, passed with little notice. It was of so little interest that William Jefferson Clinton didn't bother to fill out the appointments to the commemoration commission until long past the anniversary. The Jefferson anniversary was like trying to celebrate Christmas in July. The D-Day anniversary might have been the same if there had not been the graphic parachute drops, or if the film *The Longest Day* had been about the American Revolution and not D-Day.

Yet the importance of Jefferson to America cannot be overstated. His influence on America may even be deeper and more enduring than, I say tongue in cheek, the influence of Richard Nixon, even though Jefferson's funeral was not televised. That is what I mean by chronological myopia.

NPQ

Isn't the worry precisely that community will be anchored mainly in the vapidities of Oprah, Donahue, Geraldo, and tabloid TV that consistently fill the airwaves and cables? Isn't that shared experience closer to voyeurism than a voyage of discovery?

Boorstin

Naturally, I don't applaud that. It is clear that another tendency of media technology is that it expands to fill all available time. And in all that available time when we are waiting at the airport or sitting bored on a long flight or home from school or work, people expect more drama, excitement, and titillation than human nature in reality is capable of inventing. People seem to expect a kind of utopia of eternal amusement. But that is an extravagant expectation.

People want that iridescence of the image, that glow of gilded experience, twenty-four hours a day. Real life is just not that dramatic around the clock. Humankind is not capable of inventing as much novelty as we have come to crave. So, trivia, the weird, the strange, and the extreme fill in the space.

NPQ

So, is it the technology that creates the demand, or the other way around?

Boorstin

In my book *The Creators,* I observe that it is a characteristic of Western culture to put a special value on novelty. The Judeo-Christian religion worships a Creator God. Its sacred documents affirm that man was made in the image of the Creator. So some divinity is given to the act of novelty.

That is not the case in the great Eastern religions like Hinduism or Buddhism. There is no Creator God in the first place. There is no sense in those cultures that the ability to create something better is celebrated in the artist. Certainly, great works of art have been created in the East, but they have not had the imprimatur of novelty.

So, technology is a symbol, a symptom, and a consequence of the civilizational motive of the search for the new. Patents and copyrights are the way of protecting the benefits that people get from novelty. Technology creates endless possibilities for novelty. There are four kingdoms on earth — animal, vegetable, mineral, and now, a new one, the kingdom of the machine, where the laws of the other kingdoms don't apply.

The idea of species, a dominant idea in Western culture based on biological thought for most of Western history, was the idea of something that was identifiably discrete and fixed with distinctive characteristics. That is how Aristotle used the concept. And that is why it was very hard for Western Christian thinkers to believe that it was possible for any species to become extinct, or for a new species to come into being.

When the machine kingdom arrived on the scene it entirely changed the "fixedness" of the idea of species. Machines are not permanently fixed in their original state. They can interbreed! You can quite readily crossbreed the radio and the cellular phone with the automobile in a way you can't cross a cat and a dog.

Every technology is something that can be interbred, so there is no end to the novelty that can be created. As a result, there is a fluidity that never before existed. A natural species reacts to its environment. The machine species creates environment. The ability of the automobile to survive depends on its ability to bring forth highways. It changes the temperature in the atmosphere with its exhaust. My book *The Image* deals with only one aspect of the consequences of technology on experience, the relation of mankind to what is out there.

NPQ

Let me return to your point about *diplopia* and the double image, about the confusion between what is real and what is not. For the generation that grew up swimming in the soup of the image since they were first put them in front of the tube so Mom and Dad could take a breather, the media has virtually become the real thing, the primary realm of experience.

On the other hand, without direct experience of an event some just don't believe it is real. Speaking of the American landing on the moon, I remember that at that time many in the Soviet Union claimed it was merely a Hollywood contrivance.

Boorstin

In many Muslim countries today people still deny that the moon landing took place.

NPQ

For someone of my age, born in 1952, and certainly those who are younger, the common references are to TV series or events like *I Love Lucy* or *Leave It to Beaver*, or the first time the Beatles appeared on Ed Sullivan's show, or any number of Disney movie "classics." Hasn't this predominance of the media transformed experience?

Boorstin

It is easy to be glib when talking about reality. Isn't any experience itself an aspect of reality?

Again, let us look at the longer course of history. The first transformation of experience came with speech, and then another with writing. Writing was an enormous transformation of experience: it was possible to get a message from someone who was dead! That had not happened before writing.

Then, of course, the advent of the book made it possible to enlarge people's experience, making it possible to share an experience that you had not actually lived yourself. The reason so many medieval teachers were hostile to the book was because it destroyed their monopoly over the access to knowledge. The book created a whole new category of experience. People would read Dickens and weep over Oliver Twist. Was that experience or not experience? And, after all, the Judeo-Christian religion, like Islam, depends on The Book. Don't we call that experience? Is that unreal?

Now, I'm not talking about particular TV programs, but about technology. When we talk about technology, including "virtual reality" about which there is so much pro and con debate today, we should keep in mind the larger picture: technology enlarges and changes experience by homogenizing the dimensions of time and space. That is the way we should think about it. That is the basic point.

Yet it is important not to imply that technology is the only source of enlarging experience. The literary form that James Joyce invented in *Ulysses* was a whole new take on consciousness. The invention of biography as a literary form did not depend on technology; it was an act of imagination in ways of seeing. By definition, we can't know the categories of future novelty; otherwise, there wouldn't be any novelty.

When people worry about the vapidity of some TV programs and the tabloid trash, we must keep in mind that such material is a function of the limits of human invention. We are only capable of generating so much novelty, and apparently not enough to fill all the time that must be programmed on round-the-clock TV.

NPQ

With the explosion of cable channels, fiber-optic networks, satellites, and the coming information highway, aren't we headed for a deluge of data and trivia that will overwhelm our culture? And what are the consequences?

Boorstin

The tendency is for information to displace knowledge. That is because information consists of fragments of experience unrelated to each other and characterized by their recentness. Therefore, the reporting of them has not given anybody an opportunity to organize them. Their relevance has not been tested. The information highway is the route being built for the flow of facts that are significant because of their obsolescence.

Knowledge, however, is organized. It is structured. What cannot be related or is not relevant is discarded. The obvious force that has made information displace knowledge is the reduction of the time that lapses between when someone notices something, communicates it, and when it is received by somebody else.

In the case of television, you have an instantaneous reporting all over the world. The news reporters often haven't even been able to learn how to pronounce the names of the places they are reporting on, for example Bosnia-Herzegovina or Tadjikistan. They often don't know if it is a prime minister or a promontory they are describing.

The multiplication of bytes of information, the sheer momentum, makes it inevitable that people will be flooded by the miscellaneous. The information highway will become an expressway, accelerating this momentum even more. The invention of new machines spawns more new data than it does knowledge. This reverses the situation from earlier times, for example, the Middle Ages. There was then a scarcity of information, of data, about the heavens because they didn't have even a telescope. So there was a tendency for meaning to outrun information. Absent the invention of machines that could provide that information, people invented meaning about what went on there. They had to. Otherwise they had no structure for experience.

Now, with the multiplication of machines, of cameras ultraviolet and infrared, and all the other means to collect data from the heavens, there is a tendency for information to outrun meaning. We accumulate data. The Voyager 2 spacecraft traveled 4,429,508,700 miles during twelve years to "brush the treetops of Neptune and hurtle past Triton," as science writer Stephen Hall put it, to send back data for which we had no clue as to its meaning. That is why I call this "the age of negative discovery" — we are forever discovering the new areas of our ignorance. That is what our technology enables us to do. This, I suppose, is what it means to be human: to have more questions than answers.

Be that as it may, this dynamic of technology to create more data than meaning makes it all the more important for us to take refuge in forms of communication where there is a time lapse between when information is noted, communicated, and then received.

The flood of pseudo-events and the avalanche of trivia created by the media technology are the counterparts to this overwhelming deluge of data that outstrips meaning. The vulgarities and absurdities of so much television are only another symptom of this general dynamic.

NPQ

How is it possible, given the vast momentum of technology, to establish some equilibrium between trivia and significance, between data and meaning? Aren't you concerned that Oprah will drive out Othello?

Boorstin

It is true that television has opened the floodgates of trivia, data, and pseudo-events. But why must there be equilibrium? To talk somehow of balancing these things is what totalitarian societies try to do in their efforts to limit choice. In the Soviet Union they limited access to reading rooms and censored outside works by not translating them. They decided what were good books and bad books.

Someone once said that the Library of Congress was the world's greatest collection of bad books. To me that was just another way of saying it is the world's greatest collection of books, because a free society is one that does not presume to allow the government, or the librarian or some cultural monitor to decide what are the good books. Even the most vicious ideas must have their place in the record of human follies.

I believe in quest. Man is going in search. If you believe in freedom, you believe that there is a creative chaos in the world, and that a free society is one in which people are at liberty to wander; it is one in which there is the opportunity to be vagrant. The only answer to the concerns people have about trashy TV is to rise above that and realize that twenty-four-hour titillation is an extravagant expectation.

In this sense, the antidote to the image is the book. It is the refuge from the flood of trivia. The book remains the great source of civilization because of its durability. A book judges our experiences not by the momentary appeal of events, but by their continuing relevance. There is almost a direct relationship between the value of a work and the amount of time that elapses between when it is created, communicated, and received. The more instantaneous a work, the less likely it is to have an enduring value.

The book couldn't be further from those forms of entertainment that thrive on their evanescence. A TV series always needs a new episode. The broadcast image thrives on obsolescence. Who would watch the nightly news two days later? And who wants yesterday's newspaper? Books thrive on the test of time. Indeed, publishers still thrive on their backlists. The book is so dispersed and diffused that it would be hard to destroy it, or abolish its form.

In any case, to believe that a newer technology will abolish an older one is what I call the "displacive fallacy."

Obituaries of the book that abound today are not only premature, but foolish. Similarly, television has not replaced radio. Decades after TV was invented, there are radios in every car and we even put them in our ears when we jog. Further, to cite another example, the rise of investigative journalism in the print media can be seen as a byproduct of the preemption of spot news by television and radio. That left an unforeseen niche for the print media. New technologies don't abolish old ones; they further define, or even redefine, their function and create new spaces for them.

To affirm the book today is to affirm the endurance of civilization against the rush of immediacy. If we do that, I have confidence that in the long run there will be a survival of the Great Books and the Great Ideas and Great People that have made Western civilization what it is.

NPQ

Henry Kissinger has made the point that contemporary political leadership, particularly in the foreign policy area, is too easily swayed by the images that flash across the CNN hourly update. Absent a longer-range concept, a strategy that will see the interests of state through the emotional bumps of starving Somalis or Haitian boat people, they make decisions based upon public opinion pressure. The media feeds this. "Was Clinton standing as tall in his performance on the windswept shores of Normandy as Reagan?" they ask. "Who won the Oscar for commemorating D-Day?"

Boorstin

The media often complicates the capacity for judgment by elevating the peripheral to the prominent. But leadership is not the same as responding to television. Leadership is the quality of deciding where we must focus and what we must pay attention to.

NPQ

How has our image-dominated culture most changed since you wrote *The Image* thirty-three years ago?

Boorstin

I would say that what is most different is the multiplication of points of access, of moments and times of access, to the viewer or receiver of information; the round-the-clock homogenization of space and time, the radio in your ear, the Walkman. There is a greater self-generating momentum now that has nothing to do with need. It is this need for the unnecessary that has become so widespread.

To multiply its product without regard to the need for the product is in the nature of technology. While natural selection governed the survival of the species according to necessity, it can be said that "artificial selection" governs the machine kingdom according to the freedom of creative forces. Each elaboration of technology spawns other elaborations, and the pace accelerates. The viability of the machine depends on its capacity to create its own need and to bring forth the environment that makes it necessary.

NPQ

A final comment?

Boorstin

Human progress springs from a soul that cannot be encompassed, from a quest that cannot be contained. This requires a tolerance of the puzzling consequences of technology, of the unexpected that awaits us.

Totalitarian societies are prone to exaggerate their virtues. Free societies exaggerate their vices. It is always safer to exaggerate our vices. That is the self-insuring quality of a free society. The ultimate test of our democracy will be our power to allow the progress of paradox in science and technology as we defer to common sense in our society.

HOW THE WORLD
WORKS NOW

Normally, political and business leaders don't possess the depth of the big souls or the great minds. But their hands-on experience in shaping the world we live in more than earns them the authority to speak.

In this section we have selected just a few of the more interesting political figures from a long list of world leaders who have written for NPQ *or been interviewed for* NPQ's *weekly Global Viewpoint column, distributed by the* Los Angeles Times *Syndicate.*

More than any other Asian leader, Singapore's Lee Kuan Yew has emerged as the spokesman of the capitalist and soft-authoritarian "Asian Way." Michael Manley, twice the prime minister of Jamaica and once a socialist Third World firebrand, talks frankly about his change of mind at the end of a long career that ended in disillusion. We all know that Nelson Mandela broke the back of apartheid through decades of struggle, but what are his views as a larger-than-life statesman now that he is president of South Africa? He writes here about the weak instrument of the nation-state he now commands.

Akio Morita and David Rockefeller are not political lead-ers, but their influence has been so vast that they might as well be. In a dialogue here, they exchange views on capi-talism, East and West. François Mitterrand, who retired after two terms as France's socialist president, is less con-cerned in his remarks with opening markets as he is with distributing the wealth globally — in his view a forgotten goal of the smug consumer societies of the West. Finally, Israeli foreign minister Shimon Peres, speaking from the violent cauldron of the Middle East, declares "an end to the hunting season in history."

The East Asian Way

Lee Kuan Yew

The prime minister of Singapore from 1959 to 1991, Lee Kuan Yew is the grand old man of Asia. Under his quasi-authoritarian tutelage, Singapore was transformed from a bustling Third World port into a prosperous, orderly proto-type of East Asian modernization.

Still the eminence behind the throne, Lee Kuan Yew's formal title is Senior Minister. He talked with NPQ *Editor Nathan Gardels in late November 1992, at Istana, the former British governor's residence in Singapore.*

NPQ

Now that the Cold War is over, isn't a new conflict arising between East Asian "communitarian" capitalism and American style "individualistic" capitalism? Further, isn't this economic conflict rooted in the deeper differences between civilizations: the authoritarian bent of Confucian culture and the extreme individualism of Western liberalism?

Lee Kuan Yew

This is one facet of the problems that arise in a global economy. Latecomers to industrial development have had to catch up by finding ways of closing the gap.

As it has turned out, the more communitarian values and practices of the East Asians — the Japanese, Koreans, Taiwanese, Hong Kongers, and the Singaporeans — have proven to be clear assets in the catching-up process. The values that East Asian culture upholds, such as the primacy of group interests over individual interests, support the total group effort necessary to develop rapidly. But I do not see the conflict you describe as competition between two closed systems.

The original communitarianism of Chinese Confucian society has degenerated into nepotism, a system of family linkages, and corruption, on the mainland. And remnants of the evils of the original system are still to be found in Taiwan, Hong Kong, and even Singapore.

Hong Kong and Taiwan differ from China, of course, because Confucian ways have been moderated by one hundred-odd years of British rule in Hong Kong's case, and fifty years of Japanese rule in Taiwan. Further, because Taiwan incorporated Western ideas of universal education and the Japanese idea of competition between groups and teams — not individuals — Taiwan is better geared to prosper in the new global economy.

China itself is now in the process of sloughing off not just the communist system, but also those outdated parts of Confucianism that prevent the rapid acquisition of knowledge needed to adjust to new ways of life and work.

So, I see this "conflict" as a part of interaction and evolution in one world. Systems are not developing in isolation. For instance, Japanese companies have set up factories in America, Britain, France, and Germany, using the local work force but bringing in Japanese methods of management.

And they are succeeding: by skillfully incorporating the work force into the total production effort, the Japanese have improved productivity in the British motor industry beyond the dreams of British Leyland or even Rolls-Royce. Everybody wears the same grey or blue uniforms. They use the same toilets and share the same canteen. There are no special reserved parking lots. A sense of egalitarianism, of being equal partners in a great endeavor, pervades the work place.

Such results show that there is no reason why other British or American firms should not do likewise. In time, they will incorporate what they view as the better part of Japanese practices. What we see in today's world is one constant process of learning from, and then one-upping, one's competitor.

NPQ

No doubt there is integration and complementarity, but surely there is also conflict — not only between an economic approach that approves of vast wage differentials and one that doesn't, for example, or between collaborationist, *zaibatsu*-type corporations and the entrepreneurial style, but also between the exaggerated individualism of "The Lone Ranger" and the Confucian intolerance of free expression.

Lee

Well, I do not see the Americans sticking to a losing formula. This is a different wild west. The Lone Ranger approach is no longer the way to conquer the world. What is needed instead is a regularly constituted cavalry instead of ad hoc Lone Rangers. I'm sure the Americans will change because they don't want to lose. It is a process of action, reaction, and interaction.

NPQ

That may be so. But perhaps the differing mentalities are most clearly revealed in the approach to human rights. In one of his first statements as prime minister of Japan, Kiichi Miyazawa argued that Japan would not only continue to improve commercial ties with the post-Tiananmen regime in Beijing, but would not let "abstract notions of human rights" enter into the relationship. Subsequent leaders have made the same point.

By contrast, during visits to China, American leaders have insisted on pressing the human rights issue. "I will never accept the view that the hopes and aspirations of an *individual* in Asia should count less than a person elsewhere," U.S. Secretary of State James Baker once said. For the U.S., human rights and "freedom of thought and expression" are virtually synonymous with the "new world order" in Asia. This is still official U.S. policy.

Lee

America and East Asia are very different cultures. Chinese culture grew up in isolation from the rest of the world for thousands of years, and then extended itself into Korea, Japan, and Vietnam. From the other end of the continent, Indian culture spread out and reached as far as Thailand and Cambodia.

So, one can take a broad brush and shade East Asian culture over Korea, China, Vietnam, and Japan. Indian-Hindu culture in a very broad sense would cover Pakistan, India, Bangladesh, Sri Lanka, Burma, and Southeast Asia.

Then there is an overlay of Muslim culture, completely different from Hindu culture, which is also to be found now in Pakistan, Bangladesh, and parts of India. There are 190 million Muslims in Southeast Asia, primarily in Malaysia and Indonesia. Thailand is more Buddhist, like Burma.

Seeing the ancient, complex cultural map of this part of the world, can we all of a sudden accept universal values of democracy and human rights as defined by America? I don't think that it is possible. Values are formed out of the history and experience of a people. One doesn't learn what is right and wrong out of a book. One absorbs these notions through the mother's milk. These are the realities, so I perfectly agree with Miyazawa.

As prime minister of Singapore, my first task was to lift my country out of the degradation that poverty, ignorance, and disease had wrought. Since it was dire poverty that made for such a low priority given to human life, all other things became secondary. Moreover, as a Singaporean I do not believe it appropriate for the Japanese to speak of Western human rights, given their brutal trampling of human rights in Singapore.

I recently read a Japanese perspective on that country's actions in the Second World War. According to this view, Japan had no choice in bombing Pearl Harbor, she was boxed in: she tried to get equality of treatment, a clause on nonracial discrimination in the Treaty of Versailles, but the white answer was no. Finally, when she was faced with the oil embargo, it became apparent that she had to fight or go down on bended knees. So, because Japan had to build up its own empire, it invaded China and Manchuria. In that process — which the Japanese say was forced upon them by a hostile world — they committed horrendous brutality across East Asia.

Two weeks after Singapore was captured by the Japanese in 1942, there was a hubbub outside our lone high-rise — the Cathay Building — and I took my bicycle to have a look. It was the biggest shock of my life. Severed human heads were stuck on poles outside the building. A bare wooden board with large brush-painted characters warned: "If you do as this man has been doing, your head will end up here." And they put seven to nine other heads elsewhere all about town. The aim of the Japanese authorities was to start off their reign with everybody knowing the rules of the game. And the rules of the game were off with your head! Like everyone else, I was terrified. But there was law and order during the next three-and-a-half years of the Japanese occupation of Singapore.

Of course, the Japanese have not been the only perpetrators of this kind of brutality in Asia. Today in China one still sees televised executions. In a large stadium, the person is placed in the "take-off-flying" position with their hands tied behind their back. A revolver is pressed to the neck and they are polished off. Because the country is so vast and densely populated, there can't possibly be a policeman for each city block, so one must depend on the mass impact of this kind of retribution to bring about a semblance of order. It is probably the only way for the death threat to be effective.

So, our values are different, as they always have been. But now, television, fax, satellites, and the aircraft have brought us all into one world. After taking our separate paths for thousands of years, we now meet, and there is total misunderstanding.

I am one who has been exposed to both worlds: Singapore was governed by the British but it was basically an Asian society, so I could see what British standards were like, and compare and contrast them to Asian standards. And I was educated in Britain for four years and saw how the British comported and governed themselves. As a man of two cultures, I have learned that one cannot change core values overnight just by exposure to a different culture.

For Asia, I think that over the next one, two, or perhaps three generations (with each generation marking twenty years), there will have to be adjustments. I'm certain that the younger Japanese — those in their thirties, not the older generation who committed those crimes — already feel a certain revulsion at the idea of chopping off somebody's head and putting it on a stick. And that is because of their exposure to different values since defeat in 1945. But their process of change began in 1868 with the Meiji Restoration! So, a hundred years from now, I'm sure Europeans, East Asians, and Americans will all arrive at something approximating universal values and norms.

NPQ
_____

In terms of human rights?

Lee

Let's call it "human behavior" in general. The only exception might be the Muslims, because Islamic injunctions about how to punish adultery by stoning to death, or thieving by cutting off hands, are written down in the holy Koran. I am not sure Muslims are going to change as easily as the Buddhists or Hindus. But I cannot see them remaining totally unchanged either. After all, for them to catch up, even if only to modernize their weaponry so they can get the big bomb and blow up the Israelis, they have to train and equip a whole generation of young minds with a scientific approach to the solving of problems. Inevitably, that critical scientific mentality must bring about a change in their perceptions of core values. But it is a long and slow process. In sum, I don't think a resolution in the U.S. Congress can change China.

NPQ

In principle, do you believe in one standard of human rights and free expression?

Lee

Look, it is not a matter of principle but of practice. In the technologically connected world of today, everybody can watch the Tiananmen crackdown on TV. Today, transportation is subsonic but in another twenty years your son will be able to travel at supersonic speeds; instead of fifteen hours, in just a few hours he will be able to go from New York to Singapore.

In such a world, no society can be protected from the influence of another. But that doesn't mean that all Western values will prevail. I can only say that if Western values are in fact superior insofar as they bring about superior performance in a society and help it survive, then they will be adopted. I truly believe the process is Darwinian. If adopting Western values diminishes the prospects for the survival of a society, they will be rejected. For example, if too much individualism does not help survival in a densely populated country like China, it just won't take.

At the same time, however much Chinese leaders berate Americans because the U.S. is the world's major power, the leadership knows that the Americans have in fact been the least exploitative of China when compared to the Japanese or Europeans. This reality is deep in the historical memory of the Chinese people. The Americans left behind universities, schools, and scholarships for educating doctors.

And of course, the Americans tried to convert everybody to Christianity. In fact, today there are factions in Chinese society, not just in the Communist leadership, that believe the Americans are the most evangelistic of the whole lot: the others will just trade with you and leave you alone but the Americans will come and want to convert you. Now its not Christianity but human rights and democracy American-style! The Chinese leaders call it "human rights" imperialism.

NPQ

But wasn't the Tiananmen movement, with its replica of the Statue of Liberty and all, really a cry for "human rights and democracy American-style?"

Lee

I would not define what happened in the spring of 1989 as a movement for democracy. It was a movement for change from the total control of the Communist Party. If you had questioned a cross-section of the student leaders and others who participated, many of them would have had no clear idea of what they wanted in place of the Chinese Communist Party that governs that immense land.

Really, to these young people, democracy means, "More freedom for me!" But how does one govern one-quarter of humanity on that basis? By what principles? By what methods? The demonstrators didn't think it through. "Let's make things better." "Let's stop this corruption." "Let's stop this nepotism." "Let's have more freedom in the press and TV." "Let's have more freedom of association." That is all they really wanted.

The tragedy of Tiananmen was that the participants got carried away by the dynamics of mass emotions in a very densely populated city. Their grievances exploded into one big demonstration, and it became a frontal challenge to the Communist Party, and a personal challenge to Deng Xiaoping as leader.

As the events progressed, the slogans that were being put up became increasingly strident. I watched what was on Chinese TV and in the Chinese newspapers. The whole thing had evolved into an attack on Deng, more than Li Peng.

In my view, that was unwise. There is, after all, no tradition in Chinese history of satirizing the emperor. To do a *Doonesbury* cartoon of the emperor is to commit sedition and treason. About four or five days before the end, I read a clever little doggerel making fun of Deng. I thought, God, this is it. Either they will get away with this bit of irreverence and disrespect, in which case Deng is finished, or Deng is going to teach them a lesson. Deng slapped them down — with an unnecessary use of armor, in my view — to show who was boss.

Why such force, I asked myself? These are not stupid people. They know what the world will think. My only explanation is that Deng must have feared that if the movement in Beijing were repeated in two hundred major Chinese cities, he would not be able to control it. As with traditional Chinese rulers, he had to set up a clear, if brutal, example for all to see.

NPQ

So Deng was afraid of the prodemocracy movement erupting in two hundred cities, among the 20 percent of the population that doesn't live in the countryside, with its eight hundred million peasants.

Doesn't this point up the problem of how one central policy can't rule two Chinas — the urban and rural China — at the same time? You yourself have argued for a "twin-track" policy that allows more freedom in the cities where the educated classes demand it. Otherwise economic reform will falter.

Lee

No, not freedom. They will have to have *participation* in the way they are governed. Please, let's use neutral words, because when you use words like "freedom" and "democracy" you scare the Chinese. Since Tiananmen, these have become code words for subverting China. So when you talk to them like that, they say "Well, okay, relations with the West are off. It is them or us. And it has got to be us."

I would say this to Chinese premier Li Peng: once 20 to 30 percent of your urban population (out of each year's student cohort) has a college education, the next 40 to 50 percent are in polytechnic or technical schools, and the rest have a general education of about a U.S. tenth-grade level, you can no longer just give orders from the top down if you want to succeed in your economic development. With today's high technology, you just can't squeeze the maximum productivity out of advanced machinery without a self-motivated and self-governing work force. What is the point of having $100 million worth of machinery in a factory if you can't get 95 percent productivity or more out of it through the use of quality circles, involving engineers in the production process, as the Japanese do?

In 1980 I visited a magnificent, modern, German-built steel factory in Wuhan, in central China. It was the kind of state-of-the-art factory that one wouldn't find in many parts of Europe. But its productivity was deplorable. Hundreds, perhaps thousands, of redundant workers were just standing around idle. The plant was overmanned, unprofitable, and managed from the top down.

Compare this to an equally modern steel mill in Taiwan. A Chinese who had worked in Singapore was put in charge of the Taiwan mill. He introduced the Taiwanese adaptation of Japanese quality-control circles, dividing the entire work force into little self-governing units. Each unit produced ideas, implemented them, and was rewarded for the results. Productivity skyrocketed because the workers and engineers were governing their own work lives, which is what China needs to compete in the world.

What happens, though, when these people who have learned self-government and critical thinking pass through the factory gates and go home? As thinking, rational people, they ask, "What are they doing to me in this town where I live? Why is the traffic flowing this way and not that way? Why are the leaders acting that way, instead of this way?"

Quite naturally, the thought occurs that the same processes they brought to bear in the factory to beneficial results could be carried outside, to cope with municipal and other domestic problems. This in turn leads to a demand to elect their own mayors and town councilors. It led to the birth of environmental movements in Taiwan, and will also do so in China, where the pollution is worse.

So the process of economic advancement requires participation. One simply cannot ask a highly educated work force to stop thinking when it leaves the factory. A broader participation in the larger society must take place or the whole economic effort will collapse.

NPQ

How might such a system look in a place like China? Would Confucianism remain at the obsolete center while a kind of regional pluralism evolved?

Lee

If China wants to develop at optimal speed it has to devolve power — to the provinces, the provincial capitals, the cities, and the towns. Obviously such a devolution will take place more rapidly in the free-trade zones on China's coast — in Guandong and Fujian.

NPQ

A six-lane highway is being built from Hong Kong to Guangzhou (Canton). Four-fifths of the investment in Guangzhou is from Hong Kong. Who is taking over whom in 1997? Is China taking over Hong Kong, or is Hong Kong taking over Guandong?

Lee

When you put it in such emotive terms, "Who is taking over whom," you immediately arouse negative reflexes. After 1997, can Hong Kong take over Guandong? No, of course it cannot. It is a very small place of six million people on 450 square miles of territory. But the ideas that make Hong Kong tick are spreading throughout Guandong and are going up even into the neighboring provinces. The economic development sucks in population and penetrates ever deeper into the hinterland.

Of course there is a certain mutation of the Hong Kong idea when it implants itself in the villages and towns of southern China. But, in time, what we will see will essentially be a variation of the Hong Kong idea, an extrapolation, in Guandong.

If China is to progress, the leadership should not interfere with this process. But they can and should say what parts they don't want: the casino mentality that causes hundreds of millions to be lost every afternoon at the horse races, or the organized prostitution and drug rings. Of course, one cannot completely eliminate these things; they will happen. Freelancers cannot be stopped. But they can be checked.

For optimum development, China needs the rapid absorption of practices and ideas of the free market — plus the quick acquisition of the skills and knowledge necessary for the next stage of industrial development.

The less savory aspects of free-market societies will always be with us, but in the end Beijing can be politically in control. They can slap it down, but at a cost.

NPQ

But in the end Beijing will have to accommodate the regional devolution that will sap their central power?

Lee

In the end? Yes. Shall we say in the next fifty years? That is the amount of time it will take for the whole of China to reach the level of today's South Korea. In the process they will have produced a very widespread layer of educated men and women in the cities. And the cities will grow at least by two or three times in the next fifty years, from 20 percent of the population to 40 to 60 percent.

In these cities, with populations of 20,000 or more, a minimum of self-government at the municipal level must be set in place. Such self-governing townships would possess the participatory rudiments of the Greek city-states. China's modern version will be on a megabasis of many thousand such city-states. Around this base, one can build a pyramid of power to control larger conglomerations in the rural parts of China. This can combine with the power structure of the big cities to coordinate consumer services like transportation and communications. That is the "twin-track" approach for development that would carry Asia into modernity.

NPQ

And so in fifty years' time the kind of expectations the West has for human rights in China might be more realistic?

Lee

I am not sure that in fifty years China will have yet accepted American-style human rights. However, once they are well above the poverty level, there will be less of the kind of barbarism where a man's head is chopped off or he is shot in the back without a proper trial.

You know, sometimes we must put ourselves in Deng Xiaoping's place. Deng, who studied in Lyon, France for about four years in his youth, passed through Singapore in the 1920s on his way by ship to Marseilles. He has remarked to me what a backward place it was in those days. He congratulated me on the progress and said, "If I had only to worry about Shanghai I could have done the same as you have done in transforming Singapore. But this great weight of the peasantry in such a large land mass as China slows everything down."

When I talk to Deng, I never allow myself to forget what this man has gone through. He lost his first family, slaughtered by the Kuomintang (KMT). He fought to liberate China. Thousands of his comrades were killed by the KMT, the Japanese, disease, or starvation. When the Japanese headed toward the Northwest to capture the heart of China, the Chinese broke the Yellow River dikes to stop their advance. The following year there was famine and millions died of starvation! But that was the price they had to pay to stop the Japanese.

So, when one talks to Deng and the other leaders about human rights and about Tiananmen, where perhaps a thousand students or workers were killed, let it be against this background. Deng paid the supreme price to bring order and stability to China, and he will not stand for irreverent doggerels that could destabilize China and throw it into chaos. Who gives him the right? He gave himself the right. That is part of Chinese culture. It's in the folk saying, "I conquer the world, I rule the world." And if someone wants to challenge him, they will have to take a gun and organize and fix him! Questions of human rights in China must be viewed in those terms.

NPQ

After the Philippine Congress voted to close down the U.S. bases there, Singapore offered to be a base for the U.S. fleet. What is the *raison d'être* for a continued American military presence in Asia in this last decade of the twentieth century? Do you fear domination by the Japanese if the Americans aren't present?

Lee

Nature does not like a vacuum. And if there is a vacuum we can be sure that somebody will fill it. I don't see the Japanese particularly wanting to fill that space unless it feels that its trade routes and access to Gulf oil are threatened. If the Americans are not around, they cannot be sure who will protect their oil tankers, so they have to do something themselves. That will trigger the Koreans, who fear the Japanese, then the Chinese. Will India then come down to our seas with two aircraft carriers?

It could be a disastrously unstable state of affairs, so why not stick with what has worked so far? The U.S. presence has maintained peace on the high seas of the Pacific since 1945. The American presence, in my view, is essential for the continuation of international law and order in East Asia. We are talking about defense in the context of what threats might emerge if there is a vacuum.

NPQ

When the Japanese sent their minesweepers during the Gulf War, they sailed very conspicuously through Asian waters. The recent debate in Japan over sending their Self-Defense Forces abroad in multilateral peacekeeping mission has reportedly worried you. Are you concerned?

Lee

Allowing Japan to once again send its forces abroad is like giving a chocolate liqueur to an alcoholic. Once the Japanese get off the water wagon, it will be hard to stop them. Whatever the Japanese do, they do very well. It's part of their culture, whether the task at hand is sharpening a samurai sword or making a Sony tape recorder or compact disc. So if they start to build up an armed force, it will be the best, and it will have the most sophisticated weaponry.

Although I think the values of the younger generation have changed — they wouldn't chop off heads and put them on a pole — what proof have we that if they get into a desperate situation, for example, blocked access to oil or markets, they won't set out with the same zeal as their grandfathers did?

We'd all be happier, including the present generation of Japanese, if the American security alliance remains, leaving Japan to concentrate on high-definition television.

NPQ

So from your point of view, the American presence is vital, both in terms of warding off a security vacuum, and as a guarantee of open global economic integration?

Lee

Exactly. An Asia in which cooperation and competition increases everyone's well-being, peacefully and without recourse to arms, has been the norm. This kind of Asia, this kind of Pacific, cannot exist without America being a major economic and security presence. East Asian prosperity has been built on the global system that America built up after World War II. It would cause great animosity, resentment, and eventually conflict to shut out Asia, just as we look as if we are going to make the grade. The quiet, slow-paced world where we lived within our own national boundaries is gone forever.

In the postwar era, American idealism integrated Japan and large parts of Asia into a world that had been shut to us. Indeed, American power has largely created the integrated world in which we now live, and it would be utter madness to let it all crumble after the Cold War has been won.

No matter what happens to American power, we can't go back. One can't disinvent the aircraft or the satellite — or the global consciousness Americans have created.

Adam Smith Was Right

Michael Manley

Prime Minister of Jamaica from 1972–1980, and then again from 1989 to March 1992, Michael Manley is the vice president of the Socialist International, and has been a lifelong trade unionist. He has led the People's National Party, founded by his father Norman Manley, since 1969. A few days after his resignation on March 28, 1992, NPQ Editor Nathan Gardels spoke with him in the garden of his modest townhouse in the suburbs of Kingston.

NPQ

The night before your formal resignation as prime minister, you flew to Washington for a farewell dinner with then-President George Bush, who hailed your free-market policies and your friendship with the United States. What has happened to the man once known as a militant spokesman for the Third World, the pal of Fidel Castro who preached state control of the economy and said that Jamaican millionaires could "go to Miami?"

Michael Manley

People are accustomed to seeing a generation of leaders who dominated in the sixties and seventies die off or pass from the scene, to be succeeded by another set of leaders who understand the new realities. What seems to mystify everyone is how one leader, through nothing other than the finest tradition of self-criticism taught in British schools, could be, so to speak, two generations in one.

I find no contradiction in my life and political career, because I want the same thing now as I always wanted: I want poor people to stop being poor. I want the powerless to have new avenues to power. Is it so difficult to see that an honest man could look at reality and say "I was wrong! Things don't work that way?"

To understand how my embrace of the market and my admiration of the U.S. fits coherently and consistently with my concerns, one must first spend a moment looking at where I was before, and why. Like many leaders of the developing world just emerging from the long colonial experience, I believed strongly in the use of state power to promote social justice through the law. In this I haven't changed one iota. To this day I am immensely proud of Jamaica's peaceful social revolution, carried out from 1972 to 1980 when I was prime minister for the first time. Workers, women, and children received their rights. The doors were opened to education and literacy for all. The legacy of this revolution today stands untouched and, I believe, it will stand forever.

But I also believed, like so many others, that the state had a central role to play, not only in promoting economic development, but in directing the economy away from the colonial patterns of dependence. We exported our dearest commodities, such as agricultural goods, at the cheapest prices. Yet we paid very high prices for manufactured goods, such as machinery and autos, from Europe and America. My fear, which I shared with other leaders of developing nations, was that an independent private sector, even one made up of our own nationals, would merely reproduce this pattern and keep us forever dependent.

This set of circumstances led to a commonality of political perspective across the so-called Third World. What we all wanted to do, through the strongest state intervention, was build a kinder economic structure that was internally separate from the world economy dominated by the former colonial powers. Then, we thought, we could better grapple with our poverty and underdevelopment. The fact is we all seriously miscalculated the capacity of the state to intervene effectively. Despite the enormous sincerity we brought to the task, our nationalist and statist approach didn't work. And it didn't work for several reasons.

First, when one tries to use the state as a major instrument of production, one quickly exhausts the managerial talent that can be mobilized in the name of patriotism. Absent the profit motive, it was truly amazing how few managers one could find who were motivated solely by love of their country, and how quickly those noble souls burned out. I call this idea the "Guevarist myth." Without an equity stake or a profit motive, few men will do their best sixteen hours a day. That is an elemental reality of human psychology. "Eight-to-five" men waiting for the end of the work day weren't going to lift Jamaica, or any other developing country, out of poverty.

Second, the minute the state begins to intervene in the private sector, a terrifying backlash sets in. The Jamaican model we pushed in the 1970s never contemplated wiping out the private sector, though we were very interventionist in exchange controls, agriculture, and economic management. To establish a major state presence in the economy, we took over the National Commercial Bank. Perhaps idealistically, we thought an interventionist state and a strong market could exist in tandem, each complementing the other. But we rapidly discovered the truth. As soon as the state comes near, the private sector contracts, loses its confidence, and moves its money out.

It is now clear to me that an unfettered market, not the imposition of political control, can be the most effective instrument of opportunity for the poor — but only if the state compensates for the market's tendency to concentrate power. Left untended without checks and balances, capitalism will add more wealth and power to those who started at the head of the field to the exclusion of competitive newcomers — which is no news to anyone. The state's remaining role, then, should be to ensure fair competition and block monopoly without impeding the market incentive. If the state stimulates the inclusive, entrepreneurial process of wealth creation while checking the market's tendency to exclude through monopolization, it can remain an instrument of empowerment.

It is in this respect that I so admire the United States. The way the U.S. ensures the integrity of the competitive mechanism in the private sector is a model for the rest of the world. The way Wall Street is kept squeaky clean through the punishment of insider trading is very admirable, as is the antitrust legislation aimed at blocking excessive monopolistic practices, and the support of small business and entrepreneurs through the tax code.

Especially during the 1980s, when I was out of power, I became very impressed with how the U.S. understands the logic of the market economy. America's democratic temper senses that if one is not careful, new oligarchic structures and new concentrations of power will be created by the market.

NPQ

Where do you depart, then, from such well-known nonsocialists as Margaret Thatcher, or Mario Vargas Llosa? When he was running for president in Peru, Vargas Llosa also promoted privatizing the public sector and the creation of microbusinesses to empower the poor. Specifically, Vargas Llosa said, "I am not advocating, as the socialists would, indirect ownership through the state. We need direct ownership. Further, we need to popularize and democratize property. The privatization of the monstrous public sector should be carried out in such a way that poor Peruvians can really become shareholders and owners."

Manley

Well, I don't know that I do depart from them. I suspect what is happening is that an enormous process of convergence is taking place in the world. I discovered with total astonishment that I ended up with a lot of perspectives very, very similar to those of Margaret Thatcher. But there are some significant differences. Like myself, Thatcher would go the route of small business opportunity. Like Vargas Llosa, she too wanted to privatize in a way that brought thousands of individuals into the system as shareholders. But Thatcher could not take the extra step of wanting to empower the workers. She excluded the trade union movement. My model begins with the workers. I want the workers to become shareholders.

The worker's movement must be led out of its traditional patterns of thought. Instead of being time-clock adversaries of the owner, they should want to become owners themselves. I would like to get to the point where the workers don't need a time clock. Instead, they will come to work because they not only get a paycheck, but because a dividend payment will be waiting for them at the end of the year. My final dream is that one day there can be a society where egalitarianism means that every single person is a shareholder in the market economy.

My whole life has been a struggle to reconcile the market with the socialist objective of egalitarianism. Knowing now that one can't compromise the market model if one wants to reach the socialist objective, the best thing to do is give the market free rein while making it the vehicle of opportunity for as many people as possible. I would call this "market socialism." There is no way to eradicate poverty if one resists the logic of capitalism. That seems to me to be what Mario Vargas Llosa and Maggie Thatcher think also. Despite its weaknesses, the whole world is converging toward democracy because this political system cannot be improved upon. I believe equally that, despite its weaknesses, the whole world is converging toward the market model. One just can't improve upon Adam Smith.

NPQ

As a lifelong socialist and trade unionist who now looks to the market, what is your conclusion about what creates wealth and what creates poverty?

Manley

What creates wealth is any kind of economic model that stimulates efficient production in a context where people have the means and the will to save. Poverty is created when that process leads to a concentration of power that excludes by limiting access to those savings to which all have contributed. Ending poverty is essentially a matter of creating access to the savings that have resulted from productive activity.

NPQ

For many years, you were a prominent spokesman for the developing world as it sought a New International Economic Order. These days you seem to have far less faith in a global order of any kind. What caused your change of mind?

Manley

The international division of labor that developed as a result of colonialism defined the economic fate of much of the so-called Third World. In brief, we produced raw materials with no value added, and traded them for value-added manufactured goods. The wealth, of course, was where the value-added was. So the whole issue of the inequality between rich and poor nations was about where that value-added was located.

How could this imbalance be corrected? In the 1960s and 1970s I approached this issue from an essentially ethical standpoint: it was unjust that so large a part of the world was condemned to so little of the value-added of total world production.

And, as a matter of common sense, I and others argued that such inequality was also inefficient from the standpoint of global capitalism. If the poor had more purchasing power, they could buy more goods from the rich nations. Then everyone would gain: the poor would be less poor, and the rich nations would have more markets for their goods.

What was therefore needed, many of us thought in those days, was to introduce a measure of political management of the world economy that would equalize the terms of trade, and guarantee that poor nations would have access to technology. This was known as the New International Economic Order. The United Nations pursued this idea for two decades as a development strategy. Willy Brandt chaired the famous North-South Commission, on which sat such luminaries as *Washington Post* publisher Kay Graham, which called for this kind of global management.

But it was all predicated on a fantasy. Namely, that anyone in international politics would respond to an argument based on ethics. Surely, there were many sensible and probably quite workable proposals that emerged. But nobody was listening. Leaders from the rich North would say in private, "I would like to help, but how can I go to my electorate and say I am going to make a bargain with the Third World to regulate the globe?"

The idea was stillborn. Dead in the water. The ethical summons was not persuasive. And, certainly, one couldn't try to impose it against the U.S. Marines. The New International Economic Order was formally buried at the supposed moment of its birth, at the North-South Summit in Cancun, Mexico, in 1981. Ronald Reagan, who had just been elected, killed it with a smile. He smiled at Julius Nyerere. He smiled at Jose Lopez Portillo. He smiled at all of us and just said, "No."

In two days, twenty years of international struggle went up in smoke. Now, one can spend an entire life beating one's breast about what a terrible thing happened, in which case one should get out of politics and go teach at some marginal university. Or, one faces facts. When I saw how everyone packed up and left Cancun, confessed in their powerlessness, admonished and discharged with a smile, I said to myself, "This is obviously not the way to go."

The first alternative was to consider some type of South-South cooperation. That meant facilitating development among the poor nations by seeking economies of scale that would result from regional cooperation of complementary economies. But this, of course, is very difficult to do. To the extent that any progress can be made along this path, I have become a strong regionalist, a strong South-Southist.

But there was a recognition of greater importance that dawned on me: driven by technology, the world economy has evolved, slowly shifting the focus of production from within nation-states and dispersing it worldwide. The Ford, for example, is no longer really made in America. When a car is made in several different countries, what does it mean to talk about a national economy?

So, I asked myself logically, if the ethical argument about correcting the imbalance among nation-states didn't fly at the zenith of the nation-state's power as an economic decision maker, how can it fly in the future as nations become weaker and weaker? If I couldn't convince Washington to do something about the terms of trade, to what board of what corporate entity, in what part of the world, would I take my appeal now? Obviously, that idea is for the birds.

What is the future? Perhaps Reagan was right. Each of us has to find our niche in the global economy and pull ourselves up by our bootstraps. In the dispersed world economy, poor little Jamaica has only one choice: to find a foothold for its goods somewhere in the European Community or the eastern seaboard of the United States, and pour massive resources into educating and training its people to produce competitively for those markets. And we can make common cause with transnational companies in our country through joint ventures. That will get us into the world economy.

So, during the 1980s, I turned my ideas on their head. There is no reality to grand plans aimed at equalizing North and South. There are only states doing their small part in a decentralized fashion to hook up with a dispersed global economy.

NPQ

Do you agree, then, with the idea of one vast free-trade area from Anchorage to Tierra del Fuego?

Manley

This vision of a hemispheric free-trade zone down the road is as correct as it is inevitable. There is no other way. I can well understand the protectionist reflexes one sees these days in the United States. Everyone wants to protect their little bastion. But such protectionist sentiments are wholly irrelevant. They will be washed away in the tide of history driven by technological change.

I have always argued to my party that if we try to build our policy around the rejection of history, we do nothing other than guarantee our own obsolescence. If we want to know where history is going, forget politics and study technology. Once we align our strategy with the historical trend, we can be flexible with tactics.

We may well want to protect a sensitive industry for several years in order to prepare it to face the fierce winds of global competition. I think that is acceptable. We are buying time to face the inevitable. But the minute we get the idea that protectionist policy is forever, we only guarantee one thing: in five or six years we will be totally out of the picture. The world economy will have left us behind.

NPQ

Fidel's Cuba is staying a course directly counter to the course you have taken Jamaica, and the course being followed now by most of Latin America. Isn't Fidel getting too old to swim against the tide without drowning?

Manley

Cuba is today under tremendous pressures, which will inevitably make it more and more a siege society. Yet there are some signs of change. There are efforts to open up somewhat the political process of representation. Cuba is aggressively courting private tourism capital, including some of our staunchest private hoteliers who are just opening up business there. But I hear things are extremely tough with the end of Soviet aid.

NPQ

Why don't you suggest to your American friends that they end the trade embargo against Cuba? Wouldn't that be the paradoxical equivalent in this hemisphere of taking down the Berlin Wall? Isn't the embargo the last prop of Fidel's failed system?

Manley

I have long opposed the trade embargo against Cuba. Things would have been strikingly different without it. I even suspect that Cuba would be opening up and evolving just like the rest of this region if it hadn't had to stiffen its posture in self-defense over the years. Relations with Cuba and the U.S. should be normalized. All we have now is a source of tension that is not very good for anyone.

I do not share the view that Fidel will fall if the embargo is maintained a little longer. Those who think Fidel and Honecker are the same historical phenomenon are wildly naive. There are three fundamental distinctions between Cuba and Eastern Europe:

First, throughout all of Europe there was not one example of communism arising from a nationally based, revolutionary process. It was imposed by the Red Army. Cuban communism is the creature of the great period of postcolonial nationalist explosions that Fidel symbolized and still symbolizes. He is perhaps the last symbol. Fidel is the definitive symbol to this day of Cuban nationalism and pride. If a Cuban high-jumper sets a world record, he is "Fidel's high-jumper." There is a huge identification with Fidel that survives the suffering.

Second, unlike many if not all of the European communist dictators, Fidel has been of exemplary personal integrity. He has no Swiss bank accounts. He has not accumulated wealth for himself. Indeed, even if you think he is misguided and totally wrong, he is the very symbol of selfless service.

Third, when there is trouble in Cuba, Fidel never hides from the people behind walls and armies the way Honecker or Ceausescu did. On the contrary, when there is trouble, he goes to the people. He walks in the street. He touches. He talks. He listens. So the people don't see him as a remote tyrant. At least he is always present, always visible.

NPQ

You've modernized the means to your objective of empowering the poor. But Fidel has stayed the course. Isn't the Cuban model historically obsolete?

Manley

I happen to think so.

NPQ

What is the legacy of the Cuban revolution, then?

Manley

The Cuban revolution still resonates in the hearts of people in Latin America and the Caribbean for a very powerful reason. It was fundamentally about how a people acquire self-confidence. It was about acquiring human dignity.

Acquiring self-confidence is not necessarily a function of success. It is a function of faith in yourself, of the will to try to stand on your feet. To believe that however small you are, however impoverished your background, you are capable of anything.

You can look at Fidel's considerable failures, but still see a giant. Symbolized in this person is the will of the people. The fact that the will didn't quite work out as intended is quite irrelevant. What is important is that Fidel is an epic figure who set in motion an epic process. And even if the Cuban revolution was like a Greek tragedy, ending in disaster, we remember the epic figures that were larger than life. We remember the trials or the heroes who freed us from being condemned to the margins, even if we came from a small island that was a small part of the colonial experience.

The legacy of Fidel, like that of Marcus Garvey or Eric Williams, will never be undone. Whatever happens on the ground, that legacy will live in the spirit. These figures from our little experience in the blue seas of the Caribbean made us believe in epic possibilities. That will last longer than anything else.

Capitalism East and West:

A Dialogue

Akio Morita and David Rockefeller

The following is adapted from a dialogue between David Rockefeller, the former chairman of Chase Manhattan Bank, and Akio Morita, the cofounder and chairman of Sony Corporation. It took place at Rockefeller's New York home in late October of 1992, and was organized by NPQ's *associate paper in Japan,* Yomiuri Shimbun.

Cultural Differences
and Japan's New World Role
Akio Morita

The unification of Europe after 1992 caused great concern among many Japanese businessmen, who fear they are building a "fortress." But my view is different. We must appreciate and admire the willingness of Europeans to sacrifice sovereignty to create a greater economic region. Despite their many different cultures, languages, and traditions, and their deadly conflicts over the years, they now know that to live together peacefully, every country has to sacrifice some of its own interests for the good of the whole.

Such a decision would be very difficult for the Japanese. The Japanese are completely isolated by water from others. Thus, throughout history, we have remained virtually homogeneous and independent. We have refined our own culture, but have never had to live side by side and interact with other cultures. Very few Japanese understand just how different we are culturally from the rest of the world. And that is why so few can conceive of sacrificing some of our interests to gain harmony with others. Undoubtedly, this is the root of many of our problems today, and it is why Japan has been accused of not playing a responsible role in the world.

The origins of community and society in Japan and America are also very different. American culture is mainly Christian. When you see someone in a difficult situation, you automatically feel that you must help. Japanese culture emerges from Confucian tradition, a philosophy that is mainly about self-control and behavior: one must be modest, not too demanding. Confucianism has less to do with how you treat other people than about personal ethics. As a result, the Japanese tend to be generous to their own kind, to friends, but not to strangers. By contrast, Americans are generous to everyone.

The concept of the "nation" is also quite different. Japanese people are born Japanese. America is made up of immigrants who arrived on its shores with the will to become American. Out of the necessity of creating order in a great and open space, self-reliant communities created their own rules and hired a sheriff. Historically, then, Americans know that they create rules in their own interest. Through the experience of self-government, they know that rules are not created merely in the interest of others, but for their own good. The Japanese mentality has not been affected by such an experience. For millennia we have been governed by a government that has forced rules and regulations upon us.

Here I must also comment on another Japanese cultural difference that led to some misunderstanding when a book, *The Japan that Can Say No*, was released, in which I was listed as coauthor. I often participate in international meetings and come away concerned that the Japanese are very quiet and hesitant to argue. According to Japanese tradition, to argue with a friend is a vice, since Confucian belief dictates that if you are my friend, we should agree. A conference means something different for a Japanese than for an American. Particularly for the older generation of Japanese, going to a conference means listening to speeches and taking notes. There is no debate.

Once at a U.S.-Japan businessmen's conference, I argued with an American friend, and was later admonished by a senior Japanese colleague who said: "Your friend came from a long way, you should treat him nicely." This Japanese attitude must change. We have to be frank with our friends so we are understood.

That was the thrust of my remarks in the book *The Japan that Can Say No*. That book, however, apparently gave the impression that the Japanese are always going to say no. That's not true. My intention was simply to say that the Japanese should not mind disagreeing with Americans and others. As the Japanese become more internationalized and more willing to debate and say "no," we can play a much more significant world role.

David Rockefeller

I think your coauthor, Mr. Shintaro Ishihara, said some things that went further, which may have been what caused so much concern. Everybody agrees that the Japanese should feel free to say no when they feel a difference of opinion — on the condition that in a changed world Japan also agrees to play a more important role.

But you also raised the issue of a responsible role for Japan in the world. As Japan grows in economic strength — in some areas you are actually stronger than America, and though your population is half that of the U.S., your GNP is growing more rapidly — you need to reconsider your position and recognize that with global strength and power come responsibility. The U.S. has to be ready to accept, at the very least, a position of equality with Japan on the economic front.

It is especially critical that Japan come to terms with its role now that the Soviet threat has disappeared from the international scene. This is the historical moment to make the transition. It can no longer be taken for granted that because America is the predominant power, it must take up all the global responsibilities, while Japan just follows behind. It is important for Japan and the U.S. to work closely together. For either one to pull back and allow the other to play a too important role would cause considerable concern in the Asian-Pacific area. This is especially true if America were to pull back militarily and allow Japan to assume an increasingly dominant role in security matters.

Morita

I agree that now, as a leading economic power in the world, Japan should be more bold about becoming a world citizen. But Japan has jumped ahead at high speed economically, and it is very difficult to match this speed in changing our social system. We need strong leadership, as you say.

But leadership has many aspects: it not only means that we must have the right to say "no"; it also means that when we say "yes" we must be willing to sacrifice our own interests for the greater good of the international order. The U.S. and Japan must learn how to share sovereignty, just as the Europeans are doing during their process of integration. In Japanese we have a saying: *daido shoi,* which means "small differences are sublimated in a greater cause." That is part of what leadership implies for Japan.

Remembering Pearl Harbor

Morita

I heard the news about Pearl Harbor on a radio I had rigged to go off at 6 A.M. This was a big shock. My first feeling was that we had finally reached the point of war. Everything had been moving in that direction even though many in Japan warned against it.

Once the war broke out, as Japanese citizens we naturally felt we should do everything possible to win. At that time, it was hard for us to say whether this war was led by the military or not. All we knew was that we had to defend Japan, we had to fight. Although many people disliked the military, they generally accepted their fate. That may be the Japanese character.

I was a student in physics at Osaka University at the time, and my professor was helping the Japanese navy develop advanced weapons technology, so I volunteered to help him. My job was to help develop a heat-seeking missile. We were also involved in atomic physics. At the time I wrote an article saying that atomic energy could theoretically be used as a bomb, but that the ability to accumulate enough uranium — at the then-level of scientific technology — would take twenty years. I said atomic power could not be used during the current war.

Sometimes, when a B-29 had been shot down, its parts would be brought to our laboratory for analysis. Seeing these machines made me realize the technological gaps we faced. When I was in the navy, in the section working on airborne photography, I used a Fairchild camera. Almost all Japanese cameras were copies of Fairchilds. I knew then that, just as with cameras, we were learning everything from the U.S. So, even though Japan had victories in the first months of the war, as in Hawaii, we knew it was very dangerous because of America's technological lead.

It was a shock when the atomic bombs fell on Hiroshima and Nagasaki. From my knowledge of science, it was clear that the U.S. had jumped twenty years into the future. After the bombing, I firmly believed we had no chance. When the war subsequently ended, my feelings were complicated. We had wanted to win, but since we were so technologically behind, I knew we had no chance. Despite this feeling of distress, I was nonetheless relieved that there would be no more bombs and no more damage.

Rockefeller

I felt then, and feel now, that even though dropping the bomb meant a great many innocent people were killed, it also meant that the war would be cut short by a substantial amount of time, thus avoiding killing a great many others. How do you feel about that? Did it cause anti-Americanism?

Morita

Because the military controlled the news at the time, we knew atomic bombs had been dropped but didn't know just how much damage had been inflicted and how many people had been killed. Also, you must remember that the people in Japan never actually faced Americans as an enemy. Of course there were bombing raids from the sky, but that was just like earthquake damage caused by fate. Since we did not see the enemy face to face, we Japanese did not really develop anti-American sentiments.

The American Occupation and Postwar Reconstruction

Rockefeller

After the war, the Allied leadership recognized it was in our interest to see both Germany and Japan recover as democratic partners who would be able to sustain themselves economically, and that steps should be taken to prevent them from rearming and starting another war. History has shown that these policies were wise.

Morita

Before the American occupation forces came, we were strongly warned that they would treat us brutally. But the reality was very different. The Americans were so generous and friendly. Little things — giving us chocolates, chewing gum, cigarettes — made such a big difference in those days when our situation was very, very bad. In those harsh postwar days, all Japanese were seriously concerned about mere survival. Soldiers were coming back from the front, swelling the population. We lacked food and energy. We had no electricity or heating.

When I visited Europe in 1953, I could still see the stone and brick rubble on the streets. But in Tokyo and other cities, there was not even any rubble. Since our houses were made of paper and wood, they had burned to the ground. Nothing remained. People lived without shelter. There was no choice but to form a consensus to rebuild our nation. There was no other way to survive. The American help in such circumstances was a great relief. They supplied food and energy. That is why we became pro-American. Without America's help, we wouldn't have survived.

Of course, there was a broader agenda at General MacArthur's headquarters. His intention was to change Japan's system completely. In fact, many of the things said to be Japan's traditional way — such as lifetime employment and administrative guidance — were actually the result of American policy. MacArthur told Japan that the totalitarian system was wrong, and that we should adopt democracy and allow freedom of expression. That's why communists and left-wing trade unionists were released from prison to participate in the political process.

As a consequence, labor laws and employment customs were completely changed. Management practically had no rights to lay anyone off. This was the origin of the lifetime employment system in Japan: once we hired someone, we couldn't fire them. Today, the Japanese company is not a business organization, but a social welfare organization because we have to take care of our employees for life. Now everyone in Japan accepts this "family feeling," that we must live together and share the rewards and pains. So it is not true, as many people think, that this system comes from Japanese tradition. Before the war, anybody could be fired.

MacArthur's General Headquarters (GHQ) was also responsible for another important policy. Traditionally, democracy has meant freedom, and freedom has meant that anyone could do anything, without thinking of others — a formulation that spelled trouble for us after the war because freedom was taken to the extreme. For this reason, the GHQ gave a lot of guidance, suggesting many things to the Japanese government — orally, though, and not in writing. GHQ would say to the Japanese government, "You should be the initiator. However, we think you should do this. . . ." That is the origin of the famed Japanese administrative guidance of MITI (Ministry of International Trade and Industry). And that is why I find it ironic today when the U.S. government charges the Japanese government with too much "administrative guidance" in our policies.

Rockefeller

My first trip to Japan was in 1962, when I was chairman of Chase Manhattan Bank. By then, Japan was growing at an extraordinarily rapid pace with impressive efficiency, discipline, and organization. It was already clear then that our view of the Japanese as wonderful copiers who couldn't create anything of their own was a myth.

Morita

In 1955, Sony released its first transistor radio, and by 1961 we were the first Japanese company to issue shares on Wall Street. The Japanese prime minister at the time, Mr. Hayato Ikeda, was greatly interested in attracting American capital investment to Japan, so he pushed our efforts to raise funds from American investors to expand Japanese industry.

Rockefeller

Japan's takeoff, of which Sony was an emblem, was in fact the major factor for Chase's expanded interest — and the interest of other American financial institutions — in Asia at the time. In many ways, 1962 was the takeoff year of the "Japanese miracle."

Who's at Fault for the Trade Imbalance?

Morita

As a business leader, my assessment of the present U.S.-Japan relations begins with the trade conflict. In order to promote deeper cooperation, I hope for a discussion that includes the industries of both sides. Japanese industries are alumni of the "American school of manufacturing." We have learned our basic concepts — quality control, production technologies, accounting techniques, and all modern industrial management methods — from the U.S.

But after graduation, we would not have been good students had we failed to expand on what we learned in school. And Japanese have been good students — utilizing the knowledge we gained, adding to our creativity, and building up new industries. For example, we obtained the transistor from you, and, using the concept, created the transistor radio. But no sooner did we begin exporting in 1959 — and our production was very small — than the Electronics Industry Association in America said that the import of

Japanese transistors from Japan might be a problem for the future defense of the U.S. Because we were trying to improve the poor image of products labeled "Made in Japan," we made sure that our products were of the highest quality when we exported them. Gradually, the image of "Made in Japan" changed, and we built up our exports. Thus began the trade conflict.

Now, the American side is always claiming a trade imbalance. But what are its real causes? We used to be a large exporter of televisions. This became a big issue when the U.S. Trade Representative negotiated voluntary restraints, which we had for three years. During those three years, many companies moved their production to America. As a result, our exports have decreased greatly in consumer electronics. Even in automobiles, Japanese companies are building factories in America and reducing their exports. In the case of semiconductors, Japanese industry has sent a purchasing team over to the U.S. several times seeking to import semiconductors to Japan. By 1992, 20 percent of our semiconductors came from the U.S., as the U.S. government requested. Yet, overall, our exports continue to increase. Still, the imbalance increases. Why is this?

First, we must ask if it is necessary to pay attention only to imbalances in tangible-goods trade — such as autos or consumer products — which are the only items that appear in the numbers. Other areas — tourism, investment, financing from Japan — never appear.

Second, if we do look at the trade of tangible goods, we must study the changing composition of that trade. Even though we are exporting fewer televisions and cars, we have become a big supplier of parts to American industry, such as technological components and aircraft parts to Boeing. Not only are American high-technology industries buying many components from the Japanese, they are requesting that we develop new devices, which in turn are more expensive. Japanese and American industry are so interrelated that it makes little sense anymore to talk only about imbalances, and ignore trends and the overall structure of industry.

So, rather than always talking about imbalances, we should think carefully about future steps for mutual cooperation in industry. With the U.S., however, we have antitrust regulation problems when we begin to discuss with our American partners the future trends of technology. In Europe, the antitrust problems are much less. Top management of European and Japanese consumer industries have had annual meetings for some time now to discuss the future trends of technology.

If we develop a consensus together about the way we should go, then each company can invest money and concentrate efforts on developing new products. In ten years' time, if they advance, we won't complain; and if we advance, they should not complain. A good place to start in reframing the trade issue would be the re-examination of antitrust laws, not only from the perspective of the lawyers, but of the industrialists as well.

Rockefeller

In the last four years, as I understand it, U.S. imports from Japan have increased five-fold while exports have only increased by 10 percent. I also agree with you that the most significant figure is the balance of payments, not just the balance of trade in tangible goods. Whether there is a greater inflow or outflow of dollars is more important than whether trade is in balance.

I also agree that our antitrust laws with respect to multinational corporations need to be reexamined. We still apply the same laws as existed in the days when a company was clearly American, or clearly Japanese or German; now, so many companies are truly international. Yet, the greatest concern in our country relates to the so-called "level playing field." It is still true that U.S. markets are more readily open to Japan than your markets are to us, especially in banking and finance. Therefore, our relationship isn't balanced.

Of course, I realize that all kinds of internal political factors enter into this question of market access. Protected markets also exist in some U.S. sectors, mostly in agriculture. For example, we protect the sugar beet industry to a degree unjustified by anything other than the strong lobbying of sugar-producing states. Rice is protected in Japan. But if your consumers could buy rice for less, and ours could buy sugar for less, they would be better off, wouldn't they?

Morita

Fairness is the key to free trade. Since I started business in America, Sony has always been treated in a fair manner. I would not say that Japan is unfair, but there are many areas where we can improve our economic system in the long term. One such area is market openness. Another area is deregulation. *Gai-atsu*, or foreign pressure, will force us to change. Thus, I can understand why America has pressed Japan to change. The U.S., by contrast, is very flexible. If a new idea emerges, everyone will try it. This open nature leads Americans to think that if their idea is good, and if they have confidence in it, everyone else will naturally think it is good as well.

But it is very hard for the Japanese, or others, to follow the American pace of change in ideas. However, since we are so interdependent, it is necessary to find a point of compromise on our differing perceptions of the future. To do this, we need very strong leadership, both to convince American officials of our point of view, and to persuade Japanese officials and the general public to change. The Japanese are no fools. Many already know what we must do. But in order to realize and implement the conviction to change, we need to get through many domestic political blocks.

The present moment is politically very different than it has been for the past four postwar decades when the Liberal Democratic Party (LDP) held the majority of the Diet. In those years, businessmen didn't have to worry about politics. Unlike the U.S., where the Congress proposes legislation, Japan's ministries — really fantastic think-tanks taking the long-term view — propose legislation. And in the past, the LDP majority usually passed the bills.

Now, however, we are facing the first real political crisis since World War II. Now laws cannot pass so easily — whether concerning opening the rice market or sending Self-Defense Forces abroad as part of a multilateral peace keeping force. Japan has often been referred to as "Japan, Inc." But it has no real strong executive offices. Each ministry, like a division in a company, has strong power. But in business, top management, taking into account the future of the whole company, has the power to overrule a division manager. This is not true politically in Japan.

Kenbei and Japan-Bashing

Rockefeller

There is a lot of talk these days about Japan-bashing in the U.S. Without question there is some, and some of it is justified. But I don't think it is growing in intensity. If anything, it is subsiding. When the Mitsubishi Corporation purchased 80 percent of the stock of the Rockefeller Group, people became very worried that Japan was buying up America. Yet it seems to me there were very legitimate and proper reasons for the transaction. Contrary to what many people have thought about the Rockefeller Group deal, our family — not Mitsubishi — initiated the purchase.

The notion that this was somehow selling out to a greedy group of Japanese who were trying to gobble up American assets just isn't true. And then, there was the purchase of a Hollywood studio — Coumbia pictures. . . .

Morita

With respect to Sony's purchase of Columbia Pictures, I was shocked at some American journalism that accused Sony of buying America's soul. It was so sensational.

When RCA — to me the very symbol of American technology and industry — was sold to the French electronics company, Thomson, American journalists said nothing. Since RCA was a leader in the American electronics industry, its purchase by the French should have been the occasion for journalists to warn the American public. The biggest crisis in American industry today is the loss of its lead in exactly those areas in which RCA excelled.

Pan Am, the American flagship all over the world, is also now gone. America is losing very important strengths across the board. That's the real news. After all, we didn't remove Columbia Pictures from U.S. soil. In fact, we are improving their management. Because the movie industry is a strong exporter, it is one of the strong income sources for America. In this sense, we are helping, not hindering, American strength.

Rockefeller

To be sure, Americans were irritated about Japan's relatively slow response in helping out with Operation Desert Storm. In the end, though, Japan did put up $13 billion — a quarter of the total cost of the war. This seemed to me a very generous action. However, the substance of the final product was vitiated by the fact that it took Japan such a long time to come through. But that is often the case with Japan. For whatever reasons, political or otherwise, Japan often takes quite a long time to reach a conclusion, appearing hesitant to make any commitment, even an unsympathetic one. In the end, though, it always comes through.

Morita

The equivalent of Japan-bashing in Japan is called *kenbei*, which means a dislike of America. It has been reported to be on the rise, but I don't think it is a very serious thing.

But, to return to the criticism of Sony and myself for the Columbia purchase, maybe I touched a very sensitive nerve. The American reaction forced me to recall that when war broke out, Japanese in America — even American citizens — were forcibly interned. I had to wonder that maybe Japanese are still considered aliens and strangers by Americans, despite the massive level of our investment in the U.S., and our economic interdependence.

The only thing we Japanese can do is be good citizens in America so that we are regarded as real members of the community. Then, if American politicians were to bash the Japanese, they might lose votes. This is the way to change the attitudes of America's politicians.

Rockefeller

In the final analysis, I am optimistic about U.S.-Japan relations. There is a great deal of goodwill on both sides. While the problems we have are serious, and we shouldn't make the mistake of minimizing them, they are manageable because we have enough mutual interest to make the necessary effort.

Morita

Of course we will have serious problems from time to time. We are both big and complex countries with a wideranging set of relations. We will conflict on many points. But I think we should regard it as the inevitable friction of good relations.

The Waning Nation-State

Nelson Mandela

As president of South Africa, Nelson Mandela now must look beyond the struggle against apartheid at home to a world divided into economic light and darkness and, in Africa especially, marked by disintegrating states.

In this essay that appeared in NPQ *in the summer of 1994, President Mandela lays out his world view.*

JOHANNESBURG

We are, to use a famous phrase from another transition in history, present at the creation. Because this is so, there is a need to develop a sense of orderliness in the world. To do so, a direct link needs to be established between responsible membership of the community of nations, and global stability and progress. The converse is also true; if countries want to enjoy the rights of community, they need to act responsibly.

Philosophers teach that the rights of citizenship follow from the sharing of values in the common cause. As we prepare for the new century, each country needs to build upon a set of common properties that will aim to anchor it within the ambit of a legitimate new world order.

The test of South Africa's foreign policy in this context will be found in the quality of its domestic politics. My government wants South Africa to be a symbol of a world in which diverse people can live in peace. The quality, too, of the government will be reflected in our foreign policy itself. South Africa will be amongst those countries whose efforts are to promote and foster democratic systems of government. This is especially important in Africa, and our concerns will be fixed upon securing the spirit of tolerance and the ethos of sound governance throughout the continent.

There cannot be one system for Africa and another for the world. If there is a single lesson to be drawn from Africa's postcolonial history, it is that accountable government is good government.

It is a mistake to interpret this as Afro-pessimism. South Africa cannot escape its continental destiny; nor does it wish to do so. If we do not devote our energies to Africa, we too could fall victim to the forces that have brought near ruin to its furthest corners.

For decades, South Africa's international relations, like its domestic politics, were symbolized by the apartheid scourge. Although the Cold War was drawn into the national lexicon, the international community gradually came to recognize that the single most important issue facing the country was not the East/West conflict, but the struggle for human dignity and racial equality. The world's people contributed to ending apartheid by boycotting and isolating the South African regime. The people of South Africa themselves rose in revolt, and the political movement waged a struggle for liberation. As the 1980s closed, white South Africa was the most isolated and embattled country in the world.

But South Africa's people were never excluded from the international community. The country's contribution to the common properties of a new world order will follow from this unique experience of isolation and its opposite, embrace. South Africa's global destiny is linked to maintaining vigilance around the same precepts that united the world against apartheid, which were able to distinguish between principle and prejudice, and separated ethics from expedience, ingenuity from ineptitude.

Because the world community is in search of stability amidst uncertainty, our own experience suggests that we dare not relinquish the commitment to human rights in international affairs. Global change has, if anything, heightened the salience of the issue. The historically recent tragedies, from Sarajevo to Rwanda, whose images are the lifeblood of the influential electronic media, underpin the importance of respect for human rights in securing our common future.

While governments should be mindful of the high ideals of human rights, they should be conscious of a democratic realism that surrounds the issue, too. The neglect of human rights is the certain recipe for internal and international disaster. The powerful secessionist movements that are found throughout the world are nurtured by neglect. The erosion of national sovereignty by global forces, from trade to communications, has paradoxically been accompanied by an increase in the means to ensure its separateness: the right to differ has, tragically, become the fight to differ.

The violent breakup of states points to the horrors that face countries in Africa and elsewhere which are not prepared to accept that diversity is integral to the human condition. These failed states will fall prey to greater internecine strife that will sap, if not destroy, the potential of their people. They will fall further and further behind the great technological advances that are made elsewhere.

Many believe this fate beckons my own country. They are thoroughly wrong. Few people on earth have experienced intolerance as have South Africans. This has steeled our vigilance toward democracy and tolerance.

Even in the darkest days of apartheid and the most tragic moments of our turbulent transition, South Africans of all colors and creeds have, with great personal courage, shown respect for difference. A central goal of South Africa's foreign policy, like its domestic politics, will be to promote institutions and forces which, through democracy, seek to make the world safe for diversity. This is our vision for the twenty-first century.

Facing the twenty-first century, however, brings with it many new challenges. Since the sixteenth century, the nation-state has provided a ready guide to international politics. But these past five years have demonstrated how inadequately states are coping with global transition. Faced with the enormity of events, states appear too puny, too clumsy, to deal with diverse issues — from trade wars to public health — that now touch the lives of ordinary people. Sovereignty, once one of the central organizing principles of our world, has been profoundly disturbed.

To figure out how a democratic South Africa can fit into this new world, it is important to grasp just what has happened. Starting in the late 1960s, economic power slipped from individual countries toward an entrepreneurial pool of skills that knew no national boundaries. No longer was prosperity wedded to the domestic performance of individual countries; the fate of national economics was often being determined elsewhere.

This trend toward interdependence was speeded up by the increasing impact of communications. This revolution, associated with the miracle of the microchip, rebounded in technological break-throughs which allowed corporations to operate farther and farther offshore. Industrial production, taking advantage of competitive wage rates, scattered across the planet. The recognizable brand names become more global and less national; services rechanneled the nature of economics, dragging it farther from the national to the global arena.

As financial markets found renewed vigor beyond the nation-state, traditional forms of economic activity were reignited throughout the world. Operating around the clock, international capital markets had replaced the British Raj: they were the empire upon which the sun could never set. In this world that was increasingly losing its borders, the old East-West conflict lost its grip. The loss of national control on both sides of the divide provided the anvil upon which the events of 1989, when the Berlin Wall fell, were forged. That moment marked the turning point to a new globalized situation.

Beyond these structural changes, which have caused so much uncertainty in their sheer speed, a host of other transnational insecurities is arising. In southern Africa, and other parts of the Third World, the arc of killer diseases — tuberculosis, new strains of malaria, and AIDS — has been extended.

Acting alone, governments appear to be powerless to deal with them. As population growth rates show no sign of slowing, fears of diminished access to food loom large in Africa and elsewhere in the South. These, like the specter of water shortages, place new and often totally unimaginable constraints on governments.

Despite all this, states still pursue interests that they perceive to be absolute national interests. And, even though the nation-state still remains the focus of loyalty for millions, and is seen as the appropriate arena for the defense of the interests of ordinary people, there is at the same time a deep disillusionment with national politics in many parts of the world.

This is because something very rudimentary is happening: democratic systems that were once considered adequate have collapsed, and communities are probing new ways of conducting politics. In countries as geographically far apart as Italy and Mexico, accepted political processes have been shaken to their roots.

Certainly, economic developments have influenced these political maladies in profound ways, but economics alone offers few solutions to the plethora of post-industrial problems. The marketplace has not triumphed and the end of history has not arrived. The evidence is clear: income differentials in many capitalist countries have widened, not narrowed, and poverty and wealth levels between rich and poor countries have increased.

Today, the rich countries are living in a glorious pool of permanent economic light. Beyond this rim of light, a secondary group of countries is found; it lives in a kind of economic dusk. Farther away — beyond the pool of light and the shadow — the greater number of countries and peoples of the world live in an economic darkness. As stark as they are, images like this fail to capture the misery that these categorizations mean for billions of the planet's poor.

The international community cannot view this situation with any equanimity. A world in which a large part of the population is condemned to be excluded — cast in the darkness because they are poor — can never be secure. For the world to be at peace, we will need the rim of the light to be extended.

The countries in the shadows, like my own, have a responsibility to ensure that they help widen the arc of the world's economic lamp. Full participation in the global trading system is central to securing South Africa's international economic relations. For the sake of our democracy, we need to be in the pool of light.

The developed world must also recognize the need of the less advantaged countries to build an infrastructure, and to consolidate areas of the economy that are in their infancy. This is not to be confused with narrow protectionism. A program of trade policy reform must, however, address the levels of protection and the development of effective export incentives that are internationally acceptable.

The growth of North-based trading blocs such as the European Union and the North American Free Trade Area (NAFTA) have weakened the position of developing countries, particularly those like South Africa which are not members of any trading bloc.

In the world I have described, it is easy to understand how the leaders of nation-states will find it difficult to sustain the control they now insist on exercising over the political process within their borders. In today's world, it is no longer absolutely certain where countries end, and people begin. That is why the tyranny of the mapmakers has become a common theme among those who try to understand why it is that states fell in the 1990s, and how it is that they are supposed to survive into the twenty-first century.

© Keith Phillip Lepor

A Smug Indifference to the Global Outerclass

François Mitterrand

The former president of France, François Mitterrand addressed a symposium of forty intellectuals gathered at UNESCO to discuss "What happened to development?" NPQ Editor Nathan Gardels participated in the meeting, and obtained permission from the Elysée Palace to publish the president's private remarks.

PARIS

How can we accept that millions of men, women, and children in the poor Southern countries continue to die in front of our television cameras? If these awful sights lead us to feel compassion, that is all very well. But our reactions of late have too often been only capricious.

I fear that those of us in the richer countries of the North have gone in recent years from an embarrassed indifference to a smug indifference. Each country, it seems, is now only concerned with its own backyard. Any interest in development has dwindled. Some governments are even saying that if the poor countries cannot get out of their crisis, it is their own problem and probably their own fault because they are not trying. This is a tragedy.

The truth is that our entire planet will become uninhabitable if we buy into the illusion that we need only make it inhabitable for the few. It is foolish to believe otherwise. It first of all makes sense from the standpoint of expanding trade to incorporate everyone into the global economy; and if we create some kind of a global outerclass by excluding whole parts of the globe from growth, then feedback diseases such as AIDS, the flow of drugs, and environmental destruction wrought by massive poverty will duly exact their price on the smug in times to come. For these reasons we need to make sure the poor countries do not stay on the fringe.

Inequalities continue to grow despite the claim that the global market is the panacea for all ills. Relying on humanitarian assistance and the rules of the market alone are insufficient to cope with a situation where one-fifth of humanity lives below the poverty line.

What we need instead is a "development contract" between the North and the South. We need a single global view on development, just as there is a single global view on the environment that emerged from the Rio Summit.

Such a contract must be based on a new international ethical-moral code. I know this has been said before, and some have disparaged it. But if we do not start with that we won't get very far.

Development aid must become something more than a means to help poor countries respect their financial obligations; it must be a means to help bolster respect for social and moral contracts within societies and within the world community. It is all linked together. If no development takes place, then there can be no lasting domestic peace in these countries torn by strife. In the midst of poverty and strife, it is impossible to set up a state of law and respect human rights. If development is only considered in its financial dimension so that a country can join a world where market forces continue to rule supreme, then social equilibrium and equality will continue to be broken, and strife will continue to break out.

For its part the South, too, needs to understand that it is impossible to have economic prosperity without democratic efficiency. Only in a democracy is it possible to settle conflicts without force and violence. Only when a democratic state exists will citizens be able to ensure continuity in the management of a country.

For this reason, the developed countries have to concern themselves with the rule of law in the South. The protection of minorities under the law is something that should be a particular focal point. The new South Africa is a very good example to follow on this score. There are three elements to the development contract that I propose:

Development aid: If all the industrialized countries would commit to a goal of setting aside 0.7 percent of their gross domestic product to development aid, $130 billion would be made available for investment in infrastructure education and health in the poor countries. I am not suggesting that my own country has been perfect in this particular area, but we have increased aid by 40 percent in real terms, bringing us quite close to that goal. France has also canceled or rescheduled debts to thirty-nine of the poorest countries in the world. Here we are at least trying to clean up the obligations these countries already have that drain their resources.

The International Monetary Fund (IMF) should also make available special drawing rights for the neediest member countries. For the moment, the IMF only serves to increase profits of the rich countries that were members before 1981, and not the thirty-six newer members who need funds the most. If this injustice of the world finance system were corrected, it would make another $50 billion in hard currency available for indispensable development.

The poor countries would use these funds so that they don't have to reduce their imports — because they lack the hard currency — of goods and equipment, thereby depressing their productive capacity. There is no reason not to do this today since the risk of an inflationary backlash is extremely slight.

Mutual respect: The leaders of developing countries have made it clear that they don't want to be completely sacrificed to the intolerant liberalism of global free markets. In turn these countries must be asked to respect the rights of workers. It is unbearable to see the absence of trade unions and workers' rights in so many countries, and to see how children and prisoners are exploited. It is disgraceful to see that countries which justly struggled for independence from colonialism are themselves violating the fundamental rights of their own people. We need some common understanding between North and South on these matters.

Inventive arrangements: When the countries of the South organize themselves to seek fair market prices for their commodities — be they coffee or wood — in the world market, they are on the right track. When countries of the South cooperate with other countries of the South, they are contributing to their own success. These kinds of arrangements that will enable the South to develop by its own efforts must be encouraged.

We can no longer simply entrust the development of the world to monetary rules alone. Rather, economic security on a world scale must be part of the reform agenda of all multilateral institutions, from the World Trade Organization to the U.N. itself. We must resist the trend that aid for development is being taken off the agenda of the rich countries' policies. There is simply no grander illusion than believing we can live in a world apart.

The End of the Hunting Season in History

Shimon Peres

For decades, Shimon Peres has been at the center of Israeli political life. He has not only been both foreign minister and prime minister, but also both the shepherd of Israeli's nuclear capacity and the architect of peace with Israel's Arab neighbors.

In the following essay, first published in NPQ *in the Fall of 1995, Shimon Peres displays the visionary prowess that has made him one of the late twentieth century's leading statesmen. His most recent book is* Battling for Peace *(1995).*

JERUSALEM

The transition from the twentieth century to the twenty-first will be more than a chronological event. It will involve a change of historical period, a change of era.

The key events of the last decade, which failed to obey the standard rules of change, are a premonition of the times to come. Classic political instruments, such as armies, parties, or even superpowers, have had no role to play at all.

Thus, communism collapsed in the Soviet Union without aid from the Red Army — neither for those that supported it, nor for those who wished to rid themselves of it. As the Soviet Union was overthrown, the army remained neutral, or more precisely, on the sidelines.

One of the most captivating images during the attempted coup against Mikhail Gorbachev was that of a battalion of Red Army soldiers in front of the Russian Parliament, Moscow's "White House." The soldiers were indifferent, with a "who cares" attitude, when suddenly an old Russian woman, a *babouchka*, went up to them and said, "Children, what are you doing here? Go home!" It was almost as if the *babouchka* were the sole commander of the Red Army.

Also, the Communist Party was not beaten by another party opposing it. The Communist Party was beaten by its own children and not by its rivals. The Soviet Union did not come apart under the impact of American pressure, European intervention, or a Chinese threat. The pressure did not come from without, it sprang from within. This gigantic change in human organization occurred without the army's guns, without political parties' banners, and without superpower threats.

The same is true of apartheid in South Africa. Also, what happened in the Israeli-Palestinian conflict is very similar. It began in the darkness of calm Norwegian nights, without a single gunshot, without a single demonstration, without the dictates of a superpower. Conversely, traditional political instruments have proven completely ineffective in Bosnia, Somalia, or Burundi. The superpowers, armies, and parties which have intervened in these countries have not been successful. Is it merely chance, or are we observing the first signs of a new world that works according to rules as yet unknown to us?

Why have traditional political instruments not worked? What were the alternative means that enabled these profound changes? It is possible to answer that it is not the instruments that have changed, but rather the substance.

The armies did not move because their means of action had lost their effect. In the three above-mentioned cases — Russia, Africa, and the Middle East — the conflict was not territorial; it was not an issue of protecting the motherland, or taking land from other peoples. The issue was a struggle for a fundamental change, a change in the very content of existence. The army understood that it was not capable of protecting the supposed "status quo," because it could no longer withstand the test of reality, it could no longer endure, and there was no point in defending it. Yet, the army in and of itself was not able to bring about a new situation.

The Red Army was well aware that it could not ensure Russia's place in the new situation, because nuclear missiles and weapons had to a large extent eliminated the military option from the list of possible actions to take in order to secure a definitive advantage. The Red Army knew what the American and all other armies around the world know: missiles do not take the time factor into account (they move at a staggering speed), nor do they take into account the land factor (they care not for mountains, snow, rivers, borders, or buildings). Missiles move at a height well above that of strategic space. The nuclear weapon is an absolute weapon, against which there is no defense, and no one is prepared to accept the damage that this weapon can cause.

The elimination of weapons-based strategies has been caused by more than the new military means. The strategic objectives themselves have been profoundly changed. Power and well-being no longer stem from material sources such as territorial area, natural resources, population size, or geographic location, but from intellectual dimensions — science, technology, information. Armies can conquer only material things, and not those that are knowledge-based.

True, there are still generals who don the uniforms of the past, but they are hard-pressed to find fronts where their armies can be used. I am not arguing that danger no longer exists, or that there will be no more wars. However, I believe that the wars to come will not be those of the strong against the weak — wars of conquest — but rather wars of the weak against the strong — wars of protest. These wars will be more popular than "professional." The weapons are more likely to be stones rather than tanks, and knives rather than cannons. Whether or not the traditional army will play a central role is doubtful.

A Future Without Parties or Superpowers

Political parties also find themselves in an unexpected situation. I do not think that ideology is dead. Mankind needs ideology and belief for the elevation of its intellect. However, current ideologies, which pit East against West, and North against South, are no longer pertinent. While armies exist in order to provide protection against external threats, parties must ensure internal security, be it based on justice or on economic efficiency. Justice or the realization of efficiency thus no longer depends on the status quo, but on that which remains to be created.

Further, it has become clear that the great challenges of our era transcend national frameworks. Science knows no borders, technology has no flag, information has no passport. The new elements are above and beyond states. All countries have access, and can decide that knowledge is more important than material things, that markets are more important than states, and that iron or silk curtains can no longer stop currents of information from arriving at our doorstep. Information moves today like the air that we breathe, and it is impossible to stop it.

The lot of the superpowers is similar to those ideological parties that have become obsolete. When the Soviet Union collapsed, the United States lost its main enemy, or rather, its main challenge. It is even possible to go so far as to say that the very basis of the foreign policy of the superpower that is America has been shaken, since it was centered on the communist enemy. Foreign policy was mainly concerned with enemies. Yet, the world of enemies has disappeared, and the world of dangers has taken its place. The superpowers were accustomed to fighting enemies, large or small. They were not organized properly to cope with danger, be it from human poverty or environmental pollution.

The American president can well persuade the American people and Congress to give him the soldiers and means to fight an enemy of flesh and bone, with a known location, size, strength, and identity. Yet, the American president cannot convince his people to send soldiers to the contorted battles in Bosnia, just as he has difficulty in marshaling the means to fight hunger, terror, drugs, air pollution, desertification, or even the proliferation of nuclear weapons. It is possible to mobilize superpower-scale means, but only against another superpower. Yet, the dangers do not hail from superpowers. They seem far off and poorly defined.

The Media and Leaders

With the change in the role of the army in our era, the lack of ideological pertinence, and the increasing evidence of the weaknesses of the superpowers comes a loss of confidence in leaders, and a decrease in their importance. This is true of both those leaders that sought to arouse their people and those that sought to dazzle them. The people no longer look up, but rather, straight at the tables of knowledge.

Increasingly, public opinion tends to view leaders as if they were characters in a television program, and no longer sees them as guides capable of pointing out the path of this new era. Yet, the aspirations and needs of the people haven't disappeared.

On the contrary, contemporary change is a result of bottom-up movement. It is not imposed from the top down. If neither the armies nor the parties nor the superpowers have eliminated communism or apartheid, or resolved the conflict between Israel and the Palestinians, then who is responsible for these immense changes? It would not be an exaggeration to answer that it is television, radio, and newspaper audiences. In other words, it is the people themselves.

The Romanian cameras were intended to magnify the rituals of dictatorship. Yet, on television, Nicolae Ceausescu ceased to be frightening. One day in 1989, a few people dared to spurn the dictator on TV. It was a revelation for those who hated from a distance: true power was on their side. Ceausescu's stupor left them dumbfounded. They had not pondered any alternatives. But, he understood that his only alternative was to flee.

No doubt, in the beginning of his career, Gorbachev had a great deal of support because he was the first leader who didn't place blame for the failure of communism on his predecessors. He made the system responsible. The young people of Moscow and Leningrad sensed that he was telling the truth when he blamed the system. This negative truth did the job, but Gorbachev had no positive truth. Neither he nor his partisans were able to provide an alternative. They thought that the simple fact of liberation from the existing situation was somehow enough. No doubt they believed the old marxist slogan that "philosophers have interpreted the world in different ways, what is important is to transform it."

Outside the Soviet Union, what played an important role was not NATO's strength, but what was called, with a hint of mockery, "human rights." This subject suddenly became the cornerstone of the Helsinki Conference, and found itself at the heart of the East-West conflict. The communists did not know how to defend themselves against western accusations of human rights violations. What started as a little religious ritual quickly ended up as a powerful movement of strategic importance.

This was also true of South Africa. Frederik W. de Klerk, a man of strong religious sentiment, felt that he was going against divine will by continuing to impose the white minority on the black majority. In Israel, too, the starting point for the negotiations with the Palestinians was a moral issue. Many of us were not prepared to lend a permanent status to our domination of another people against its will. Never in our history have we dominated another people. We have always thought that the highest expression for a people is self-mastery. To us, the true hero is the person who can master his instincts.

The power of governments was largely due to the monopoly they had over the flow of knowledge. But, ever since knowledge has become available to all, a new dynamic has been set in motion that can no longer be stopped. Each and every citizen can become his own diplomat, his own administrator, his own governor. The knowledge to do so is available to him. Also, he is no longer inclined to accept directives from on high as self-evident. He judges for himself.

Today, it is over the radio — or TV, cable, and the Internet — that revolutions are made. They are broadcast, modemed, cabled, and faxed directly into people's homes. Governments are not always aware of the fire that is smoldering, or the smoke rising from the flames. This revolution is a perpetual one, not an institutional one. It cannot be stopped, and does not rest for a minute. It moves forward, changing things that have been set since time immemorial.

The poor peoples of Asia have understood that by adopting new economic rules, they too can soar to economic peaks as successfully as the peoples of North America and Europe. They have learned that there is no "southern" or "northern" economy, that there is no white, black, or yellow people's economy. There is a good economy and a bad economy. All can and must choose the good. Rather than putting politics above the economy, they have understood that it is better to put the economy at the very heart of politics.

This is because the economy is in the service of people, while in most cases, politics serves states and ruling elites. This is especially so since it has become apparent that a fair economy is not purely mechanical. The economy is also based on deep human values. There can be no flourishing economy without an education system for the entire population. There can be no flourishing economy without an ever increasing level of science and technology; there can be no flourishing economy without freedom of research, without freedom of movement, and freedom of speech. There can be no flourishing economy without equality of men and women — because if only half the population participates in development (compared to economies where the majority of the population cooperates in the effort), there will be no economic prosperity. There can be no flourishing economy without democracy. The economy is first and foremost a human issue.

The Challenge of Imagination

For all of these mindbending transformations, we have seen not the end of change, but only the beginning. The extraordinary revolution that appeared during the twentieth century started with the technological revolution, which carries the electronic one at its core: both have had consequences at a strategic political level, and at an economic one. However, it is already obvious that yet another revolution awaits us, even more laden with consequences: that of genetic engineering.

Genes are being mastered in order to change man, to change the environment, to change the world. The electronic and technological revolution caught us short. We were not intellectually prepared, and we still hesitate to get our feet wet. The genetic engineering revolution will find us even more perplexed. Morally and intellectually, we have been primarily concerned with what should be done with these new technologies. Henceforth, it will be necessary to consider what we will do with ourselves.

It is difficult to rid ourselves of preconceived ideas, to accept the new situation. It is so pleasant to yield to memories. What we remember is that of which we are conscious. If something is unpleasant, one quite simply forgets it. It is much more difficult to imagine. He who thinks along the lines of the future realizes that he is impotent because he does not know. Furthermore, where the future is concerned, one must never forget anything; it could be dangerous. We probably have no choice but to leave the places in history that we have known and move into the exhibition halls of the new world, even when it is difficult to know what awaits us there. One thing is certain: anyone who wishes to buy a ticket for the twenty-first century need not arm himself with a bow and arrow, or even a cannon and guns. The hunting season is over.

There is no longer any need to hunt because the real attractions are no longer venison, so to speak, but our spirit of creation. The real calories we need to live as human beings will be created by our ability to innovate. To enter the twenty-first century, we must go as human beings, flashing not our hunting permit, but our act of birth.

During the hunting era, food was lacking. Men had to dominate beasts to put food on the table. They also had to fight their fellow hunters to ensure a larger share of the food. Today, we are discovering that the breadth of material and spiritual sustenance is a function of our intellectual capacity.

We are no longer on hunting ground, but rather in a scientific space. Poor peoples can help themselves if they know how to eliminate preconceived notions, obsolete wars, and their backwardness in the area of education. They can help themselves more than can the rich peoples, as long as they avoid waste and gear their resources to their true potential.

The great wastes of our times are the arms race, government by dictators, and cultural blindness. It is no longer possible to get rich through war: dictatorship is a waste of resources to glorify the head of state. Cultural blindness prevents the young from tasting the fruit of the tree of science.

There is not much left to learn from the blood of Abel shed by Cain, nor from the adventures of Nimrod the hunter. Perhaps the few lines engraved on the tablets of law brought down from Mount Sinai by Moses are still truly of possible help to us. Even the tablets were broken — their message floats on the winds of the future. In the twenty-first century, mankind will have to face conditions unknown to him. Yet, it is only then that he will be able to fully play the role for which he is destined.

© Shimon Peres

For NPQ subscription information contact:

New Perspectives Quarterly
10951 West Pico Boulevard, 3rd floor
Los Angeles, California 90064
800-336-1007 or 310-474-0011
Fax: 310-474-8061